SECOND EDITION

Concepts and Issues in Comparative Politics

An Introduction to Comparative Analysis

Frank L. Wilson
Purdue University

Prentice Hall

Upper Saddle River, New Jersey 07458

Library of Congress Cataloging-in-Publication Data

Wilson, Frank Lee (date)
    Concepts and issues in comparative politics: an introduction to comparative analysis/
Frank L. Wilson.—2nd ed.
        p. cm.
    Includes bibliographical references and index.
    ISBN 0-13-095020-3 (alk. paper)
        1. Comparative government.   I. Title.

JF51.W614 2002
320.3–dc21   2001046156

VP, Editorial director: Laura Pearson
Senior acquisitions editor: Heather Shelstad
Assistant editor: Brian Prybella
Editorial/production supervision and
    interior design: Barbara Reilly
Copy editor: Sylvia Moore
Editorial assistant: Jessica Drew
Prepress and manufacturing buyer: Ben Smith
Marketing manager: Claire Rehwinkel
Cover art director: Jayne Conte
Cover design: Bruce Kenselaar

This book was set in 10/12 Baskerville Book by ElectraGraphics, Inc.,
and was printed and bound by Courier Companies, Inc.
The cover was printed by Phoenix Color Corp.

© 2002, 1996 by Pearson Education, Inc.
Upper Saddle River, New Jersey 07458

Printed in the United States of America
10   9   8   7   6   5   4   3   2

ISBN: 0-13-095020-3

Pearson Education LTD., London
Pearson Education Australia PTY, Limited, Sydney
Pearson Education Singapore, Pte. Ltd
Pearson Education North Asia Ltd, Hong Kong
Pearson Education Canada, Ltd., Toronto
Pearson Educación de Mexico, S.A. de C.V.
Pearson Education—Japan, Tokyo
Pearson Education Malaysia, Pte. Ltd
Pearson Education, Upper Saddle River, New Jersey

To Carol

Contents

Preface

Young Americans who visit abroad as tourists or as students are always surprised at how much their counterparts in other parts of the world know about the United States and its government and politics; international youth are amazed at how little we Americans know about their countries and politics. In a world that is shrinking in size as a result of the electronic and communications revolutions and that is increasingly interdependent economically, politically, and socially, knowledge about other countries around our world is essential for contemporary students from all disciplines. Yet American students are among the least well informed about what is going on in other countries. Introductory courses in comparative politics are designed to help overcome that weakness and to provide the basis for a lifetime of learning about the world around us.

The introduction to comparative politics is a challenging course for both the student and instructor. The challenges come from the dual nature of the course: to introduce beginning students to the comparative method of analysis and to provide background on politics in several different countries. Both these goals are necessary. Comparison is an important approach to gaining insight into social science, but information about a number of "cases" or countries is necessary in order to draw such comparisons. Students in courses that deal only with a series of country studies, one after another, usually fail to learn to make the comparisons; students in courses that focus more on a thematic approach and comparison tend to end up feeling that they have been hit by a flood of unconnected facts.

The task of giving students enough information to engage in comparative analysis without overwhelming them with too many isolated facts about many countries they have barely heard of is a real challenge for those teaching introductory comparative politics. This short textbook is designed to assist in that task by focusing on the challenge of comparison. It can be used with traditional textbooks that deal with several countries in a single volume; it can also provide a comparative framework for instructors who wish to use a series of single-country textbooks. It can be used alone in conjunction with readers on issues in comparative politics or intensive use of international news sources.

The book addresses a series of issues and themes in comparative politics by making comparisons from a limited set of countries. I hope to introduce a number of basic features of politics around the world that are important for students to understand as they become interested and informed citizens: the nature of sovereignty, parliamentary systems, proportional representation, political culture, political party systems, and so on. Such information will assist citizens in understanding the nature of their own country's political system and in finding other ways of remedying problems they may find in that system. Another goal is providing introductions to the conceptual and theoretical issues that are likely to be important as preparation for more advanced courses in comparative politics: democratization, economics and politics, military intervention, and so on. Students will thereby acquire the vocabulary and rudimentary theoretical basis for discussing these issues in depth in future course work in comparative politics.

In order to limit the flood of facts for introductory students, I have drawn most of the comparisons from a set of ten countries: Britain, Canada, China, France, Germany, India, Japan, Mexico, Nigeria, and Russia. These countries are sufficiently prominent that they appear regularly in our newspapers. They are also the countries that are most often used in introductory courses in comparative politics because of their international stature or the particular political features that they illustrate. The countries offer a range of political experience that allows comparisons of issues such as historical impact on contemporary politics, development, change, legitimacy, democratization, and political performance.

I acknowledge first of all my debt to over thirty years of students in courses in comparative politics who have helped me to learn how to make politics abroad interesting and important. Their eagerness to learn about the world and to see how foreign experience can better enable them to understand their own political system is impressive and makes the task of preparing a textbook such as this a daunting challenge. I hope that those who read this book will appreciate how much their predecessors have taught me about comparative politics.

I have also benefited from the suggestions and corrections of those who reviewed this text in manuscript form. For the first edition, Harvey Fireside, Arthur B. Gunlicks, Richard L. Merritt, Andrew Milnor, and Thomas Nichols provided useful guidance. For the second edition, I received helpful suggestions from Kathryn Hochstetler, Colorado State University; Alice B. Hashim, University of Louisville; and Rodger M. Govea, Cleveland State University. The staff at Prentice Hall and Barbara Reilly did an outstanding job of production. Above all, I appreciate the love and patient support of my wife, Carol W. Wilson, on this and many other projects. I dedicate this volume to her.

Frank L. Wilson

PART I

BACKGROUND TO COMPARATIVE POLITICS

The study of the governments and politics of the world is usually referred to as *comparative politics*. The term means little to the beginner but suggests both a subject of study and a means of approaching that study. As you begin this introduction to comparative politics, it is important that you learn the meaning of this and several other basic terms used by political scientists, journalists, and other observers of world affairs.

In the past, those who studied foreign governments tended to focus on the nature and history of the formal institutions of government: constitutions, parliaments, presidents and prime ministers, judicial systems, and bureaucracies. But the world of politics is much richer than simply these formal institutions. Today's politics is inevitably affected by a country's historical legacy and the political attitudes and values that have been formed in the past. A country's government must always struggle with the challenges and resources provided by its geographic location. Politics in all countries is intimately connected with their economies and societies. While these are all issues that might well be studied in history, geography, economics, or sociology courses, they are also important to the student of politics. As a result, we start our survey of the concepts and issues of comparative politics with a quick look at the background factors to politics.

Chapter 1

The Study of Comparative Politics

The first day or so we all pointed to our countries. The third or fourth day we were pointing to our continents. By the fifth day we were aware of only one Earth.

Discovery 5 Space Mission

Many of us listen to compact disc players made in Taiwan; nearly all of us wear athletic shoes from Korea or China; our watches come from Switzerland or the Philippines; and our shirts or blouses are imported from Central America. An effort in the early 1990s to legislate a required disclosure of how much of an automobile was produced in the United States foundered when American auto makers realized that even their cars would bear labels indicating substantial foreign production, with tires from Italy, electrical wire harnesses from Mexico, partial assembly in Canada, and so on. U.S. producers sell passenger aircraft to airlines around the world; new production techniques in France reduce the ability of American farmers to sell their poultry in Europe. Bankers in Paris follow the latest exchange rates of the dollar and Wall Street brokers begin their day by reviewing the overnight performance of the Nikkei average in Tokyo. In a few seconds we can dial around the world with a connection as clear as if we were talking to a friend a few blocks away; in seconds we can send a facsimile of a document we hold in our hands to Australia; e-mail allows us to shop anywhere in the world. More Americans travel abroad than ever before, and similar records are set by foreign tourists enjoying the beaches in Florida or the national parks in Utah. The arguments of German ecologists inspire environmental activists challenging acid rain in the United States; a new political agenda from an American president gives ideas to political leaders in Russia or Britain. A construction strike in Japan slows

U.S. lumber exports; ethnic clashes in Northern Ireland lead to protests by Irish Americans on the streets of Boston.

All this suggests the increasing global interdependence of our economic, social, and political lives. What happens in one part of the world affects other parts hundreds of miles and continents away. Interdependence means that Americans at the start of the twenty-first century cannot ignore what is going on in the world around them. It is important for us to understand the political processes and institutions of countries around the world. We need to be aware of the social and economic forces that bring political changes in far-off settings. Just as it is important for well-informed citizens to know more than the current events and constitutional provisions to understand American politics, it is also important to know the interaction between society and politics, general patterns of political behavior, and theories of how political parties and other political groups work in order to have a more complete understanding of politics abroad. This is the heart of *comparative politics*. It is the search for knowledge about underlying political forces and processes by comparing political phenomena in one country with those of other countries.

WHAT IS COMPARATIVE POLITICS?

Comparative politics involves both a subject of study—foreign countries—and a method of study—comparison. By tradition, most American scholars of comparative politics direct their attention to foreign countries while making at least implicit contrasts with U.S. politics. The focus on foreign political entities allows us to improve our understanding of politics around the world. Often, however, the study of foreign governments tends to focus too much on descriptions of the features and peculiarities of a single government. This may make interesting and sometimes amusing reading, but it misses the richness of insights that come when the comparative methodology is used as well.

The Comparative Method

Physical and biological scientists use laboratories to reproduce experiments in their search for scientific laws and facts. Political scientists generally cannot conduct such laboratory experiments in their search for generalizations about politics. Through comparative studies, they can compensate for the lack of laboratory experiments by comparing political experiences and phenomena in one setting with those in other settings. By looking at similar political phenomena in several contexts, they can discover some elements of the nature of politics. In so doing, they make the world their laboratory in seeking fuller knowledge not just of one country but of the essence of politics that will be useful in understanding many countries.

There are three steps in careful comparative analysis. *First,* political forces, institutions, and practices are examined in several different settings in order to discover similarities and differences. For example, British political parties are quite different in organization and style from parties in the United States. *Next* comes the attempt to explain why similar political phenomena assume varied forms in different countries. It is also often useful to explore why they are similar when the settings are so diverse. We might explain the differences between British and American parties as coming from U.S. federalism and Britain's parliamentary system. *Finally*, good comparative analysis involves efforts to examine the consequences of these political differences. To use the British-American contrast again, the looser organization of American parties leads to a lesser ability of Americans to use party labels as simplifiers when making voting decisions.

Such comparative analysis based on the experiences of several countries rather than several lab experiments may enable us to predict or at least understand disparate patterns of social and economic policies, political activities, and change. It is unusual for social scientists to be able to state firm "laws" in the way that physical and biological scientists propose "laws of science." The variability of human behavior makes it very difficult to enunciate such scientific laws in the social sciences. But comparative analysis does enable political and other social scientists to make many propositions and predictions that have a high probability of being accurate and durable.

This search for continuity and predictability is what distinguishes good comparative politics from journalism. News analysis centers on current political developments and activities. Good journalists can explain why the French Center-Right lost the 1997 election or how Russian president Vladimir Putin won the presidential election in 2000. Political scientists look beyond these current events to explore the broader causes and implications of the decline of social democratic parties or the use of referendums in building public acceptance of a regime. Journalists look at public opinion polls to see the current popularity of a leader or a policy; political scientists focus on polls that probe deeper orientations to the political system and patterns of political behavior. Often in comparative politics there is an implicit, if not explicit, desire to identify political trends that will not only explain the present but also foretell the future.

Approaches to the Study of Comparative Politics

There are a variety of specific methods used by those seeking to make comparative politics as "scientific" as possible. Many comparative political studies devote considerable attention to historical patterns. Historical analysis is based on the notion that developments in the past affect contemporary politics. There have been a number of comparative historical analyses that have been very useful in understanding the divergent courses of political development in different countries.[1] Institutional analysis focuses on descriptions of political parties and groups and on the operation of the legislature, executive, and bureaucracy in the political process. It involves much more than describing the institutions in one country; it compares the structure and organization of these institutions in a variety of settings.[2]

Other approaches to comparative analysis focus on cross-national opinion survey research. This involves efforts to compare political attitudes and values in different countries by asking the same questions of population samples in two or more countries. Such research is costly, and there are often problems in assuring that the same question measures the same attitudes in the different countries. For example, one of the most important cross-national survey research projects, *The Civic Culture*,[3] was faulted for gauging intensity of partisan commitment by a question on how the respondent would react to a son or daughter's marriage to a spouse belonging to another political party. That question worked well in measuring party commitment in the United States, but it measured social class more than partisan intensity in Britain. Of course, the problem of equivalency becomes even more important when the questions must be translated into two or more languages. Cross-national survey research remains nonetheless an important tool for comparative politics.

Still another approach utilizes the growing quantitative data that we have on contemporary countries. Statistics on economic performance, education, health, population size and composition, communications, and many other patterns of social and political interaction are readily available to scholars. In addition, there are many specialized data collections providing figures that are more specifically political: number of parties in countries, legislative activity, duration of governments, electoral results, political revolts, incidents of terrorism, and so on. These statistics can be analyzed in cross-national studies to show correlations between, for example, economic performance and electoral results, level of education and voting turnout, or ethnic diversity and political revolts. The results are often impressive, with seemingly irrefutable statistical results. But there are problems with these cross-national empirical studies. Often the statistics are inaccurate in spite of the best efforts by those who collect them. Other problems emerge as we try to use statistical measures of abstract qualities. For example, electoral turnout may be used as a measure of political alienation–the lower the turnout, the greater the alienation; but turnout is affected by many factors other than political alienation.

For other political scientists, the best way to study comparative politics is through rational choice theory. Based on theories developed by economists for the study of microeconomics, rational choice theory has spread broadly among those studying political science. In this approach, political actors, even institutions such as political parties or legislatures, are assumed to be purposeful in their actions. Further, their acts are assumed to be rational and driven by their own self-interests. By recognizing patterns of rational behavior, the analyst can understand what is happening and even predict the future of politics. A good example of this was Anthony Downs in his *An Economic Theory of Democracy*.[4] He argued that voters tended to group at the center of the political spectrum. As a result, political parties could be expected to move from their ideological "homes" on the left and right to converge at the center where they could best attract the largest number of voters.

Rational choice approaches to comparative politics are much more elaborate now and include detailed deductive models and mathematical equations that purport to indicate the probability that actors will choose one course of action or another.[5] For some, rational choice is the cutting edge of the discipline in its promise to provide generalizations and scientific theories about political life. For others, assumptions of rationality and purposefulness in politics are risky. They also contend that such abstract deductive analysis misses the heart of politics that can only be understood by understanding the history, cultures, and institutions of a state.[6]

By far the most common form of comparative study is the case study. In case studies, scholars look at a specific political feature in a single country, such as a study of political parties in India or select committees in the British House of Commons. The analysis of this one country, however, is informed by explicit or implicit comparisons with other countries. My own scholarly work includes a study of interest groups that was devoted entirely to French politics.[7] It was enriched, however, by contrasts between the French groups and American lobbies, British groups, and German corporatist bodies. The same is true of many other case studies. A study of British parliamentary committees, for example, would be aided by contrasts with the experience of American congressional committees. Such case studies are usually eclectic in approach, utilizing historical and institutional analysis alongside available statistics or opinion survey findings.

As a result of the wide variety of approaches and the prevalence of case studies on single countries and narrow subjects, there is a pressing need to draw broader conclusions from these separate studies. Comparative politics scholars often work at separate tables with inadequate communication among them to make sense of the broader themes and theories of comparative politics.[8] Contemporary comparative politics needs greater attention to finding ways to synthesize and integrate the growing body of knowledge about politics around the world.

An earlier effort to find such an integrative theory of politics was the notion of the *political system*.[9] This involved an application of systems analysis to political science. See Figure 1.1. *Systems* are goal-seeking entities with complex but interrelated parts. They interact with other systems in their environment. The airplane, the human body, a heating system, and a stereo set are examples of systems. *Social systems* are enduring patterns of human relationships such as those found in religious groups, economic networks, and the pattern of international relations among

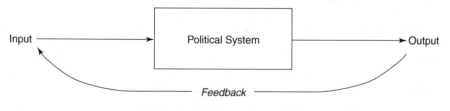

FIGURE 1.1   The Political System

states. Such systems pursue certain goals and perform specific tasks to meet human needs.

In the 1950s and 1960s, several scholars attempted to apply systems analysis to political science and especially to the study of comparative politics. It was a way to escape the rigid historical analyses and descriptions of formal political institutions that had characterized earlier efforts to study governments around the world. In practice, when systems analysis was applied to concrete cases, the theory proved inadequate to explain the reality of the political process. Few political scientists use a formal systems approach now. But many political scientists and political commentators continue to find the notion of a "political system" a useful reminder of the interrelationships between the state and society. It reminds us that politics needs to be understood as part of a broader social system with the state as an entity affected by its environment and affecting in turn other parts of society. It is in this loose, generalized sense that the term *political system* has acquired wide usage by political scientists and general political observers.

AN INTRODUCTION TO THE VOCABULARY OF COMPARATIVE POLITICS

There are few things more sterile than debates over the precise meaning of academic jargon—and this is true for scholars as well as for introductory students. But accepted definitions for our terms are needed for clarity in our analysis. What follows is a brief attempt to define some of the key terms that will be used throughout this and any other book on comparative politics.

Power and Authority

A simple definition of *power* is that it refers to the ability to get someone to do something that they would not otherwise do. This power can be exercised by persuasion, influence, the threat of force, or compulsion. A father exercises power when he sends his child to bed. When power is used, the resulting act must be something that he or she otherwise would not have done. Thus, the child who tells her father to go to sleep as he nods off while reading the newspaper has not exercised power over her father; he would have gone to sleep whether or not she told him to. Power is present in all aspects of life from the home, school, church, or social club to the national government. It is more interesting, though, to study power at the national level because its consequences are more important than in local, school, or business settings.

National politics emerges from the competition among various actors for the power to control the lives of others. The scope of political power is broad in the sense that the actions of many are determined by those few holding power. It is also broad because governments have great effects on their citizens' lives: their economic well-being, health, education, and security from threats at home and abroad. National governmental power is also more intense than other kinds of powers because of its broader capabilities to enforce decisions. Governments of all kinds have the ability to assure their power over their citizens by compulsion: imposing penalties, confinement, and in extreme cases, inflicting injury or death on those who resist them.

The term *power* often connotes firm enforcement by compulsion or the threat of sanctions. You might obey a thug who demands at pistol point that you give over your wallet in a situation of naked power. But many other relationships lead to voluntary compliance with those who exercise power. Thus, you may willingly hand over the contents of your wallet to a government you believe should be obeyed. *Authority* is usually employed to denote power that is viewed as proper and is voluntarily accepted by those who are governed. In many settings, those who are ruled by others accept that rule as rightful and comply freely with the directions of those with power. Instead of the threat of compulsion, authority involves the sense that those who rule do so rightfully and should be obeyed.

Legitimacy

Where people freely accept those who wield power over them, power is *legitimate*. When power is regarded as legitimate, the governed not only acknowledge the power of their governors but the ruled feel that the power wielders ought to have power and they ought to be obeyed. The German sociologist Max Weber identified three sources of political legitimacy: tradition, charisma, and rationality/legality. Sometimes power is accepted as legitimate because of tradition, as when monarchs in the past were viewed as ruling by hereditary divine right, or even today where village elders are viewed as legitimate rulers because they always have ruled in the past.

Some power wielders acquire legitimacy because of their charismatic appeal. Charisma means more than simple popularity or attractiveness; it involves a mystical, even religious link between rulers and ruled. The ruler's power is legitimized by a shared sense of leader and followers that it is the leader's destiny to rule and the followers' duty to obey. There are few pure, modern examples of such leadership, although many leaders benefit from their personal attraction for their followers. The legitimacy of Hitler's rule, especially in his first five years, is often traced to his charismatic appeal to the German people.

The most common contemporary source of legitimacy is in the rational/legal strengths of the leaders. Most contemporary leaders derive legitimacy from the fact that they have acquired power in the ways prescribed by constitutions or other established rules. They maintain their legitimacy—or gain it if they did come to power by abnormal channels—by meeting the expectations of the ruled that their rulers will provide economic well-being and security from domestic and international threats of violence. The power of democratic leaders acquires legitimacy through their electoral victories, which show that they are supported by the most people. Authoritarian leaders are also legitimized by rational/legal means when they come to power through the expected ways and when they meet popular expectations about their performance.

In our times, however, legitimacy is increasingly linked with observance of democratic principles. The trend toward more democracies is driven by recognition of political leaders and grass-roots citizens that democracy is the basis for legitimate government. In the last two decades, democracy has won acceptance in most parts of the world as the ideal form of government. This trend is referred to as a new wave of democratization that in the view of some is sustained by a deep, slowly rising tide of public demand for democracy. Of course, definitions of democracy vary widely according to cultural backgrounds. But the presence of a government accountable to the people and observant of their basic human rights is now seen widely as essential for legitimacy. Autocratic regimes now find themselves under much stronger pressures to move toward democratic standards than was the case fifteen years ago. On the other hand, democracy alone is not a guarantee of legitimacy. Democratic regimes may lose their legitimacy in the eyes of their citizens if they are ineffective, corrupt, or unable to maintain public order.

Legitimacy is a key factor in understanding the survival of regimes. For example, in Nigeria widespread electoral fraud and political corruption in 1983 deprived the leadership of its legitimacy, and the regime was easily toppled by a military coup. The Soviet Union retained its legitimacy as long as it was able to meet its people's expectations of economic growth and order. When the Soviet economy faltered in the 1980s, the regime lost its legitimacy and collapsed. The absence or loss of legitimacy does not always lead to the fall of the regime. Sometimes illegitimate regimes may survive because they use coercion to prevent revolt or because no credible alternative regime is present.

The Sovereign State

Legitimate leaders are viewed as exercising power over the people within specific geographic limits. These political entities are usually referred to as *states*. The state includes a set of political institutions—legislatures, executives, bureaucracies, and armies—as well as those who rule—leaders and powerful groups—which make authoritative and binding decisions over the people in a specific geographic area. The use of the term *state* causes some confusion for Americans who use "state" to refer to the various political subunits making up our federation. But the term *state* used to refer to national governing entities avoids the confusion of alternative words. *Nation* more accurately denotes an ethnic group whether or not it has its own political entity. *Country* refers simply to a geographic area whether or not it has a political entity. *Regime* refers to the set of leaders and institutions holding power in a state.

Traditionally, a state has been regarded as *sovereign* or all-powerful over its people and territory. Its decisions are final and cannot be overruled by other states. This is the heart of the notion of *sovereignty*. In the past, sovereignty was held by monarchs ("sovereigns") who often justified their rule as a hereditary right or even as divinely ordained. Today, there is widespread acceptance, in principle if not always in practice, of *popular sovereignty* as the basis of legitimate political power. Popular sovereignty is the doctrine that those who govern derive their authority from the people. It becomes the basis for democratic rule in that the people choose those who govern.

The notion of state sovereignty is today very much contested by actual developments. In a world that is as tightly interdependent as ours has become, decisions made in one state often have implications for many other states whose people and rulers are unable to affect those decisions. For example, an increase in Japan's interest rates may draw funds from around the world that otherwise might have been invested in Europe or the United States. Renewed Muslim fundamentalism in Nigeria may promote similar religious fervor in surrounding African states. European restrictions on immigration and asylum may affect population movements around the world. Sometimes states make deliberate efforts to affect the domestic policies of other countries by their own decisions. Thus, in the 1990s, the United States hoped to encourage moderation among Chinese leaders by threatening to end trade advantages for the Chinese if China dealt too severely with its political dissidents.

Beyond this interdependency among states, there are a number of supranational bodies that also impinge on the sovereignty of individual states. One of the most important is the fifteen-member European Union (EU), whose member states have voluntarily transferred sovereignty over many domestic and economic decisions to Union institutions. For example, virtually all economic policies in the EU states are now set in Brussels rather than by the separate state governments. The United Nations sometimes asserts its rights to protect people from their own governments. It has done so in recent years by authorizing interventions in Somalia and the former Yugoslavia. Non-governmental organizations (NGOs) such as the World Bank, the International Monetary Fund (IMF), and the World Trade Organization (WTO) exercise influence over domestic policies around the world. For example, concerns that the IMF might refuse to renew its loans led Russia to abandon certain social and economic policies in the late 1990s that Russian leaders and the Russian people had wanted to impose.

Interdependence may be entirely informal. There is no doubt that international economic forces shape public policy with or without the pressures of international NGOs. As an example, advanced industrial democracies have reevaluated many of their labor policies to enable them to be more competitive with less regulated labor markets in the developing world. Of greater significance, informal norms now foster the development of democracy and respect for human rights that make autocratic rule and manipulated elections more difficult in the new century. The norms may be vague and international in their origins but they are effective in limiting the powers and tenure of dictators. This was illustrated in the 2000 elections in Serbia when the autocratic president, Slobodan Milosevic, was forced out of office by mass demonstrations when he tried to distort or ignore his loss in a presidential election.

It is likely that the growing global interdependence will further curtail national sovereignty in the future. Governments are increasingly unable to pursue economic or political policies at home that are inconsistent with international practices. National governments are discovering that their actions at home are limited by the need for harmonizing domestic economic and social policies with the rest of the world. And they are finding their domestic policies influenced by international bodies such as the IMF, the World Bank, regional associations like the European Union, and the United Nations. They even see their actions limited and directed by informal and unorganized but still important forces such as international public opinion or the international business and financial community.

This reduction in the ability of a state to determine its own domestic policies raises problems in maintaining the reality of popular sovereignty. In democratic states, the problem is even more acute since control over decisions that affect people's lives is shifted from elected national officials to unaccountable international bodies or forces. For example, how could Russian citizens protest the IMF's veto of their government's proposed economic policies? Or how could the French, who had elected a socialist government in 1997, react against the international economic climate that forced their government to retreat from its social welfare programs? These problems of popular sovereignty and democratic control are likely to increase as national sovereignty wanes. There is little interest in "democratizing" international bodies such as the IMF or the UN: To do so would only provide the basis for these bodies to increase their impact on internal decisions of the separate states. Of course, it is impossible to "democratize" the informal forces of interdependency, such as the international banking community, that produce the major intrusions into state sovereignty.

Democracy

The term *democracy* has been applied by many countries to their political systems. Nearly every regime claims to be democratic. Even Stalin claimed that what most others saw as a ruthless totalitarian dictatorship was simply an "improved" version of democracy. Democracy is a Western idea, but it has achieved near universal acceptance as the desired form of government. At the beginning of the twenty-first century, democracy has become the most desired form of government in ideal if not always in practice. Peoples everywhere seek democracy.[10] Third world countries with little experience or acceptance of Western values in general strive toward Western concepts of democratic rule. In the aftermath of communism's fall in Eastern Europe and the Soviet Union, some twenty new regimes have emerged, nearly all claiming to be democracies but with a wide range of actual political practices that do not always coincide with what most of us see as democratic.

What is meant by democracy? In its simplest sense, democracy is best defined as self-government as citizens directly or indirectly govern themselves. But that gives us only the general feeling that the people should rule. In modern terms, democracy is nearly always indirect in that the people select representatives to govern on their behalf. That makes the presence of free elections essential to modern, representative democracy. A second requirement of democracy is the guarantee of civil liberties and human rights to all citizens. Third, democracies nearly always have limited governmental powers. These three elements—free elections, respect for human rights, and limited government—are the essence of the Western form of democracy sought in so many different settings as we begin a new century.

Free elections depend upon the existence of several characteristics.[11] First, elections must be held on a regular basis for the key policy-making positions in national politics. Second, the elections must involve alternative candidates representing different political viewpoints. These candidates need to be free to explain their programs to the public through the mass media, open meetings, and individual contacts. Third, voting should be universal for all adults. Balloting should be through secret ballot with the electorate able to make their choices without fear of sanctions. Fourth, the election results must be honestly tabulated and those elected brought into the appropriate offices.

These are ideals, and even states that virtually everyone acknowledges as democratic sometimes fall short of meeting some of these conditions for free elections. For example, in Japan, the bureaucracy often rules behind the façade of a less powerful, popularly elected parliament. Citizens may be deprived of the right to vote by literacy requirements or effectively barred from participating by traditions of exclusion, such as those in the U.S. South until well into the 1970s. Vote fraud is often a problem in regions of otherwise democratic countries such as in France's Corsica, Mexico's rural areas, or—until very recently—the U.S.'s Chicago. To point to these or other faults is not to deny the democratic nature of these countries but to point out the usual gap between democratic ideals and actual practices.

Competitive elections are not enough for modern democracy. Another important feature of democracy is the *rule of law*. The rule of law means that all inhabitants of a country are subject to a set of laws established by common accord. A president, prime minister, or other leader cannot arbitrarily rule without legal authority to do so. The laws are applied equally to rulers and the ruled, to wealthy and poor, and to all ethnic groups within the country. Indeed, the rulers can be brought before the bar of justice to be held accountable under the law for their actions. The rule of law implies the existence of a neutral judiciary with the ability and willingness to enforce the laws equally on all. There, justice, fairness, and the protection of the laws are available to all.

Democracies are committed to the observance of a long list of human rights and civil liberties: free speech; right to assemble; freedom of the press; freedom of religion; freedom from discrimination on the grounds of race, sex, religion, or social class; right to a speedy and fair trial when accused of crimes; and right to vote. These are the basics; they ensure citizens of protection from the government. Increasingly, democracies are adding social rights to the traditional list of political rights. Nearly everywhere, the right to an education is regarded as a fundamental civil right. In many democracies, the right to a job, retirement security, and medical care have become important civil rights. These social rights are designed to protect the citizen from the worst effects of a free market society and to promote political equality in settings of economic inequality.

We often see these rights and freedoms as fixed and absolute. In fact, they evolve over time and change from one culture to another. In the nineteenth century, most people regarded the exclusion of women from the political process as normal and accepted; very few hold that view in the twenty-first century. Today, in many countries people see more progress toward economic equality as the next and natural step in the evolution of democracy. There are real limits to how well political equality can be achieved in societies where there are great economic inequalities; the wealthy usually end up with more possibilities of influencing government than do the poor.[12] There are also important cultural differences about the nature and relative importance of these civil rights. For example, a Southeast Asian friend who immigrated to the United States recently wondered aloud to me about how we could call this "the land of the free." She had just had an unpleasant encounter with her neighbors and eventually the police because she had let her chickens run free in her front yard—a "freedom" she had enjoyed in her homeland.

Nearly all countries have accepted the United Nations Declaration of Human Rights and thereby committed themselves to a long list of civil rights. Even the most autocratic regimes pay lip service to these rights. What sets democracies apart is that there the rights are not only stated, they are enforceable through legal and political means. The proof of the enforceability comes from courts that at least occasionally find against the government and in favor of individuals and groups who feel that their rights have been violated by the state.

Finally, democratic government is limited government. There are limits on both the scope and the means of government. In democracies, not all social, economic, and cultural decisions are made by the political rulers. Democratic governments share the making of important societal decisions with independent bodies such as churches, private enterprises, trade unions, associations and clubs, private and public schools, and mass media. The presence of numerous autonomous entities that divide power over society with government is called *pluralism*. Instead of a single party or government making all decisions in a society, under pluralism decision making is shared by many independent and conflicting groups. Churches set moral values and shape policies on marriage, divorce, and family relations; businesses decide what to produce and establish prices for their goods and services; labor unions bargain with employers over wages, working conditions, and social benefits; professional groups establish their codes of ethics, training requirements, and professional standards; social clubs organize recreational activities. The result is the fragmentation of society into many overlapping and sometimes conflicting entities. This fragmentation makes it difficult for any single group or force to dominate all of society. This sharing of decision making reduces the risk of absolutism by government.

Democratic government is also limited in the powers that it can use. These limits come from the existence of a set of accepted norms and procedures of government. They are accepted as the appropriate procedures and they are followed in practice. Deviation from these standards by government is dissuaded always by fear of public reaction to such abuse of power and ultimately by fear of court action to sanction those who broke with the established norms and procedures. But the presence of a constitution is not evidence that it is observed. Stalin enacted a constitution with democratic procedures and extensive rights, but it remained only a window dressing for his arbitrary and personal dictatorship. The standards and codes need not be in a formal constitution; Britain has a well-functioning democracy even though it does not have a written constitution. What counts is the commitment on the part of those who rule to observe an accepted set of norms and the willingness of the public to force political leaders to observe them when they deviate.

CONCLUSION

In our increasingly small and interdependent world, it is important to improve our knowledge of the politics and society of other states. Comparative political analysis can help us to understand what is happening in other countries. It assists us in finding greater knowledge about politics everywhere. It can also help us better understand the strengths and weaknesses of our own political system. Through the examination of the experience of other states we can often find solutions to the political problems in our own country.

With the rather dry task of defining terms now behind us, we will move forward to more interesting topics of comparative politics. The focus will be on concepts and theories that have emerged from the many studies of separate countries. We will be looking at the broader ideas that seem relevant beyond a single country and may be building blocks to the theories that assist us in making reliable explanations of the past and proposals about the future. Two overarching themes of our times will recur frequently: democratization and globalization. As we have seen, these represent powerful trends as we move into the new century.

NOTES

1. Theda Skocpol, *States and Social Revolutions: A Comparative Analysis of France, Russia, and China* (New York: Cambridge University Press, 1979), Samuel Huntington, *Political Order in Changing Societies* (New Haven, CT: Yale University Press, 1968), and Barrington H. Moore, *The Social Origins of Dictatorship and Democracy: Lord and Peasant in the Making of the Modern World* (Boston: Beacon Press, 1966).

2. See, for example, Arend Lijphart, ed., *Parliamentary Versus Presidential Government* (Oxford, England: Oxford University Press, 1992) and Gerhard Loewenberg and Samuel Patterson, *Comparing Legislatures* (Boston: Little, Brown, 1979).

3.   Gabriel A. Almond and Sidney Verba, *The Civic Culture* (Boston: Little, Brown, 1962).

4.   Anthony Downs, *An Economic Theory of Democracy* (New York: Harper & Row, 1957).

5.   Robert H. Bates, "Comparative Politics and Rational Choice: A Review Essay," *American Political Science Review* 91 (September 1997), 699–704.

6.   For a balanced assessment of the strengths and weaknesses of rational choice, see Michael Coppedge, "Thickening Thin Concepts and Theories: Combining Large N and Small in Comparative Politics," *Comparative Politics* 31 (July 1999): 465–476.

7.   Frank L. Wilson, *Interest-Group Politics in France* (Cambridge, England: Cambridge University Press, 1987).

8.   Gabriel Almond, "Separate Tables: Schools and Sects in Political Science?" *PS* 21 (December 1988): 828–842.

9.   David A. Easton, *A Framework for Political Analysis* (Englewood Cliffs, NJ: Prentice-Hall, 1965).

10.   Samuel P. Huntington, *The Third Wave: Democratization in the Late Twentieth Century* (Norman: University of Oklahoma Press, 1991; Harry S. Rowen, "The Tide Underneath the 'Third Wave,'" in Larry Diamond and Marc F. Plattner, eds., *The Global Resurgence of Democracy,* 2nd ed. (Baltimore: The Johns Hopkins University Press, 1996); and Richard Rose, William Mishler, and Christian Haerpfer, *Democracy and Its Alternatives: Understanding Post-Communist Societies* (Baltimore: The Johns Hopkins University Press, 1998).

11.   Adapted from Robert A. Dahl, *Polyarchy, Participation, and Opposition* (New Haven, CT: Yale University Press, 1971).

12.   Robert A. Dahl, *Democracy and Its Critics* (New Haven, CT: Yale University Press, 1991).

Chapter 2

The Background to Politics

The past is never dead. It's not even past.

William Faulkner

It is unwise to look at the politics of a state in isolation from the many other activities that have shaped the current pattern of politics. There is little doubt that the political system is affected by the past history of a country in different and important ways. Contemporary politics is also very much influenced by the country's geographic setting. We look to the historian for the full details of a country's history and to geographers for the full analysis of topography and climate. But political scientists also must be aware of a country's past and its geographic setting in order to fully understand the nature and issues of a state's contemporary politics.

THE IMPACT OF HISTORY ON POLITICS

In 1993, French news magazines and newspapers devoted many pages to the execution two hundred years earlier of King Louis XVI. Distinguished jurists participated in mock retrials of the king; schoolchildren at all levels probed the reasons for and the excesses of guillotining the king; opinion pollsters asked people across France about their views of the guilt of the king and the appropriateness of his execution; psychologists pontificated on the lasting traumas of regicide; and the opinion pages of local newspapers were filled with the judgments of ordinary citizens who wrestled again with their ancestors' involvement in the execution. Royalist movements held public meetings to promote the restoration of the monarchy. In the meantime, as the anniversary of the king's death approached, Paris police took special measures to control demonstrations at the site of the decapitation. An execution two hundred years earlier had played an important part in subsequent French political development; it had returned to become a contemporary political event.

French memories of the Revolution of 1789 suggest how history may leave behind a legacy of division over what that history means. More than two hundred years later, the French are still divided by the events of their revolution between those who see the Revolution as the beginning of democratization not only in France but in many other countries and those who see the violence and excesses of the Revolution as the source of France's continuing political divisions and instability. Americans do not argue over the desirability of the American Revolution, but public opinion polls in France still show a substantial part of the population who feel that their revolution was a lasting disaster.

Americans are often said to be ahistorical in their ignorance of history and its effects. As a new country with an almost entirely immigrant population and with highly mobile citizens who more often than not move away from the communities where they were born, the United States lacks the historical roots that most other countries feel. Growing up in California, I rarely saw a building that had been constructed before 1945. Over half my great-grandparents had been born in other countries; most of my friends had been born in other states and moved while young to the West. As a result, none of us felt much emotional attachment to our past. In contrast, young people in most other parts of the world grow up in the houses where their parents and even grandparents were born. Most people of the world spend their lives in the towns or villages where their parents and grandparents were raised. They daily walk by sites of historical significance dating back two, three, or more centuries. There is clearly a much closer attachment to historical roots among these peoples than is typical in the United States.

The Political Legacy of History

The impact of history on contemporary politics, however, goes much beyond this emotional link with people's roots. Even ahistorical Americans cannot escape the impact of history on their contemporary politics; the impact is even greater in countries with greater historical awareness. There are a number of legacies history has left behind in every country: a set of political ideas, attitudes, and values; political symbols; political institutions; and durable political and social problems.

To a large extent, the *political culture* of a state is the product of the past. Political scientists refer to political culture as the attitudes, orientations, expectations, and values that people have about politics. In Chapter 4 we will look more closely at the consequences of political culture on politics. Here it is important to note the frequent pattern of inheriting political culture from the past. What people want from government, how they expect their rulers to behave, and how they feel that they should respond to the directions of those who lead are often orientations that they inherit from the past. The experience of their parents affects their orientations;

their own experiences more often than not simply reinforce these inherited patterns based in their country's history.

A few examples will illustrate the historical roots and lasting impact of political culture. Many observers believe that the willingness of the Russian people to accept the rigid authoritarian rule of the communists was founded on traditional patterns of autocratic authority that had established themselves centuries earlier as the Russian state was emerging. Westerners are often critical of the apparent corruption of nepotism in developing countries such as Nigeria. Yet the strong links of Nigerians to the extended family and village throughout history produce behavioral norms that explain the prevalence of favoring family and friends in handing out government jobs and contracts. What outsiders decry as corruption among contemporary Nigerian politicians is simply the reflection of strong extended family and communal values present throughout history. German traditions of obedience to authority explain the general reluctance of Germans to revolt. Lenin once scoffed at the Germans, saying that they could never start a revolution because before they rushed to occupy the railway stations they would first buy the ticket required for admission to the platforms. While this was an exaggeration, it caught a lasting orientation toward authority that has long affected German politics.

History also passes on important political symbols with deep emotional power. These symbols can tie people to the state. For Americans, the Stars and Stripes is a legacy of our revolution and its persistence in battles makes it a powerful symbol. When abroad, the flag waving in the wind at an embassy or consulate unleashes strong feelings of love of country. When demonstrators burn the flag, we sense strong, even irrational anger toward those who would defile our national emblem. In a similar way, the monarch has become a powerful symbol in Britain of the continuity and dignity of the country. The misdeeds of the royal children may titillate the public, but most feel that the Queen represents what is noble, good, and lasting about Britain. In China, Mao Zedong's long leadership made him a national hero and a political symbol. Even after his policies have been repudiated, Mao buttons, tie clasps, pendants, and good luck charms remain popular tokens. Such human and inanimate symbols derived from the past give dignity to the modern state and stir emotions that encourage its citizens to make sacrifices on behalf of the country.

Political institutions often come from the past. The obvious example is Britain, where deliberate efforts have been made to perpetuate past institutions even as they have evolved to accommodate the needs of democracy and a modern industrial state. Parliament can trace its origins back over seven centuries, but it is a very different body than it was a hundred years ago or even fifty years ago. Its functions and powers have changed, but the British carefully preserve the historical weight behind this institution. As an illustration of how these traditions are perpetuated, British members of parliament (MPs) sit in party groups that face each other across a center aisle, just as they have since the Middle Ages when they first met in an old English chapel that had facing pews. Even today there are white lines sewn into the carpeting in front of both banks of benches. The line was originally drawn in medieval times to keep opponents beyond sword distance when debates became intense. Of course, contemporary members of Parliament no longer wear swords, but the careless MP who strays across the line in front of his bench while making a speech will draw catcalls from the opposing bank and a reprimand from the Speaker.

This persistence of the past in contemporary politics is universal. Even when institutions and practices evolve over the years, it is important to know the past in order to fully comprehend the present. The Japanese Diet originated in the nineteenth century and many of its formal procedures date from that authoritarian era. Now it serves as the centerpiece of Japanese democracy. Often, however, inherited institutions persist with few alterations even when there have been dramatic changes in politics. In much of Nigeria, for example, there is a system of Islamic law and traditional Islamic courts that date back several centuries. Contemporary systems of local-level clientele politics in Mexico are unchanged from what they were 150 years ago. Many former colonial powers have inherited important political institutions such as the bureaucracy, parliamentary structure, or military from their colonial masters. India is a good example of a state with many institutions that were set in place during the colonial era, including a vast bureaucracy that has persisted with few changes in the institutions and practices left behind by imperial rulers over fifty years ago.

Finally, history bequeaths unsolved problems from the past. Divisive issues often take decades to resolve, and some issues are so difficult that they are not resolved but passed on for future generations to muddle through. For example, the failure of American political leaders after the Civil War to assure equal treatment for African Americans created a legacy of racial antagonism that contemporary leaders are still struggling to overcome. The current struggles between Irish Catholics and Protestant loyalists in Britain's Northern Ireland reflect battles begun three centuries ago when settlers from England and Scotland established themselves in Northern Ireland at the same time that other Britons were establishing plantations in Virginia and the Carolinas. Each summer in Northern Ireland the "marching season" brings both Catholics and Protestants into the streets to commemorate 300-year-old battles and martyrs and to reopen old wounds for contemporary politicians to heal. Much of the contemporary conflict in the Balkans comes from centuries-old animosities that are perpetuated by local folklore and history.

It is not only the issues that carry over but often the approaches to them as well. Many of a state's challenges remain constant over the years. As a result, current leaders can see how their predecessors have dealt with the issue in the past. Contemporary politicians sometimes inherit policies and precedents that are difficult to change. Or they can examine the successes and failures of previous approaches to long-lasting problems in order to assist them in shaping their new policies. A good example of this comes from our American views of the world. As America tries to redefine its role in the post-cold war world, we invoke earlier experiences with isolationist and interventionist approaches to assist in shaping policies for the twenty-first century.

History usually provides a mixture of positive and negative legacies to contemporary politicians, some that strengthen the contemporary state and others that weaken it. Because of this mix, contemporary politics is not determined by the past. Skilled leaders can build on the positive historical features and try to ignore or overcome the negative ones.

Shaping History: A Means of Contemporary Politics

In reviewing these historical influences on contemporary politics it is important to remember that history is rarely objective. It can be manipulated by skilled politicians as they seek to shape the collective memory of the past to serve their own interests. What counts for contemporary politics is less what actually happened in the past than what is believed to have happened. Most Americans, for example, regard the War of 1812 as a battle for freedom of the seas forced on their ancestors by the seizure of American sailors for service on British warships. An impartial historian might conclude that the war was more accurately described as an American attack on Canada motivated by those on the frontier who wanted more land. The latter, more accurate view of the War of 1812, however, has little effect on the popular version of the war—a war that provided the new country with the very powerful symbols of a national flag and the national anthem. What counts is not history in the abstract but history as it is perceived.

In the Soviet Union under Joseph Stalin, textbooks, histories, and encyclopedias were rewritten to provide Stalin's view of the "correct" interpretation of the past. Russians who grew up during the 1930s recount how they often were told to cut out the pictures of individuals who had fallen from the graces of Stalin and obliterate the text on these individuals to ensure that future students would not even know about their existence. More recently, as the spirit of *glasnost* (openness) spread at the end of the 1980s, Mikhail Gorbachev urged libraries and bookstores to stop circulating existing histories. These books, he and other reformers felt, contained inaccurate views of the past. But in doing so, Gorbachev was doing as his predecessors had done: providing histories to support their views of the past. Thus, history becomes not simply a source of influences on the present from the past but also the reflection of contemporary politics.

In effect, any country's history offers many different legacies. Usually, the overall heritage is so diverse that it would be of little use in looking to history to understand contemporary political events. History alone does not determine politics, but it clearly has important effects on the present day that cannot be ignored.

Historical Approaches to the Study of Comparative Politics

Among the most fruitful approaches to understanding the evolution of political history have been those efforts to use the history of one country to explain changes occurring elsewhere. Some interesting and important studies have sought to understand the modernization process. They draw on the experience of those countries that have achieved modern and stable political systems in the hope of identifying keys to the development of newer countries. However, there is little agreement on what those key factors are. The underlying assumption is that there is a linear process toward political development and that by looking at those farthest along this line of development we can find the processes and changes less developed states must make to move toward greater development.

One of the most influential of these historical analyses is that of Samuel P. Huntington.[1] Drawing on the experience of political development in Western Europe and the United States, Huntington placed emphasis on the political dimensions of development. He noted that economic and social modernization often created tensions that hindered the achievement of political order and stability. Huntington contended that orderly change was most likely when states were able to develop strong political institutions before experiencing social and economic modernization. Among the most important of the political institutions were political parties. Huntington found less importance in whether there were one or several parties than he found in the fact that there was a political party in place to encourage and channel political participation as social change brought more actors onto the political stage. Where those political institutions were in place, the tensions of social change could be better managed and directed to durable modernization.

Another influential approach to understanding political development is offered by the dependency school.[2] Dependency theory contends that imperial rule by West European powers since the sixteenth century has established durable patterns of dependency for many once powerful and wealthy cultures. Historical dependency continues into the present with neoimperialist economic relations that benefit powerful economic interests in dominant states and the national elites in both dependent and core states. This pattern of international economic relations determines internal politics for the dependent states.

Dependency theory divides the world into the core economic areas—the industrialized, free enterprise countries of Western Europe and North America—and the periphery—or countries geographically or economically isolated from economic influence. Even though these peripheral countries have formal autonomy and independence, their economic dependence on the core countries leaves them in a condition of de facto dependency or colonialism. States on the periphery of the world economy—and this includes all third world or developing states—are dependent on the world economy and especially on the core economic powers for their economic well-being and political futures. International economic forces shape domestic politics in dependent countries and deprive them of political autonomy. As a result, third world governments lack the strength and autonomy needed to control their own resources for their own drives to economic and political modernity.

A final example of the use of comparative history to understand current developmental trends is the extensive literature on revolution and change. Theda Skocpol[3] has analyzed revolutions in France, Russia, and China to understand why political change assumed a revolutionary character. She finds in each case that the revolutions were not simply extreme forms of individual or collective behavior but distinctive conjunctures of social and historical structures and processes. In France, for example, Skocpol points to the simultaneous collapse of the central administration, peasant uprisings, and the political movement of nationalist radicals in the middle class. By comparing the causes and courses of revolution in one country with similar developments in other countries, comparative historians seek to better understand past events and perhaps to foresee similar events as they unfold in the future. The dynamics of one revolution help in understanding others and perhaps in predicting future revolts.

Another important issue in recent years has been the attempt to find historical sources of democracy. With many countries now seeking to build democracy, there is great interest in identifying those factors most likely to produce stable and effective democracies. Traditionally, scholars interested in this have looked at the record of Western Europe and North America and found important historical anchors to successful democracy. However, few countries can remake their histories to resemble U.S. or British experience to assist in constructing democracy. Happily, there is more and more evidence that a variety of historical backgrounds can be compatible with establishing democracy. Democracy can be found in some most unlikely settings: There are durable democracies in Japan and Germany, where democracy was imposed by foreign occupation forces in the wake of military defeats, and democracy thrives in India and Costa Rica in spite of the historical absence of economic modernization. This does not mean that all efforts at democratization will succeed, but it does suggest that there are a variety of historical paths to successful democracy.

These are only a few of many attempts to use history to understand contemporary politics. We will return to some of them in later chapters as we explore issues of political change and democratization. Here they are used to illustrate not only the importance of the endeavor to link past history with today's politics but also its limitations. Each scholar finds different—and even conflicting—themes and theories in his or her search through history. There is no doubt that history is important in understanding contemporary politics, but it is often more useful in identifying historical roots of modern changes only after the changes have occurred.

POLITICAL CULTURE

I have noted that all countries are affected by the political cultures they have received from the past. The political culture refers to the attitudes, values, and orientations that people have about politics.[4] Because these underlying values and orientations affect how people behave in their political actions, they are important to understand. It is widely accepted that a country's political culture is an important determinant of how well the political system functions.

Among the most important dimensions of political culture is the people's general orientation toward political power: Are power wielders to be feared or welcomed? How should they react to decisions made by the regime? In some states, Britain for example, people have a deferential attitude toward political leaders and regard it as important to comply voluntarily with government policies. In other countries, in France for example, people have a natural suspicion of those who wield political power and see it as their civic duty to challenge them periodically. These attitudes are reflected in the differing political experiences in these two countries. Britain has seen gradual evolution in its political development, while France is still vulnerable to revolt. In still other countries, such as Mexico or Nigeria, people living in remote regions are barely aware of the national political entity and simply ignore its existence.

Political culture also includes how proud individuals are of their country and its politics. Satisfaction with the quality of life and the political system are important indicators of general orientations and support for the regime. Table 2.1 provides information on public attitudes toward the way democracy works in several West European democracies. Note that those indicating high or fair satisfaction with democracy are quite high and they are higher at the end of the 1990s than in earlier years of that decade. The low levels of satisfaction with democracy in Italy reflect both the general tendency of Italians to criticize their government and the crisis in public confidence provoked by scandals, failed political reform, and the collapse of the Italian party system. In countries that are still undergoing democratization, the level of trust in democracy is generally lower. For example, in 1994 only 36 percent of Russians gave positive marks to the way government was working then under democracy compared to 51 percent who thought it was working well in the past under the former communist regime.[5]

The evidence of general public satisfaction with the operation of democracy in these countries and others is, however, paralleled by polls that show growing levels of public mistrust in politicians and political institutions.[6] Citizens of most advanced democracies indicate growing skepticism about the integrity, competence, and effectiveness of those who lead them and even in the institutions—such

TABLE 2.1   Satisfaction with Democracy in Britain, France, Germany, and Italy in 1993 and 1999

Question: "On the whole, are you very satisfied, fairly satisfied, not very satisfied, or not at all satisfied at the way democracy works in your country?"

	Britain		France		Germany		Italy	
	1993	1999	1993	1999	1993	1999	1993	1999
Very satisfied	7%	12%	3%	7%	6%	15%	1%	3%
Fairly satisfied	42	52	38	52	45	52	11	32
Not very satisfied	31	18	36	27	36	24	39	41
Not at all satisfied	17	7	20	10	10	6	49	23
No reply	5	11	3	4	3	4	1	2

Source: Eurobarometer: 39 (1993) and 51 (1999).

as legislatures, bureaucracies, and political parties—that govern them. This trend has multiple sources, including the decline in general levels of social trust, better and more critical media coverage of politicians, heightened public expectations about the conduct of their leaders, limits on governments' abilities to shape policy because of internationalization, and general doubts about the effectiveness of government action in meeting social needs. The trend toward greater mistrust of government focuses more on individuals and institutions than on the principle of democratic governance. People support democracy even as they are critical of those people and institutions that make democratic government.

These are only a few of the many dimensions of political culture. We usually expect that there is a linkage between a people's underlying attitude toward politics and the kinds of political action, if any, that they engage in. Someone who does not believe participation has any political effect is unlikely to make the effort to be involved in politics. Those who believe that government decisions should be obeyed are likely to comply with laws even when they disagree with a specific policy.

Political Culture and Political Stability

Political stability is measured by the durability of a particular constitutional order or regime, the presence or absence of turmoil and violence, and how long key political leaders stay in office. Countries are unstable if they constantly change entire governmental systems, if they experience great political turmoil, or if the leadership changes very frequently. They are stable if the regime is durable, violence and turmoil are limited, and leaders stay in office for several years. Most see political stability as desirable and as a measure of the performance of a political system.

Because of the importance of underlying attitudes and values, political culture is particularly important in explaining why some countries are more stable than others. Thus, analysts are likely to explain the more turbulent course of democracy and the many regime changes in France by pointing to the French distrust of political authority. Nigeria's troubles with making democracy work are attributed to communal values that seem to promote what others see as corruption. The survival of communism in China is explained at least in part by Chinese traditions of "kowtowing" to authority.

Most agree that political culture is closely linked to political stability. But it has limited value in explaining much about the dynamics of political stability. For example, most Sovietologists found strong cultural roots for the acquiescence of Russians to authoritarian power. This view of Russian political culture seemed useful in explaining the durability of the communist government. But it contributed to the failure of most observers to recognize the impending fall of Soviet communism in the late 1980s. Few believed that postwar Germany had the kind of political culture needed to support democracy, but over the years the German political culture was remade into one that sustains democracy.[7] Because of the difficulty of using political culture to understand these dynamics, culture cannot be used alone to explain political stability.

Furthermore, reliable descriptions of a country's political culture are very elusive. While we can readily accept the notion that underlying attitudes are important in explaining a political system, it is much more difficult to define what those attitudes are. The most "scientific" way to identify dimensions of a country's political culture is to use survey research of public opinion. But while public opinion polls are good for measuring opinions on specific issues and personalities, they are not very useful in identifying deep-seated values. For example, the polls cited in Table 2.1 reflect the respondents' evaluations of specific leaders and policies at a given point in time more than they measure durable and underlying attitudes about democracy.

As a result of the difficulty in precisely identifying a country's culture, political culture descriptions are often simply the impressions of close observers of a country's history and contemporary politics. Such subjective descriptions are only as good as the observer, and even the best of them fall victim to misperceptions of underlying attitudes and orientations. The danger of such subjective descriptions is that the study of political culture is reduced to simplified caricatures of diverse peoples: heel-clicking, obedient Germans; riotous French; deferential Britons; Confucian Chinese; hard-working Japanese; macho Mexicans; and so on. Such stereotypes are unreliable and misleading indicators of a country's political culture or anything else other than the observer's own biases.

In sum, it is difficult to identify and describe a country's political culture and shifts that take place, sometimes rather quickly, in what seem to be durable orientations and values. In addition, the correlation between political attitudes and actual political behavior is not automatic. The fact that an individual has democratic values does not mean that he or she will always behave in a democratic manner. Consequently, those interested in understanding political stability are better off avoiding explanations of stability based on political culture.

The Acquisition of Political Values

Political attitudes are not innate in human behavior; they are learned. The process of developing political values, orientations, and values is known as *political socialization*. Under normal circumstances, political socialization passes values and orientations from one generation to the next. Much of this is accomplished during adolescence. However, political socialization is an ongoing process that persists throughout life as the individual's attitudes change to conform to his or her political experiences.

The individual's first exposure to political stimuli is through the family. Basic political values, and sometimes party preferences, are developed unconsciously in the home and retained by many people throughout their lives. The following description of the socialization of French children illustrates the process:

> Growing up, a child learns with what symbols his family identifies itself. Beyond the limits of the family he becomes aware of groups of people, of *cercles* with which he

and his family are either associated or not. He recognizes the associations through many symbols, some small, some important, some obvious, some hidden from all but the initiate.[8]

The school is another agent of political socialization. In most countries, the schools are places where conscious efforts are made to instill in young people the political values and orientations deemed important for the political system. History and civics courses are usually mandatory, and the state often stipulates which textbooks can be used. The classroom may be used to train young people for the kinds of citizenship roles desired by the state. In the United States, for example, the daily flag ceremonies in public schools instill national pride and loyalty; election of class officers teaches democratic choice of leaders. In some countries, military drills prepare students for service in the armed forces. In other countries, community service projects help inculcate the ideal of voluntary civic service.

Another important agent of socialization is the peer group. As a result of the basic urge to conform, those who surround the individual at school or at work help shape his or her political orientations. People usually seek to cooperate with peers and to bring their attitudes into line with others. There are still other important agents of socialization: mass media; social groups such as clubs, churches, or unions; and the person's own political experience.

With so many diverse sources of political socialization, people usually receive different and conflicting values that they must sort out for themselves. For example, children in developing countries often learn traditional values (service to the family and loyalty to the kinship or ethnic group) at home and secular values (civic responsibility and loyalty to country) at school. The choice any individual makes among the various versions cannot be predetermined.

Culture Shifts

Most underlying political values are durable and last through an individual's entire life and are even passed on to the future through the socialization processes. However, there are cases where the political culture has changed in important ways in relatively short periods of time. Some of these culture changes have occurred as a result of deliberate efforts to reshape a political culture that is not deemed to be supportive of the kind of political system desired by the political elite. Other shifts in political culture occur spontaneously as individuals react to sudden or even gradual changes in their life conditions and political experiences without anyone trying to change their political views.

A good example of the deliberate efforts to change the political culture can be seen in China after the Communist Revolution. The leadership undertook a major effort to build political values that would support their regime. The schools were directed to inculcate communist values among the young. Massive reeducation programs utilizing the mass media and person-to-person contacts were designed to purge the adults of traditional political attitudes and to replace them with attitudes in keeping with the new social and political order. The Chinese did not shrink from using force and sought to achieve party control over all agents of socialization. The result was the rapid appearance of a new political culture that, at least outwardly, reflected the values approved by the regime.

Other cultural shifts can occur unconsciously. Some see such a shift in political culture taking place in today's industrial democracies.[9] Long-term prosperity and the growing sense of security from foreign wars allow most individuals in Western Europe and North America to attach lower priority to government attention to material necessities and defense. Citizens are shifting their focus from "materialist" concerns with protection and basic needs to newer "postmaterialist" concerns about promoting self-expression and equality, protecting and enhancing the environment, and achieving their aesthetic potential. Younger people, growing up during the postwar economic boom and without a fear of war, are especially prone to express these new postmaterial political values. No one is orchestrating this culture shift, but it is likely to have important political consequences. Many observers believe that the new values will bring different priorities to government in much of Western Europe in the coming years as these postmaterial younger generations reach the age where they dominate politics.

GEOGRAPHY

A century ago, *geopolitics* emerged as an important field of study for geographers and political scientists. Those interested in geopolitics asserted that geographic features such as topography, natural resources, climate, and human settlement patterns virtually determined a country's political situation with respect to other states and even internally. Geography also imposed a narrow range of options on domestic politics. A couple of examples will illustrate how geopoliticians saw politics as determined by geography.

The broad, flat plain that spreads across northern Europe from Russia through Germany and the Low Countries to the west coast of France became an "invasion alley" through which armies could move easily. As a result there was near continuous warfare through this plain for over a millennium. By facilitating warfare, the north European plain brought political instability as towns and regions were fought over and annexed by rival armies. This topographical feature thus promoted a sense of insecurity in the peoples of the region that brought about the tolerance of strong, authoritarian leaders who seemed most able to protect people from invasion and destruction.

In the Nile delta and in many parts of China, the climate was often arid and the population large. Agriculture to produce the food for these populations depended upon the development of large and complex irrigation systems. The building, maintenance, and use of these irrigation systems in turn required strong, central governments. As a result, these areas saw the emergence of powerful and despotic governments while other parts of the world still were governed loosely by local satraps, religious leaders, and village elders.[10] Elsewhere in the world, the impact of government on people's lives was still small, but in these systems based on irrigation needs, control of the vital resource of water gave government extraordinary power over people's daily lives. Some see the origins of our modern totalitarian states in these "oriental despotisms."

During the first third of the twentieth century, geopolitics focused on the geography of international politics. Various schools of geopoliticians sought to identify key mountain passes, vital ocean straits, and other strategic geographic positions needed for world conquest. Their thought, often distorted by those who used it, inspired the wartime strategies of Nazi Germany and Japan. As a consequence, geopolitics fell out of intellectual favor after the Second World War. But we do not have to accept the determinism and the strategic viewpoints of prewar geopolitics to see the very real impact that geography can have on the domestic politics of nearly all states.

One of the best examples is Britain. The fact that it is an island shielded its political regime from the destabilizing effects of foreign invasion for nearly a thousand years. Unlike its neighbors sitting in the continent's "invasion alley," British regimes were not toppled as a result of military defeats and its border remained unchallenged. Its island status brought concentration on a strong navy for its military, and this meant that there was rarely a large ground army to threaten intervention in domestic politics. Although the British Isles are small, they provided the resources needed for early industrialization: water for power, coal, iron ore.

Other examples of the importance of geography can be seen in Japan and Nigeria. Like Britain, Japan was sheltered by its island status from invasion and from the political ideas that swept through other countries. Unlike Britain, however, Japan lacked most of the resources needed for economic development and had to seek them through aggression. In Nigeria, dense tropical forests cut off the coastal regions from the influence of Islam that after 700 A.D. brought change and civilization to what is now northern Nigeria. Later, the same disease-plagued jungles blocked the influence of western colonizers and religions that brought modern education and institutions to southern Nigeria after 1860.

While acknowledging geographic effects on politics, it must be stressed that geography is only one of many factors at work in shaping contemporary politics. As an example, I noted that Britain's island status helps explain the absence of a strong political role for the military. However, the island status of Japan has not prevented the development of a centuries-old tradition of militarism in that country. Geography influences but does not determine politics.

CONCLUSION

This chapter has examined briefly some of the important historical and geographic background to politics and noted the several ways in which past events and geography affect today's politics. There are other important background factors that also affect politics. Of particular importance are the economic and social systems. We turn now to a consideration of these influences.

NOTES

1. Samuel P. Huntington, *Political Order in Changing Societies* (New Haven, CT: Yale University Press, 1968).

2. See Immanuel Wallerstein, *The Modern World System I: Capitalist Agriculture and the Origins of the World Economy in the 16th Century* (New York: Academic Press, 1974), *The Modern World System II: Mercantilism and the Consolidation of the European World Economy, 1600–1750* (New York: Academic Press, 1980), and Robert A. Packenham, *The Dependency Movement* (Cambridge, MA: Harvard University Press, 1992). For a contrasting view, also embedded in historical analysis, see David S. Landes, *The Wealth and Poverty of Nations: Why Some Are So Rich and Some So Poor* (New York: Norton, 1999).

3. Theda Skocpol, *States and Social Revolutions* (New York: Cambridge University Press, 1979).

4. Oliver H. Woshinsky, *Culture and Politics: An Introduction to Mass and Elite Political Behavior* (Englewood Cliffs, NJ: Prentice-Hall, 1995).

5. Stephen White, Richard Rose, and Ian McAllister, *How Russia Votes* (Chatham, NJ: Chatham House, 1997), p. 45.

6. Pippa Norris, ed., *Critical Citizens: Global Support for Democratic Governance* (Oxford, England: Oxford University Press, 1999), and Susan J. Pharr, Robert D. Putnam, and Russell J. Dalton, "Trouble in the Advanced Democracies: A Quarter-Century of Declining Confidence?" *Journal of Democracy* 11 (April 2000): 5–25.

7. Kendall Baker, Russell J. Dalton, and Kai Hidebrandt, *Germany Transformed: Political Culture and the New Politics* (Cambridge, MA: Harvard University Press, 1981), and David Conradt, "Changing German Political Culture," in Gabriel A. Almond and Sidney Verba, eds., *The Civic Culture Revisited* (Boston: Little, Brown, 1980).

8. Lawrence Wylie, "Social Change at the Grass Roots," in Stanley Hoffmann et al., *In Search of France* (New York: Harper & Row, 1963), p. 231.

9. Ronald Inglehart, *The Silent Revolution* (Princeton, NJ: Princeton University Press, 1977), and Ronald Inglehart, *Culture Shift in Advanced Industrial Society* (Princeton, NJ: Princeton University Press, 1991). See also Russell J. Dalton, *Citizen Politics: Public Opinion and Political Parties in Advanced Industrialized Democracies*, 2nd ed. (Chatham, NJ: Chatham, 1996), pp. 89–110.

10. Karl A. Wittfogel, *Oriental Despotism: A Comparative Study of Total Power* (New Haven, CT: Yale University Press, 1957).

Chapter 3

❖❖❖❖❖❖❖❖❖❖❖❖❖

Society and Politics

How comfortable would it be to have islands of prosperity in a sea of poverty?[1]

A recent study estimated that the gap in the per capita income between the richest of the Western industrialized countries and the poorest developing countries was about 400 to 1—a German, for example, had a per capita income four hundred times that of a Mozambiquean. That is a startling gap between wealthy and poor countries. Even more startling is the fact that this gap is of relative recent origins. Around 1750, the gap between the income of the poorest and the wealthiest was about 5 to 1; the gap between average income in Europe compared to China or India was about 1.5 or 2.0 to 1.[2] There are similar gaps between the wealthy and the poor *within* countries, and this inequality too has widened historically, particularly in recent years. Such huge disparities pose problems for international relations and for domestic politics in wealthy and poor states.

This is only one of many indicators of the importance of understanding a country's economy and social composition in order to grasp the reality of its politics. This chapter focuses first on the economic dimensions of politics and then turns to an examination of the impact of society on politics.

ECONOMIC INFLUENCES ON POLITICS

The relationship between the economy and the state has always been intimate and complex. In traditional societies, economic power was often combined with political and religious powers in the hands of the tribal chieftains or village elders. As societies modernized, the various social powers separated into distinct political authorities, economic actors, and religious leaders. However, the link between politics and economics has remained strong. Economic structures and performance affect the state, and the state shapes the economy through its policies. *Political economy* refers to this complex interrelationship. In the past two decades, the political economy of individual states and of relations among states has attracted great attention from political and social scientists.

At the start of the twenty-first century, people everywhere expect their governments to provide them with economic security and growth. This is true whether their economies are free enterprise, capitalist ones with minimal role for government intervention, or state-directed economies. The regime's responsibility goes beyond achieving economic success. Even in societies where the economies are based on free enterprise, citizens expect the state to moderate the effects of economic cycles of recession and boom, and to provide social programs to protect those who are disadvantaged by the free play of market economics.

The economic accountability of the state in the eyes of its citizens remains strong even as globalization reduces the ability of any single state, even a large and economically powerful one, to determine its own fate. More often than not, national political leaders are forced to contend with international economic trends that are beyond their control and may force them into policies that they oppose on ideological or domestic political grounds. For example, as Japan's economy suffered in the 1990s due to increasingly intense competition from countries with low labor costs, Japanese political and business leaders were forced to abandon Japan's tradition of ensuring lifetime employment to many employees.

While a state's success in providing economic growth is not alone sufficient to keep the incumbent leaders or regime in power, economic failure nearly always contributes to the weakening of the political regime's legitimacy. In democratic countries, economic problems often lead voters to oust the governing party. As an example, the crushing defeat of the French Center-Right government in the 1997 legislative elections was due in large part to the failure of that government to fulfill its earlier campaign promises to reduce unemployment and economic stagnation. One scholar has even developed a model that predicts the outcome of French national elections based on growth, unemployment, inflation, and other economic indicators.[3] His model also works well in other Western industrial democracies.[4] In nondemocratic countries, economic malaise can bring the toppling of the regime. The fall of the Soviet Union in 1990, for example, is closely linked with that country's economic collapse.

Politics and Types of Economic Systems

There are two basic and competing notions of how to organize the relationship between the economy and the state. Under *capitalism* or a free enterprise system, the economy is based on the private ownership of all property, industry, and commerce. Economic decisions on what to produce, how much to make, the sales price, and the cost of labor are made virtually automatically by the interplay of supply and demand for goods and services. Government's role is minimal. It should only provide such essentials as a currency and ensure fair play. Decisions on how much and where to invest capital are made privately by individuals holding these monetary resources. Economic equality is not seen as a useful goal; rather the free competition of economic actors will result in a natural disparity of wealth.

Socialism is an economy based on the collective ownership of nearly all property and means of production. The collectivity owning and controlling property is usually the state. Under socialism, the state is the primary economic actor. Its task is to identify the community's economic objectives and to manipulate prices, wages, resource allocation, and investment in order to achieve these objectives. This usually involves the development by the government of short- and long-term economic plans to guide the economy. Socialism is also seen as offering the best way to achieve economic equality among members of the society.

In reality, few states have achieved either of these pure forms of economic systems. Most communist states were based on government ownership of the means of production and centralized planning, but there were often important economic activities left in the hands of individuals. For example, well before the fall of communism, the majority of fresh meat and vegetables sold in most of the Soviet Union came from the "private plots" of collective farmers. Economic plans were often visionary rather than realistic. And the state's economic power that was designed to promote economic equality was usurped and used for its own advantage by a narrow political elite.

Most Western industrial countries come close to the capitalist model, but the state is usually a far more important economic actor than is envisioned by doctrinaire capitalism. Indeed, many states developed *mixed economies* from 1945 to 1980, based in part on privately owned enterprises and in part on state-owned enterprises. These countries had extensive *public sectors* of economic enterprises owned and operated by the state as well as the predominant *private sector* of the economy. The state-owned enterprises were often in key economic activities such as banks, railroads, airlines, public utilities, and coal mining. In addition, nearly all major industrial countries developed vast systems of public welfare to assist those disadvantaged by the free play of capitalism: pensions, health care, unemployment and disability insurance, job training programs, child labor laws, and job health and safety laws.

In mixed systems, the state played an active role in the economy. Much government economic action has been based on the thought of John Maynard Keynes, a British economist who argued that governments could lessen the impact of economic cycles by intervening in the economy. *Keynesianism* called for government intervention both in bad and good times. When the economy faltered, Keynes contended, government should have spent more and lowered taxes even if it meant budgetary deficits in order to prod the economy. When good times came, government should have reduced its spending and raised taxes to cool inflationary tendencies and to pay off the deficits incurred in bad times.

There are other forms of intervention used in the mixed economies. In some cases, the state intervenes to impose wage and price controls, limits on foreign exchange, tariffs on imports, and other trade limitations. Finally, states help their companies to be competitive with foreign firms by sponsoring research and development. Many primarily free enterprise countries, notably Japan and France, have developed "industrial policies." These industrial policies foster technological research and investment in enterprises deemed to be important for future economic competition. In short, even in free enterprise countries, the state is an important economic actor. Its policies affect the growth and nature of the economy. The success of political leaders is based to a large degree on their skillful management of the economy.

The developing countries are another setting where mixed economies have been predominant. Large portions of the economy have come under the control of the state. This is in part due to the socialist convictions of early leaders in these countries as they began the task of building their countries' economies. But it is also due to the absence of private capital and individual entrepreneurs in most third world countries. Many of these countries emerged from colonialism impoverished; very few people had enough capital to begin to build modern economies through private investment and enterprise. Most leaders in these countries did not want excessive foreign investment, which they rightly saw as a new way of creating colonial dependency. As a result, the state became the major actor in the efforts to rapidly develop the economies of third world countries.

From the Postwar Consensus to a Neoliberal Agenda

From 1945 through the mid-1980s, a "postwar consensus" favoring a mixed economy and a social welfare state dominated politics in most industrial countries. That consensus had support from business, trade union, and political leaders as well as popular majorities in most industrialized economies. It reflected an informal and sometimes a formal agreement that while the economy should remain largely in private ownership, the state should actively intervene in the economy to promote growth, promote full employment, and control inflation to the extent that was possible without producing unemployment. Most of these industrial democracies established mixed economies, engaged in some forms of state-guided economic planning, and adhered to Keynesian economic policies.

They also accepted the notion that the state should provide a "safety net" for those disadvantaged by the vagaries of economic cycles. In addition to programs designed to help the poor and unemployed, democratic governments in Europe and beyond introduced broad social welfare programs for all such as subsidized housing and transportation, full medical benefits, aid to the disadvantaged, pensions and retirement benefits for all, and a host of other programs. In Britain, people talked about the government's care for its citizens as extending "from the cradle to the grave" or "from the womb to the tomb." The state's role in the economy steadily grew. (See Table 3.1.) The United States, with strong traditions of free enterprise

TABLE 3.1   Government Spending as a Percentage of Gross Domestic Product (GDP)

Country	1870	1920	1937	1960	1980	1990	1999
Britain	9.4%	26.2%	30.0%	32.2%	43.0%	39.9%	39.3%
Canada	n.a.	13.3	18.6	28.6	38.8	46.0	40.2
France	12.6	27.6	29.0	34.6	46.1	49.8 ·	52.2
Germany	10.0	25.0	42.4	32.4	47.9	45.1	45.6
Italy	11.9	22.5	24.5	30.1	41.9	53.2	48.3
Japan	8.3	14.8	25.4	17.5	32.0	31.7	38.1
United States	3.9	7.0	8.6	27.0	31.8	33.3	30.1

Source: IMF figures, reported in "Survey: The World Economy," *The Economist,* 20 September 1997, p. 8. The 1999 figures are from *OECD Economic Outlook,* No. 67 (2000), Paris: Organization for Economic Cooperation and Development.

and a fear of big government, was among the few industrial democracies to fail to participate in most of the programs that came out of the postwar consensus.

By the 1980s, most industrialized democracies had begun to retreat from this postwar consensus. High costs, public deficits, stagnant economies, and the need for more flexible, market-responsive economic policies to deal with growing international trade competition led these countries to reexamine their old policies. There are several factors that account for this change in priorities. First, during the 1970s many highly developed economies developed simultaneous high inflation, economic stagnation, and high unemployment. These problems did not respond to the usual government economic manipulations. Furthermore, Keynesianism faltered because few elected politicians had the courage needed to raise taxes and curtail government spending in inflationary periods as Keynes had urged. As a result, large national debts accumulated with little effort to reduce them by taxes or spending cuts.

At the same time, there was a renaissance of neoliberal economic thought stressing the virtues of unhampered, free enterprise.[5] While in the United States we usually associate "liberalism" with big government, the term *liberalism* in other countries refers instead to the nineteenth-century notions of free enterprise and parliamentary democracy. In the United States, liberal means to be on the political Left; in other countries, liberal is usually "conservative" and on the Right. Thus the conservative economic policies championed by Ronald Reagan and the American Right are regarded as *neoliberal* everywhere else in the world. The explanation for this confusion comes from the fact that the United States has never had a powerful socialist movement. In Europe and elsewhere in the world, the socialists became the Left and the liberals were pushed to the Right on a broader political spectrum than developed in the United States, where the term *liberal* came to represent the more moderate Left.

The revival of neoliberalism, or conservative economic policies, since the early 1980s marks a retreat from the mixed economies that had been popular in Europe and other industrial democracies. It involves a return to economic policies that are driven by market forces rather than by government decisions. Neoliberalism found expression in the economic strategies of leaders such as Ronald Reagan in the United States, Margaret Thatcher in Britain, and Germany's Helmut Kohl. Governments in these countries and elsewhere loosened their economic controls and left more to the free play of market forces. In several countries, such as Britain and France, large portions of the public sector were *privatized*–sold to private investors.

The dominance of neoliberalism was also promoted by the economic and political failures of communism in Eastern Europe and the Soviet Union that discredited the socialist economic model. Socialism did not work there, and many saw that as proof that it would not work anywhere. In the aftermath of the collapse of socialism, most East European countries turned to more capitalistic approaches to structuring their economies. At the same time, mixed economies in both developed and developing states experienced problems. In Western Europe, states found that their vast social welfare systems were costing too much. They struggled with ways to cut back on these very popular programs or to limit their costs. In developing countries, there were growing doubts about the ability of government to lead their countries into economic modernity. Many of these countries opened up their economies to greater private entrepreneurship, both to their own people and to foreign firms.

Neoliberalism soon spread to less developed countries. International agencies, such as the World Bank, the International Monetary Fund (IMF), and the World Trade Organization (WTO) promoted free enterprise and free trade. Countries with large foreign debts were compelled to open their economies and to cut back on domestic spending in order to get guarantees or renewal of their loans. For example, when Mexico faced economic decline in the early 1990s, international pressures encouraged austere economic policies and the sale of some government-owned enterprises. In India, the government of Narashimha Rao was forced to cut public expenditures in order to qualify for new loans from the IMF. In addition to these pressures from world organizations, less developed countries have also been pressured toward greater free enterprise by international investors. Investment from abroad has been an important source of economic growth in these countries but private banks and investors are unwilling to send money to countries whose governments decline to allow their economies to respond to market forces.

Thus, the 1980s and 1990s were years when economic neoliberalism or capitalism spread. It is nevertheless too early to speak of a "triumph of capitalism." First, in spite of brave rhetoric to the contrary, few countries have cut back on their welfare programs. They are too popular to eliminate, especially in democracies where voters are likely to remember and punish parties that reduce their health care or pensions. Second, the figures for 1990 and 1999 in Table 3.1 illustrate how little government's share of the Gross Domestic Product (GDP) has actually declined. In some countries, government spending as a share of the GDP has actually increased since 1980. Second, while neoliberal ideas are dominant, they do not reflect a broad public or elite consensus. Market economics, free trade, and limited government dominate the political agendas of most countries, but their leaders and people still see and sometimes hope for the return to an active role of the state in the economy and further social and welfare programs.

Politics and the Level of Economic Development

Too often, we categorize countries into two broad groups: developed and undeveloped. In fact, the process of economic development is an ongoing one as technology, resources, state policies, and people's attitudes and values constantly reshape the economic system. Nor is there uniformity even within countries of this process of economic change. Even in highly developed countries such as those in Western Europe, it is not unusual to find areas where economic development has lagged well behind the rest of the country. For example, there are areas in rural southern Italy where farmers still use horse-drawn plows and wagons in bare subsistence farming. On the other hand, many countries that we would label generally as undeveloped have bustling cities with many of the problems of large cities in highly developed countries. Lagos (Nigeria), New Delhi (India), and Mexico City are all examples of crowded urban areas with the traffic, pollution, housing, and employment problems of cities in more highly developed countries. China offers an extreme example of uneven development. In coastal areas that the state has designated as "special economic zones," economic growth has been very impressive and has brought prosperity to the inhabitants. Elsewhere in the rural interior of China, people still live in primitive conditions. This "uneven development" causes major political and social challenges in both highly industrialized and developing countries.

We use a number of different terms to refer to those countries whose economies lack the industrial, consumer economies found in North America and Western Europe: undeveloped, less developed, developing, southern hemisphere, or third world.[6] Choice of which term to use depends more on personal taste than on any significant differences in meaning. While many of the countries that fall into these categories are "developing" economically and politically, there are some that may be deserving of the label of "*non*developing." The economies of these countries have stagnated or even deteriorated because of foreign debt, corruption, internal political conflict, or natural disasters. In addition, rapid population growth in these parts of the third world absorbs much, if not all, of the benefits of any economic expansion. Bangladesh, Democratic Republic of the Congo (formerly Zaire), and Liberia are current examples of such troubled countries.

Some people object that all of these terms reflect the Western bias that industrial development and economic growth must be along the lines of what occurred in Western Europe and North America. This is no doubt true in part. However, while the values placed on economic growth and development may be Western in their origin, they are now nearly universal among the leaders and peoples of virtually all countries of the world.

There are reasons to raise reservations about the universal desirability of economic development. Nearly always, it entails the shift of human resources from agriculture to manufacturing and commerce. In many cases, this seriously undermines the ability of a state to feed its people. Nigeria, for example, was a food-exporting country before its independence in 1960; by 1985, it was a net food importer and barely able to feed its population. There are also social and political problems that come from uprooting rural peoples and thrusting them into industrial settings. The family, clan, and village loyalties that once provided emotional strength and economic support in bad times are weakened. In such settings, radical and extremist groups often find ready recruits. Finally, economic development often ruptures the harmony of nature and humankind that is valued in many traditional societies. Pollution and the despoilment of the land replace the care that people accorded their environment in more traditional economies.

Many of the developing countries face huge international debts. As their peoples learn of the consumer benefits enjoyed by others, their demand for Western-produced goods increases. These countries often attempt to finance these imports and their own economic development plans with receipts from the sale of their natural resources. Then they face an additional problem: The international markets for natural resources are highly volatile. The demands and prices for resources shift wildly and unpredictably. This has consequences for countries trying to use the receipts from the sale of their resources to finance economic development.

Again, Nigeria offers a good example of the problems. There are important oil deposits in southeastern Nigeria. During the 1970s, when an international oil shortage pushed the prices for petroleum very high, Nigeria rushed the development of its oil industry. In 1980, Nigeria was producing 2.1 million barrels of oil a day and marketing it at $40 a barrel. The government decided to use the resulting revenue to finance broader economic development and launched an ambitious and expensive program based on expected oil profits. Foreign banks anted up billions of dollars to support these development plans. Then the oil shortage became an oil glut. By 1981, Nigeria's oil production fell to only 500,000 barrels a day at $30 a barrel; by 1985, the price for petroleum had fallen to less than $10 a barrel. The government's economic development plan was left in shatters; huge international debts accumulated; the economy was nearly destroyed. This economic failure contributed to the military coup at the end of 1983 that toppled the Nigerian Second Republic.

Nigeria's experience is similar to that of many other developing countries that based economic development plans on projected income that did not materialize. Demand for raw materials—such as tin, rubber, and copper—varies much more rapidly and more widely than does demand for other products. This leaves these countries highly vulnerable to economic shifts in the already developed world.

A group of scholars, many from Latin America, developed the "dependency approach" as a way to explain seemingly enduring patterns of dominance of third world economies by developed countries and multinational corporations.[7] Adapting Marx's theory of imperialism to the twentieth century, these scholars claim that a world economic system has emerged between the "core" developed countries and the "periphery" of underdeveloped and dependent countries. The result is a new colonialism or neocolonialism that binds presumably independent states to powerful industrial economies every bit as tightly as did classical imperialism. The resources of dependent states are thus used to the benefit of the wealthy states. This dependency relationship not only perpetuates economic underdevelopment but shapes the internal social and political realities within each underdeveloped country. It sustained the political and social control of traditional elites in developing countries and blocked both economic development as well as political reform in these countries.

In the 1970s and 1980s, dependency explanations of the third world were dominant among academics. They have become less persuasive as we move into the new century. Dependency theories placed blame for economic and political failure on the world economic system and denied internal causes of underdevelopment within the peripheral states. This neglect became evident as these states undertook successful internal economic and political reform. Dependency also denied the possibility of countries breaking free from the economic and political limitations of its approach. But by the end of the 1980s, there were numerous examples of newly industrialized countries (NICs) that had broken out of the allegedly permanent bonds of dependency. South Korea, Taiwan, Singapore, Thailand, the Philippines, and later Argentina, Brazil, and Mexico broke into the ranks of modern industrialized countries, developed worldwide markets for their products, and raised the standard of living of their peoples. In many cases, they also moved forward in achieving democratization.

The challenge of explaining why some countries are wealthy and others are poor is a continuing one. As the new century begins, the dependency view of blaming colonialism for the impoverishment of many parts of the world and the liberal economists' notions that the market economy and a democratic political system are needed for development are no longer fashionable. Many scholars now point to a country's culture for explanation of its economic status.[8] For these analysts, societies' differing cultural values on interpersonal trust, individual achievement, tolerance, openness to innovation, and personal freedom explain the different levels of economic development. Critics of the school of "culture matters" viewpoint assert that the measurement and definition of these values are often unclear and stereotypical. It promotes racism by labeling certain cultures as "inferior" in providing for economic development. The critics also fear that this cultural approach to explaining prosperity leads to cultural determinism and omits the important effects of political structures, geography, climate, and historical patterns.

Even "developed" countries experience transformations in their economies. Most of the richest countries of the world are shifting from economies based on labor-intensive industrial production to economies centered on high technology and services. This evolution to postindustrial economies places importance on knowledge and technical skill rather than on large amounts of capital or manual labor. This change has important political consequences, and not all of them are good.[9] It is in large part responsible for the long-term unemployment that plagues political leaders in countries such as France, Germany, and Italy. The decline of heavy industry and the increased mobility of workers lead to the decay of neighborhoods around the factories and shift political power to new suburbs. The postindustrial changes bring new issues to the political agenda.[10] For example, environmental protection is much more important for a state that has acquired high technology than for one still reliant on polluting, heavy industry.

Economics and Democracy

I noted two basic economic structures earlier in this section: capitalism and socialism. In theory, neither of these models dictates a particular form of government. It is possible to conceive of a successful democracy with either a capitalist or a socialist economy. Similarly, authoritarianism may be equally at home with either of these economic forms.

However, some have claimed that democracy is facilitated by a capitalist economy. Indeed, in the past decade, many have seen the emergence of free enterprise in former communist states as a sure sign of their democratization. There are some aspects of capitalism that do promote some features of democracy. Notably, the state's powers are by definition limited under capitalism. Competition among powerful autonomous groups settles key social issues such as production, price, and wages. This automatically produces the political pluralism upon which democracy thrives. Others dispute these claims and point to the inherent inequalities of capitalism. However helpful capitalism may be to democracy, it is by no means a sufficient condition to build democracy. During the twentieth century, there were far more capitalist dictatorships than capital democracies. Nor does the introduction of capitalism necessarily promote democracy. China is a good example. A market economy is well under way, but it has had little effect on democratizing the dictatorial, communist regime. Another concern is the difficult question of whether or not we can have the political equality that is a key feature of democracy in societies with great economic disparities.[11]

Some have even argued that economic liberalization (moving toward a more capitalist economy) is detrimental to democracy because it needs a strong central government to guide that transition.[12] As a result, the involvement of the general public, interest groups, local and regional governments, and the national legislature in decision making is strictly limited. Once liberalization is completed, there is a strong, authoritarian government with little interest in opening the process to more democratic participation.

The simultaneous imposition of both democracy and capitalism often produces high levels of political turmoil and uncertainty.[13] Such political and economic disorder coming from simultaneous political and economic liberalizations may well lead to a popular rejection of democracy. This is a current danger in the postcommunist changes of Russia and several East European countries. Political leaders have been unable to control the great economic dislocations produced by the move to capitalism from highly centralized, state-run economies. The economic problems have brought political turmoil and left many Russians and East

Europeans longing for the economic certitudes and political order of the past. This shows the uncertain relationship between economics and politics.

Nor is there any necessary link between democracy and the level of political development. Many highly developed countries are democratic, but there are also many developed states that still have authoritarian regimes. Certainly, economic development itself does not bring automatic democratization. Many of the newly industrialized countries have achieved economic modernization and still maintained oppressive regimes that have made few if any concessions to democracy in the political realm, and have made little progress toward democracy. South Korea, Thailand, and Taiwan have prospered with free enterprise economies but struggled in attaining democracy. Singapore—the most successful of the newly industrialized states—is far from reaching even minimal democratic standards. This again illustrates the complex nature of the interaction between economics and politics: There is interaction, but its direction and consequences are not always predictable.

SOCIAL CLEAVAGES AND POLITICS

In the past decade, India has experienced serious political turmoil that brought the assassination of two of its prime ministers. In addition, massive riots have occurred on several occasions in various parts of this large nation, resulting in thousands of casualties. These clashes in India were not over government policy or ideology but rather over the influence of various religious groups: Hindus, Moslems, Sikhs, and others. Such communal violence is common in many parts of the less developed world. But it is by no means restricted to developing countries. Britain, for example, has experienced over twenty-five years of conflict and near civil war in Northern Ireland where Irish Catholics and Ulster Protestants contest for power. The degree of violence and the resulting political instability in India and Britain as well as many other countries demonstrate the close interaction between society and politics.

All societies are divided by a number of social cleavages: social differences that not only distinguish between groups within the state's population but also divide it into conflicting groups. The most universally important lines of social cleavage are socioeconomic class, ethnicity, religion, and region. These social divisions lead inevitably to conflicts among groups over allocation of resources. Such conflict is normal since resources are always less than needed to meet everyone's desires. In many cases, the conflict is healthy in that it develops interdependence among the various groups in society and prevents stagnation. Much of this conflict takes place outside the political realm. For example, rarely do governments find it necessary to intervene in the competition for adherents among different religions. On other occasions, as in India, these social conflicts explode into violence and disorder that challenge the very existence of the state. Thus, the political system is strongly influenced by the presence of conflicts based in social cleavages that the state must manage or resolve.

Even where the level of conflict is low, social cleavages have important political consequences. They often serve as the basis for building ruling coalitions in both democratic and authoritarian regimes. For example, in the United States politicians usually target specific social classes, religions, and ethnic groups as they seek to put together a presidential election coalition; Chinese leaders rely on a coalition of the military, party workers, and government economic bureaucrats. Often social groups acquire distinctive patterns of political behavior—preferring a specific party and using particular forms of political action. For example, the upper middle class often aligns with right-of-center parties and relies on informal, personal ties to influence politics, while the working class links up with the leftist party and may have to resort to strikes or protests to get its voice heard by politicians.

Socioeconomic Cleavages

Socioeconomic or class cleavages are social distinctions that reflect the stratification of society according to income and social position. There are, in the most simple formulations, three broad social classes: the working class, the middle class or bourgeoisie, and the upper class. Usually, these classes are pictured in a pyramid form with a large working class, a smaller middle class, and a much smaller upper class. In reality, the structure of social class divisions in any country is far more complicated. The working class is divided among skilled workers, unskilled workers, and "underclasses" of unemployed people who are only on the margins of society. The middle class includes small independent business people, employees in large enterprises, civil servants, professional people, and engineers, but also clerks, salespeople, secretaries, and so on. The traditional upper class of propertied nobility has virtually disappeared and blends in with the upper middle classes.

The nineteenth-century German social historian Karl Marx drew attention to the importance of social class in understanding politics. He believed that class was the essential characteristic of society and that all other social divisions were manifestations of class conflict. Marx believed that the old propertied upper class had been replaced by a strong middle class or bourgeoisie of entrepreneurs whose power was based on their capital or monetary wealth. Under the capitalist system, they were driven to lower prices and in doing so pressured their workers into lower salaries and dangerous working conditions. As a result, tensions between the bourgeois employers and proletarian workers would inevitably increase as the proletariat's misery and size expanded. Eventually, this would result in a spontaneous revolution. In the aftermath of the revolution, a new socialist state based on the nearly universal working class would do away with all classes in the triumph of the proletariat.

When Marx developed this thesis in the mid-nineteenth century, there were good reasons to believe it was accurate. His critique of the potential shortcomings of capitalism at the time was perceptive, and many believe that it still points to social and political weaknesses in contemporary capitalism. Class divisions were clear-cut at that time, and they were reflected in sharp distinctions among people in jobs, housing, dress, diet, and recreation. The working class was truly oppressed, and there was tremendous inequality between the haves and have-nots in most of Europe during the emergence of the industrial society. However, in the past fifty years, class conflicts have diminished in the Western democracies and the possibility of a proletarian revolution is virtually nil. Class awareness has declined; the working class has shrunk and the middle class has greatly expanded; class hostilities have nearly disappeared as the benefits of growing economies have been widely shared. These changes have reduced the value of the old Marxist notions of class and class conflict.

In nearly all industrial countries, there is little awareness of social class. For example, in Britain in 1990, less than half of the people expressed a sense of belonging to any class[14]—and this in a country widely regarded as having one of the most class-ridden societies.

There are a number of explanations for the decline in the sense of belonging to a class. First, most developed countries have seen a leveling of society since the Second World War. The postwar economic booms brought a broader sharing of wealth and a spread of consumer goods among people of all classes. Progressive income taxes and extensive social welfare programs have diminished the impact of income differences. Education and, with it, upward social mobility are now available to people of modest backgrounds. Second, strong trade unions have helped to integrate the working class into the broader society. They have become respected and listened-to advocates of the working class. Third, industrial societies have changed and become more complex. The decline of heavy, labor-intensive industries in Europe and North America has undermined working-class awareness and solidarity. Workers often commute to their jobs from distant neighborhoods, reducing their availability for joint action.

Taken together, these developments have produced what some call the "embourgeoisement" of society in Western democracies. Instead of the usual pyramid of class, some contend that what is found now is a diamond of class with a vast middle class. In this diamond, there is only a small lower class and an equally small upper class based on achievement. (See Figure 3.1.) The middle class is diverse in its composition and includes well-paid and skilled workers from what used to be regarded as the working class.

Some critics of modern society contend that this vast middle class shares many of the problems of the old working class. The new middle class is made up of employees whose jobs, salaries, and futures are at the discretion of their employers. The modern institutional employer, some argue, is even less concerned with the welfare of employees—blue collar, white collar, even middle-management—and more willing to exploit employees than were the classic, property-owning capitalists of Marx's time. The new middle class is made up of employees of large, impersonal corporations who are subject to the whims of their employers and lack control over their destinies. This is indeed a different middle class than the bourgeoisie of independent capitalists in classic Marxist views of social class, but one that critics see as still producing social tensions. These critics argue that today's

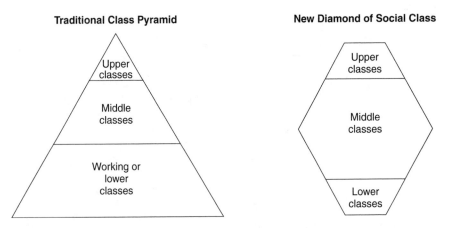

FIGURE 3.1　Models of Social Class in Industrial Democracies

problems of employee exploitation and inequitable distribution of society's resources are as great now as they were in the past.[15]

However, most observers see embourgeoisement as producing an era of relaxed class relations in Western industrial democracies. So far there is little to suggest that this new middle class sees itself as a class, as deprived, as sensing common interests, or as in need of mobilizing to defend its interests. In an era of relative affluence and a wide sharing of that affluence, social class has lost salience. People are disinterested in class-based conflict or political appeals based on class interests. As a result, many see class as playing less and less of a role in the politics of industrial democracies.

With these shifts in the nature and salience of social class, most industrial democracies experience little of the class conflict foreseen by Marx. Even the less conflictual elements of class differences have diminished. Voters no longer vote as strongly along class lines as they once did. In Table 3.2, you can see the decline in class voting in Britain. In 1964, voters tended to support the party most closely identified with their class; by 1992, party vote was distributed with only a hint of the old class/party alignments. The Liberal Democrats drew nearly equally from all social classes; the Conservatives had increased their appeal to working-class voters; and Labour had increased slightly its appeal to middle-class voters. The results from the 1997 elections confirm the basic trend but may be anomalous because of the vast swing to Labour in its landslide victory.

While the political consequences of class have moderated, they are not absent in industrial democracies. Some scholars see a reshaping and redefinition of social class but an enduring impact of class on voting patterns and political behavior.[16] Others see the potential for a revival of traditional class politics in societies where the economy is stagnant, unemployment high, and trade unions weakened.

Social class divisions were supposedly abolished in communist states. In fact, social hierarchies reflected in prestige, influence, and economic benefits pervaded

TABLE **3.2**   Social Class and Voting in Britain

	1964		1992			1997		
	Conservative	*Labour*	*Conservative*	*Labour*	*Liberal Democrat*	*Conservative*	*Labour*	*Liberal Democrat*
Higher managerial	86%	14%						
Lower managerial	81	19	59%	16%	21%	36%	36%	21%
Supervisory	61	39						
Office and clerical	61	39	59	27	20	31	46	18
Skilled workers	29	71	38	41	18	28	58	9
Semi- and unskilled	25	75	30	50	15	24	58	12

Source: 1964: Samuel H. Beer, *Britain Against Itself* (New York: Norton, 1982), p. 81; 1992 and 1997: Anthony King, et al., *New Labour Triumphs: Britain at the Polls* (Chatham, NJ: Chatham House, 1998), p. 11.

the former communist countries in Europe; they exist as well in the few remaining communist states of China, North Korea, and—to a lesser degree—Cuba. The party elite, factory and farm managers, and other valued groups had access to consumer goods, medical care, travel privileges, better housing, and other benefits that ordinary people did not. Indeed, the existence of these privileges and the elite's inability to hide them contributed significantly to the downfall of communism.

Class divisions usually are less important in third world countries. In most of these countries, the overwhelming majority of the population are still small farmers. The working class—the social class most likely to become aware of class distinctions and to be mobilized for class action—is small. Other cleavages, especially ethnic differences, usually override class feelings in political alignments and conflict. In Nigeria, for example, poor and wealthy Ibos band together to defend their interests against Yorubas or Hausas. The importance of the ethnic division leaves little opportunity for the poor to challenge the privileges of the wealthy within or between ethnic communities.

Although traditional worker-versus-employer class conflicts are usually not important political factors in less-developed countries, there are still very important class tensions and cleavages. Where the ethnic issue does not overwhelm them, these tensions are reflected in the conflict between landless peasants and property owners and between marginalized, often peripheral, groups and those that are enjoying more of the benefits of economic development. A good example of the importance of these tensions came in the mid-1990s when Indians in the Mexican state of Chiapas revolted just as Mexico was celebrating its entrance into the world economy as a result of the enactment of the North American Free Trade Area (NAFTA). The impoverished peoples of this region sensed that their needs were forgotten. While the open rebellion eventually waned, there are periodic violent episodes to remind us of the alienation of the Indians in Chiapas and elsewhere in rural Mexico. The Mexican situation is similar to that in many other third world countries where uneven development and the continued deprivation of important sections of the population perpetuate social class tensions that may be explosive.

In many societies, class tensions are eased by movement up and down the social ladder according to the individual's abilities. The sons and daughters of lower-status parents can often move into more affluent situations than those of their families. Education and the individual's achievement are the keys to upward mobility. Such mobility prevents the attribution of social standing to the fortune or misfortune of one's birth.

On the other hand, India's 3,000-year-old caste system stands as an illustration of rigid structuring of society based on an ascriptive (defined by birth) social hierarchy. At the very bottom of society are the "untouchables" and "tribals" (aborigines) who make up almost one-fourth of the billion people in India. In 1950, the newly independent India formally outlawed the untouchable designation, but it remains a reality of Indian social and political life. The untouchables are limited to cleaning latrines, handling the dead, and other menial tasks. They cannot escape their untouchable status nor can they hope that their children will do so. Above this bottom of the hierarchy are four broad castes or orders and some 2,000 sub-castes. Borders between these castes are carefully maintained. In 2000, newspapers carried the tragic story of two young lovers who were both in lower or "backward" castes, but the 19-year-old woman was a couple of degrees higher than her lover. They eloped and married in Delhi. When they returned to their village, the family of the 21-year-old man hanged him and burned his body; the young woman's family did the same to her. As a cousin of the young man explained, "We can only marry from our own caste. It is not possible for one to marry outside his caste. This does not happen in our society. It is not possible."[17] With such strictures, it is not surprising that one observer notes that "Caste is India's social reality reflected in all phenomena of life, in marriage, in voting, work, and social relations."[18] Such a social cleavage clearly limits India's ability to develop economically and to achieve democracy.

Ethnic Cleavages

At the start of the twenty-first century, ethnic cleavages are clearly the most divisive and explosive social cleavages in countries at all levels of development. Ethnic divisions are important not only in developing countries where colonial rule brought many peoples within the same country but also in the older Western countries where the political integration of different peoples had seemed to be resolved centuries ago. Ethnic clashes are the cause of several full-scale civil wars in the former Yugoslavia, some of the former USSR republics, and African countries such as Liberia, Rwanda, and Angola. Ethnic conflicts are the source of terrorism and near civil wars in Northern Ireland, Lebanon, Israel, and India. They fuel separatist feelings in Quebec, Corsica, and Scotland. They are reflected in employment, housing, and political discrimination in many other countries.

Ethnicity is manifest in other more benign ways in politics. It is often the source of political coalitions. People everywhere tend to "vote for their own kind" in free elections. This is why multiparty politics often is a failure in countries with deep ethnic cleavages. When the parties are distinguished only by ethnicity, the only way to increase electoral support is to maximize the turnout of the party's ethnic group. To do so, ethnic leaders sometimes enhance the sense of danger from other ethnic communities in order to stimulate voter turnout. Nigeria's first experiment with democracy in the early 1960s illustrates this. There were three major parties, each closely tied to one of the major ethnic communities. Elections in 1964 were expected to be very close, and party leaders irresponsibly urged out their voters by claiming the other parties/ethnic groups were out to get their people, even to commit genocide against them. While such extreme warnings produced high turnout, they also provoked ethnic tensions that brought two military coups and a tragic civil war that left millions dead.

Ethnic conflicts in Eastern Europe and the former Soviet Union have become major problems in the past few years. For several decades, strong, decentralized, and authoritarian governments simply suppressed virtually all manifestations of ethnic differences. National minorities in the USSR, Yugoslavia, and other East European countries were allowed to preserve their languages and folkloric traditions but not permitted political autonomy. Once the communist states collapsed, ethnic groups throughout the region renewed old demands for autonomy and sought revenge for grievances accumulated during the communist era. These are not new conflicts; Imperial Russia used to be referred to as "the czar's prison of nations," and the nationality conflicts in the Balkans have long been a source of conflict and international warfare.

In many industrial nations, immigration of workers and refugees from all parts of the world is creating a new ethnic cleavage. In countries such as Britain, France, Germany, Switzerland, Canada, Australia, the United States, and elsewhere, literally millions of immigrant workers and political or economic refugees have sought political freedom and economic advancement. At first, most of these immigrant workers were invited to industrial countries that experienced shortages of unskilled labor in the 1960s and early 1970s. But as unemployment became a problem in the 1980s and 1990s, these immigrants were no longer welcome. Others arrived as refugees when decolonization took place. Many of the new immigrants were racially distinct from the indigenous peoples: North Africans in France, East Indians and West Indians in Britain, Turks in Germany, East Asians in Canada and Australia, Hispanics in the United States.

As more immigrants have arrived and those already there have brought in family members, the size of the racial minority of immigrants has grown to account for a large percentage of the total population. (See Table 3.3.) In addition, these immigrants stand out because they have generally refused to assimilate with the native population and because they are concentrated in large urban centers. As

TABLE 3.3   Immigrants as a Percentage of Total Population in Selected Countries, 1997

	Percent Immigrant Population
Australia	21.1%
Britain	3.6
Canada	17.4
France	6.3
Germany	9.0
Japan	1.2
The Netherlands	9.2
Switzerland	19.0
United States	9.3

Source: "Survey: The United States," *The Economist,* 11 March, 2000, p. 5.

the number of immigrants has grown, resentment toward them has increased in many industrial democracies. They compete with native populations for scarce jobs, housing, education, and social services. They are blamed, usually unfairly, for rising crime rates and the deterioration of once grand cities.

The political consequences have been several. First, there have been increasing incidents of racial violence directed at immigrants. Most are isolated and individual attacks, but some have been mob actions against unwanted immigrant neighbors. The number of racial incidents varies widely by country but the trend is upwards in several major countries. For example, in Germany at the end of 2000, there were over 1,000 anti-immigrant or anti-Semitic incidents a month, compared with less than 700 incidents a month a year earlier.[19] Second, extremist parties on the far Right have used resentment against immigrants to recruit supporters. The major parties have generally proved willing to defend the civil rights of immigrants and avoided anti-immigrant appeals. Parties of the far Right, such as France's National Front or Germany's Republican party, have not hesitated to make demagogic appeals to racist sentiments. Third, in a few countries where the immigrants have been around long enough to become citizens they have become important sections of the electorate. In Britain, for example, second and third-generation East and West Indians and Africans are now courted by the major parties for their votes and for aspiring leaders to run for public office.[20] Fourth, immigrant peoples are often among those who have suffered most from the economic disruptions in the past. As a result, they are often very discontented and have on occasion aired their grievances with demonstrations and violence. Britain experienced several such manifestations of unrest in non-White neighborhoods of industrial cities during 2001.

There is no doubt that a major source of political violence during the new century will be ethnic conflicts. These conflicts are widespread in all types of political systems and in countries at all levels of development. The prevalence of ethnic conflict feeds on itself. There is international contagion as the achievement of independence for Estonians leads Croats to seek their own country; as Croats gain independence, the Slovenes and Bosnians want theirs; the achievement of independence for ethnic communities in Eastern Europe renews interest in separatism among Scots, Corsicans, and French Canadians. There are very few countries that are ethnically homogeneous. Wherever there are two or more ethnic groups coexisting in the same state, there will be a need for people to learn and practice tolerance. And that will not be an easy task for governments to achieve. Governments can pass laws against discrimination, but it is much more difficult for them to achieve the change in attitudes necessary for different peoples to live together peaceably.

Religious Cleavages

Religious differences are often closely intertwined with ethnicity. The various ethnic groups often differ in their religious commitments. For example, the conflict in Northern Ireland has a strong religious dimension, with the Irish nationalists being strong Catholics and the loyalists strong Protestants. The verbiage of this conflict in Northern Ireland often sounds more like a religious war than an ethnic struggle. Similarly, in India, religious differences are the focus of conflicts between Hindus, Moslems, Sikhs, and Christians as well as between extremists and moderates within these religions.

Religious differences can also exist among people of similar ethnic backgrounds. Historically, the conflict between Catholics and Protestants in Germany was a central feature of earlier centuries. Religion is still a significant factor explaining voting behavior in many countries including Germany and the United States. In some cases, religious differences have served to buffer the state from popular discontent. For example, in the eighteenth century much of the unrest in Britain was channeled into religion, with disadvantaged people expressing their discontent by joining dissident religious groups rather than political movements.

There are also conflicts among people professing the same religion but with varying levels of commitment. One of the most serious current sources of religious violence comes in Islamic countries where devout Moslems have declared a holy war, or jihad, against their Moslem brothers and sisters who have made too many religious compromises. In several countries where the Catholic Church is predominant, there have been conflicts between anticlericals and clericals over the proper role of the church in politics and society. In the past, these conflicts were often intense; now they are mostly over and reappear mainly in debates on education and family matters. But even now, the most reliable predictor of the vote in France and Italy is religious commitment. The stronger the individual's attachment to the Catholic Church, the more likely he or she is to vote conservative.

Regional Cleavages

Another politically significant cleavage is the division of a country along geographic or regional lines. In many modern states, differing political values and attitudes characterize people living in different geographic regions. These populations compete for scarce government resources such as money, jobs, and development projects. Italy offers a good example with sharp economic and cultural differences between a prosperous and well-developed North and a rural, poor South. The North has become increasingly resistant to the shift of the benefits of its prosperity to develop the poorer South, and this is reflected in the birth of new parties in the North to support its regional claims. In general, concerns about regional problems are greatest for large countries that have a core area and many remote, outlying regions. For example, the benefits and political influence enjoyed by people living in and around Moscow and St. Petersburg are far greater than those of Russians living in remote, eastern Russia.

Regional differences are often linked to varying degrees of economic development. In nearly all countries, economic growth is spread unevenly among the various regions. Regional cleavages are likely to be deep and to become explosive if one region's viewpoint regularly prevails or if it receives a disproportionate share of the government's offerings. If such a cleavage becomes bitter, there is frequently a danger that the deprived region will secede. Disparities in the economic development of the North and South in the United States were a primary cause of the American Civil War. Similarly, in Nigeria, regional conflicts coming in large part from economic inequalities resulted in the secession of Biafra and a tragic civil war.

Another dimension of regional cleavages is the division between urban and rural areas of a country. The distribution of political power, and ultimately of government resources, is a source of tension between urban and rural populations. This is particularly true of states undergoing the transition from a predominantly rural to an urban society. Rural areas are likely to resist their loss of political influence; urban areas complain about delays in shifting political power to accord with new demographic realities. Rural-urban cleavages are especially important in developing countries where modern cities have emerged and leaders seek to promote industrialization. Rural people then feel left on the margins of politics. Contemporary Japan faces real challenges in integrating people still in rural areas with those in rapidly modernizing urban centers. The gap between rural and urban needs and interests contributes to political divisions and tensions in Japan.

The Political Relevance of Social Cleavages

There are many divisions in society that may have political significance. The ones discussed above are those that most frequently cause division in contemporary states. Over time, older cleavages wane and new ones emerge as society itself evolves. Some cleavages are more important politically than are others. Division and conflict are not necessarily bad in themselves, but when the cleavages become deep and create unreconcilable differences among people in a single state, they can endanger the stability and even existence of a political system.

There are a number of factors that determine the political relevance and consequences of social cleavages. First, the depth of the cleavage is affected by the extent of differences that are determined by a societal cleavage. The greater the discrepancy in the access of segments of society to available resources such as goods, prestige, and power, the deeper the cleavage and the greater the political significance of that cleavage. The greater the deprivation or discrimination along the lines of social divisions, the more likely it is that the cleavage will be politically relevant and dangerous. When an ethnic group, region, religious community, or class sees the majority of the state's power, wealth, and prestige in the hands of rival groups, they are likely to feel deprivation on the basis of the cleavage and to seek redress against the other groups.

A second important factor affecting the salience of social cleavages is the pattern of divisions in society. Table 3.4 illustrates two hypothetical countries. In Country A, all social cleavages coincide so that the ethnic division aligns the same groups against each other as do regional, religious, and class cleavages. In such so-

TABLE 3.4   Patterns of Social Cleavage in Hypothetical Societies

Country A: Coinciding Lines of Cleavage

	Ethnic Group A	Ethnic Group B
Region		
North	100%	0%
South	0	100
City	100	0
Rural	0	100
Religion		
Protestant	0	100
Catholic	100	0
Social class		
Middle class	100	0
Working class	0	100

Country B: Cross-Cutting Lines of Cleavage

	Ethnic Group A	Ethnic Group B
Region		
North	30%	70%
South	70	30
City	75	65
Rural	25	35
Religion		
Protestant	40	50
Catholic	60	50
Social class		
Middle class	60	45
Working class	40	55

cieties where there are *coinciding lines of cleavage,* the divisions are likely to be explosive, since every dispute aligns the same groups against each other. The task of government in managing social conflict in such a polarized setting is very difficult.

In Country B, there are *cross-cutting lines of cleavage* that divide society into many potential groups that may conflict on one issue but need to cooperate on another. This tends to keep social conflict to more moderate levels. Thus, some city dwellers in ethnic group A will want to cooperate with urban ethnic group B people when the issue relates to city matters; workers from both ethnic groups will want to form a coalition to deal with industrial relation policies; and so on. These coalitions will shift from issue to issue, and the need for cooperation with a variety of different groups serves to moderate conflict over any single issue. For example, religious disputes are likely to be kept moderate in order to allow Catholics and Protestants to ally on other issues.

Of course, these are hypothetical countries. In the real world neither pattern is likely to be found in a pure form. But we can see societies that come close to these abstract patterns. Nigeria, for example, approaches the coinciding-lines-of-cleavage pattern with Ibos living in the South, interested in industry and commerce, more affluent, and Christian, while Hausas in the North are more agrarian, less well-off, and Moslem. The result created a sharp polarization, an attempted secession by the Ibos, and the tragic Biafran War. Britain and France resemble the pattern of overlapping cleavages with many different lines of cleavage creating the need for multiple and shifting coalitions to affect government decisions in the different policy areas.

A third determinant of the political salience of social cleavages is the general state of economic well-being. When the economy is prospering, it is possible to spread benefits widely among various groups to meet their demands. Everyone can enjoy the resources of the state. When the economy is in difficulty, the state has fewer benefits to distribute and competition among various social groups for the state's resources becomes more intense and volatile. For example, part of the explanation for the sudden rise in social tensions in Russia can be traced to the economic collapse. With growing shortages even in essential goods and virtually no ability of the Russian government to meet the grievances of the many deprived groups, competition among sections of society increased and became more intense and even violent.

A fourth factor is the attitude of the various social elites. Political and social leaders play a large role in moderating or building social tensions. The motives underlying the leaders' choice of strategies vary from personal ambitions to the needs and dynamics of the social group. But it would be wrong to underestimate the importance of the elites in exacerbating or easing social cleavages.

For example, in some parts of India where the religious leaders have attempted to stem the rise of fundamentalist sentiments, tensions between Moslems and Hindus are lessened; in other areas, the leaders have fanned the flames of holy war. In Northern Ireland, loyalists proclaim their fear of "papism" and "rule from Rome" if they allow greater involvement by the Catholic nationalists and heighten tensions in that grim conflict. A good contrast of elite attitudes and the resulting pattern of class cleavages can be seen in France and Germany. In France, labor leaders continued to use the imagery and rhetoric of Marxist class warfare long after the reality no longer corresponded to such a scenario, and this kept social class tensions in the workplace. In Germany, labor leaders dropped class warfare imagery and agreed to work within the existing capitalist structures, with a notable decline in class tensions. It is clear from these examples that the attitude of the leaders has an important effect on the salience of social cleavages. Leaders can moderate conflict by the rhetoric they use or they can enhance conflict and keep alive cleavages that are disappearing by their words and symbols.

Finally, the importance of social cleavages can also be affected by international influences. In this era of easy travel and vast communications networks, events in one country affect other countries through a process of international contagion. A good illustration can be seen in the rise of extreme right-wing groups in many European countries to express protest against immigrant populations. Inspired by examples in other countries, these movements often take the same names and use similar tactics. They have spread racial tensions from areas of greatest problems (for example, France or Germany) to other countries where attitudes toward the immigrants have not been as hostile (such as Italy).

Together, these various factors determine how deep the cleavages will be, how much tension and conflict they produce, and how difficult it is for government to manage social divisions. They illustrate how cleavages become more or less salient to political leaders.

CONCLUSION

It is surprising that, as we enter the twenty-first century, many of the social cleavages with the most direct political consequences are class, religious, ethnic, and regional divisions originally established before the beginning of the twentieth century. These cleavages have found reflection in political parties, governments, bureaucracies, and the political dialogue in all types of political systems, democratic and authoritarian. They seem to perpetuate themselves even after social change removes much of the meaning of these old cleavages. Religion still dominates politics in Northern Ireland. Caste still dominates the political, economic, and social affairs of India. Class remains a powerful indicator of how British and German voters make their electoral choices. Ethnic divisions rooted in centuries-old conflicts still predominate in Russian politics.

It is not that there are no new divisions worthy of reconciliation in the political arena. There are conflicts between people working in advancing and declining economic sectors, cleavages over the use and abuse of new technologies, moral and ethical debates related to the nature of life, and divisions over conflicting sets of materialist and postmaterialist values. But these new cleavages have been slow to find reflection in political debates and in political parties. Political battles continue to be defined by the old cleavages and only rarely incorporate the new ones. Will that change as we continue to move into the new century? It is still too early to say. Yet these very old socioeconomic cleavages, some of which have little relevance to the reality of life in the new century, still have explosive power. One insightful observer notes that highly organized wars among industrialized countries, the kind of warfare that dominated the twentieth century, are unlikely in the new century.[21] But that does not mean world peace. Instead, we are likely to see these *inter*state, even world wars replaced in the twenty-first century by *intra*state wars. The new conflicts will be small, civil wars. More often than not, they will be devoid of idealism or ideology but brutal, nihilistic violence pitting neighbors against each other in unwinnable conflicts. The new century has dawned with several such conflicts in full force: in Chechnya, the Democratic Republic of Congo (formerly Zaire), Kosovo, East Timor, Sri Lanka, Palestine. Certainly, such conflict poses challenges for any kind of government; internal wars make democracy virtually impossible.

NOTES

1. Paul Kennedy, *Preparing for the Twenty-first Century* (New York: Random House, 1993).

2. David S. Landes, *The Wealth and Poverty of Nations* (New York: W. W. Norton, 1999), p. xx.

3. Michael S. Lewis-Beck, "Introduction: The Enduring French Voter," in Michael S. Lewis-Beck, ed., *How France Votes* (Chatham, NJ: Chatham House, 2000).

4. Michael S. Lewis-Beck and Tom W. Rice, *Forecasting Elections* (Washington, DC: CQ Press, 1992).

5. Desmond S. King, *The New Right* (Chicago: Dorsey, 1987).

6. The term *third world* distinguishes those countries that were not part of the "first world" of Western democracies or the "second world" of communist states. Originally, the term included the notion that these states were unaligned in the cold war conflict between East and West, but this diplomatic sense of the term yielded to a more economic definition of less developed states even before the disappearance of the "second world."

7. Fernando Enrique Cardoso and Enzo Faletto, *Dependency and Development in Latin America* (Berkeley: University of California Press, 1979), and Immanuel M. Wallerstein, *The Modern World System*, 2 vols. (New York: Academic Press, 1980).

8. Lawrence E. Harrison and Samuel P. Huntington, eds., *Culture Matters: How Values Shape Human Progress* (New York: Basic Books, 2000), and Landes, *The Wealth and Poverty of Nations*.

9. Samuel P. Huntington, "Post-Industrial Politics: How Benign Will It Be?" *Comparative Politics* 6 (January 1974).

10. Ronald Inglehart, *Modernization and Postmodernization: Cultural, Economic, and Political Change in 43 Societies* (Princeton, NJ: Princeton University Press, 1997).

11. Robert A. Dahl, *Democracy, Liberty, and Equality* (New York: Oxford University Press, 1986), and Robert A. Dahl, *On Democracy* (New Haven, CT: Yale University Press, 1998).

12. Adam Przeworski, *Democracy and the Market* (Cambridge, England: Cambridge University Press, 1991).

13. See the special issue of *Journal of Democracy* 5 (October 1994) on "Economic Reform and Democracy."

14. *British Politics Group Newsletter,* No. 22 (Fall 1990), p. 10.

15. For a good presentation of both sides of arguments about the waning of social class, see Terry Nichols Clark and Seymour Martin Lipset, eds., *The Breakdown of Class Politics: A Debate on Post-Industrial Stratification* (Baltimore: The Johns Hopkins Press, 2000).

16. Geoffrey Evans, ed., *The End of Class Politics: Class Voting in Western Societies* (Oxford, England: Oxford University Press, 1999).

17. Reported in the *FT Weekend,* 22–23 July 2000, p. I.

18. Ibid.

19. *The Financial Times,* 12 October 2000, p. 4.

20. Jessica R. Adolino, *Ethnic Minorities, Electoral Politics and Political Integration* (London: Pinter, 1998).

21. Hans Magnus Enzensberger, *Civil Wars: From Latin America to Bosnia* (New York: The New Press, 1994).

PART II

POLITICAL ACTORS

At the heart of politics in every country is a set of political actors: individuals and groups that become involved in the political process either as occasional, amateur participants or as full-time professional politicians. Aristotle claimed that "Man is by nature a political animal." In fact, under normal circumstances, most people tend to have limited interest in civic affairs. Some, however, become very active in politics, and there seems to be a common set of factors in all countries that determines who these political activists are. It is important to look at individuals as political actors: their motivations and the forms of their political involvement as citizens. Since elections seem to be among the broadest forms of political participation, it is especially important to look at how citizens vote and why they select the candidates that they do.

The British playwright, and sometimes amateur politician, George Bernard Shaw expressed doubts about human interest in politics: "It is very doubtful whether man is enough of a political animal to produce a good, sensible, serious, and efficient constitution. All the evidence is against it." Because of their individual low level of political interest and sophistication, people tend to combine for political action. The two most common forms are political parties and interest groups.

Political parties are key elements in making contemporary, representative democracy work. Even where democracy has not emerged, parties serve as means of organizing and structuring political action by otherwise isolated individuals. As a result, they have attracted much attention by political scientists and other observers. Interest groups are often maligned as self-serving lobbies whose actions distort the national interest and pervert the morals of public officials. In fact, however, interest groups are essential political actors that allow those with similar views and those affected by certain aspects of public policy to voice their concerns in public forums. Group action varies from the formal petitions and lobbying of well-organized and financed groups such as the National Rifle Association to the informal notions of students as a section of society affected by changes in student loan programs or the future job market. In all kinds of political systems, groups play key political roles and cannot be ignored.

Chapter 4

❖❖❖❖❖❖❖❖❖❖❖❖❖

The Citizen in Politics

. . . government of the people, by the people, for the people . . .

Abraham Lincoln

These stirring words from Lincoln's Gettysburg Address capture the essence of democracy and identify its key requisite: that government be of and by the people. They convey the sense that citizens in democracies have a right and duty to be involved in making the policies that govern them. As democracy spreads in the new century to new lands and peoples, it is striking that the older, well-established democracies are experiencing an era of public disillusionment with their political institutions and leaders. Free, competitive elections are the hallmark of modern representative democracies but voter turnout is down almost everywhere; citizens are cynical about the intentions and procedures of their leaders; trust in political institutions has declined.[1] These trends have led many to see a new crisis of democracy[2] and to search for new ways of popular involvement in the democratic political processes.

Prior to the democratic revolutions of the eighteenth and nineteenth centuries it was not unusual for most of a country's population to be totally ignorant of and apparently unaffected by the government that ruled it. The individual was a passive *subject,* not a participating *citizen.* The spread of democracy in the nineteenth century made people participants in the political process. Also at this time, new forms of warfare demanded mass armies of volunteers and conscripts instead of smaller numbers of mercenaries. As a result, even authoritarian regimes recognized the benefits of transforming their subjects into citizens. Today, average people in nearly all states are aware of and clearly affected by their governments. They are generally encouraged to participate in some way in the political process. So widespread is the norm of mass political participation that it is regarded as one of the principal features of the modern political state, in contrast to the nonparticipatory traditional polity.

One reason for the increase in political involvement on the part of the general population is the common acceptance of *popular sovereignty* as the basis of legitimate political power. Since nearly all regimes base their power on the fact that the people are sovereign, it is natural that citizens should be involved in politics to exercise their sovereignty. Even authoritarian states attempt to involve their citizens in controlled forms of political involvement as a means of legitimizing their rule.

Political involvement can occur for a variety of purposes. The most obvious goal is to give citizens influence over the course of policy making. This, of course, is the central goal of participation in democratic states. Participation with the goal of controlling government comes through elections to select leaders and through other means of expressing individual and group views on proposed government policies.

Secondly, political participation can have the goal of controlling the citizenry. In many authoritarian countries, the governments promote participation in acceptable and controllable forms. Involvement, even in a token form, can bring a commitment to the regime and its policies and reduce the risks of revolt. An illustration from college life will help explain this. An instructor may give the class a chance to vote on whether or not an exam should be open-book or closed-book. The instructor's motivation may be to give students their choice, but the effect is also to limit opposition to the decision. Those who feel disadvantaged by the decision cannot complain, because they were allowed to voice their opinions. Thus, involvement becomes a way to enhance the prospects of broad acquiescence to state policies.

A third end of participation may be to extract services that otherwise would have to be performed by the state at a greater cost. From the *levée en masse* (mass mobilization) of military conscription, regimes have found other ways to extend their resources through volunteer services by their citizenry. A heavy snowfall in Beijing, China, leads to tens of thousands of people who, as a voluntary act of civic engagement, go into the streets to remove the snow. The same happens in Western democracies where volunteer civic activities perform many of the duties of the state. One example is the use of volunteers to clean the sides of highways or remove graffiti from walls and bridges. The volunteers feel that they have performed a civic duty, and the state saves the money it would have had to spend to assign paid monitors or police officers.

A fourth goal of participation is to legitimize the regime and its policies. In an era when popular sovereignty and mass participation are the universal norms, political leaders of all kinds of regimes want to involve their citizens in politics in one way or another in order to legitimize their rule. Often the participation is token or ceremonial: voting in elections with only a single candidate; turning out for a parade or a rally; attending political education meetings. Nevertheless, the individual gains a sense of involvement that accords legitimacy to the regime.

Most countries have all four of these motivations at work in various modes of political participation. Democratic regimes generally emphasize the notion of citizen control over government, while nondemocratic countries use participation to control their citizens and to extract services from them. But all four are present in all regimes. Whatever the underlying motivation, mass political participation has become an accepted norm for all forms of government.

INDIVIDUALS AND POLITICS

Political participation involves commitments of time and energy that most people give only grudgingly, if at all. Political action competes with a number of other ways that people can use their leisure time–sports, television, reading, church activities, social clubs, sightseeing, concerts, theater, films, and so forth–and it usually loses out to these other pursuits. Given the choice of how to spend their leisure time, most citizens choose something other than politics. In nearly all societies, the actual number of active political participants represents only a small percentage of the total adult population. Even in those countries where operating democracies make citizen participation important, the level of interest in politics on the part of the population in general is quite low. Usually, less than half of the people in Western democracies express any interest in politics.

Who Participates in Politics

In most societies, participation is correlated most closely with the *level of education:* The higher an individual's level of education the more likely it is that the individual will be an active participant in politics.[3] In third world countries where illiteracy is high, participation is generally low because much of the population is unaware of what is going on in politics. As the education level rises, so does the overall participation in politics. This is not simply a question of overcoming illiteracy. The educated citizen is more likely to engage in the political process than is the uneducated citizen. Such a person is more likely to follow political developments, to see how they affect people's lives, to have opinions on a broader range of political issues, to engage in political discussions, and to become involved in political activities. As a result, in developed countries, there is a strong association between more education and more interest and involvement in politics: High school graduates are more likely to participate than are dropouts; college graduates are more likely to be involved than high school graduates.

While level of education is the most important determinant of participation, there are other factors that influence the degree of an individual's political involvement. Some of these are *personal* factors related to the person's own attitudes, beliefs, and personality. For example, the individual's disposition toward social activities, sense of political efficacy in dealing with government officials, intensity of political attitudes, and perception of civic duties will influence the extent and nature of his or her political involvement. This reflects people's attitudes and their past experience in political action.

Another set of factors influencing involvement relates to the *political setting*. Public interest and involvement are affected by mass media exposure, personal contacts, government efforts to increase or limit participation, and accessibility of political institutions. Of special importance is the degree to which the political decisions affect the individual. The more immediate the impact on the individual, the more likely he or she will become involved. It is always those most affected by zoning changes or planned sanitary disposal sites who circulate petitions, write their legislators, attend meetings, or demonstrate in the streets. This is the NIMBY effect ("not in my back yard") and it is a very powerful political mobilizer. In a broader sense, when people perceive a real crisis in their public affairs—an economic crisis, widespread corruption, uncontrolled street violence—they are more likely to become mobilized for all types of political action. In normal times, they feel less urgency in political action.

Socioeconomic factors—such as social class, occupation, wealth, gender, ethnicity, and age—also influence the extent of participation. Generally, the more affluent are more active than the less affluent; men have been more active than women—but that is rapidly changing now in most countries; dominant ethnic groups are more active than minorities; and older people (except the very oldest) are more active than the youngest people.

Finally, the likelihood of participation is also affected by the individual's own *political beliefs*. Those who hold strong political views or who have accepted an ideology are more likely to become involved in politics than those whose political views and commitments are less well-developed. Participation is also heightened where there are movements or leaders who seek to mobilize citizens behind their causes. Often the level of participation rises as such movements succeed in transforming generalized discontent into a focused political or social movement. Charismatic leaders are sometimes able to mobilize otherwise uninterested people by their personal, even messianic, appeal.

Forms of Political Participation

In the United States, legalized abortion has stimulated strong and emotional political involvement. In attempts to influence public policy, we have seen letter-writing campaigns, displays of posters and bumper stickers, legal action, petitions, electoral politics, public meetings, rallies and demonstrations, sit-ins, boycotts, and even acts of violence by those mobilized around this issue. The abortion debate illustrates the wide range of different modes of participation and also the fact that a single issue may evoke action in many different forms. A wide spectrum of political activities, ranging from nonparticipation to public office holding, is available to the citizens of most states. Figure 4.1 illustrates how the more intense the participation in terms of commitment and time, the fewer the number of people who engage in that activity: the farther up the pyramid, the fewer participants.

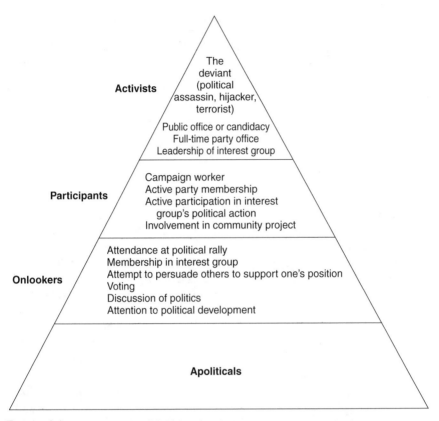

FIGURE 4.1   Pyramid of Political Involvement

Source: David F. Roth and Frank L. Wilson, *The Comparative Study of Politics,* 2nd ed. (Englewood Cliffs: Prentice-Hall, 1980), p. 151.

In well-organized authoritarian regimes, such as past and present communist systems, political participation is often extensive, involving nearly all the population in some form of political action. Authoritarian leaders recognize the dangers of suppressing all forms of participation and instead channel political action into forms that they control and choose. For example, China frequently has resorted to "mass campaigns": party-directed efforts to mobilize the vast population toward objectives set by the party leadership. The theme of the mass campaign varies and has included civic action as mundane as a campaign against flies to the complex political, economic, and social goals of the Great Proletarian Cultural Revolution of 1966–1968. Other forms of unchanneled participation are frowned upon or repressed. Thus, the regime cracked down on the "democracy wall" of political posters in 1979, the student pro-democracy movement of 1989, and demonstrations since 1999 by a quasi-religious sect known as the Falun Gong.

Political scientists distinguish between conventional and unconventional modes of participation.[4] Table 4.1 presents the usual differentiation into conventional

TABLE 4.1   Conventional and Unconventional Modes of Political Participation

Conventional	Unconventional
Voting	Petitions
Election campaign activities	Protests and demonstrations
Group actions	Strikes and sit-ins
Party membership	Boycotts
Meetings with political leaders	Political violence
Letter writing	Terrorism

and unconventional participation. Conventional political actions are those where the individual goes through public officials using channels of participation—such as electoral politics, letter writing, and interest group activities—approved by the elite. Unconventional actions are those where the individual bypasses the political elite through direct action that challenges or bypasses that elite.

The division into two sets of participation modes is misleading because most political actors do not make that distinction as they engage in politics. People see the various forms of participation as a range of activities that may be used according to the response of policymakers, the nature of the issue, or the intensity of their feelings. Sometimes the more direct modes of political action are seen as extreme forms to be used only after other types of action have failed to produce results. More often, concerned citizens see all modes as part of coordinated efforts to affect public policy. Antiabortion activists, for example, have used most of the modes of participation and frequently used them simultaneously.

What is conventional and unconventional varies from country to country. Petitions, for example, are a normal part of American politics but may be unconventional in Britain. Demonstrations may be antiregime and intended to oust the rulers in India but designed only to influence elected officeholders in France. Modes of participation also vary over time within the same country. For example, the building of barricades was once a common form of political action in France; today, barricades are unusual but farmers or truckers regularly clog cities with their tractors or trucks to protest policies that they do not like. It is useful to think of a broad repertoire of political activities that individuals and groups might use in their efforts to influence policy decisions or to reshape the regime.

The effects of the broader repertoire of political actions on democracies is a matter of debate. Some argue that the shift to these forms of direct action are important new means of influence for those citizens who are often left on the margins of the usual political process. Demonstrations, boycotts, unofficial strikes, and other direct actions allow minority groups—ethnic, religious, and political—and the disadvantaged to make their views heard in the political process. Others contend that the use of unconventional forms of participation may well increase the inequalities in participation that already work against the disadvantaged.[5] Still others worry that direct action will be harmful to stability and public order in democracies, especially in the newer ones.

Voting

In spite of the wider repertoire of political action, voting remains the most common form of political participation. This is especially true in democracies, but elections are also an important feature of many authoritarian regimes. Because of the importance of elections as a form of participation, it is important to examine how people choose as they vote and how the structuring of the vote affects the outcome of elections.

Americans need to bear in mind that few other countries offer their voters the chance to elect as many public officials. U.S. voters typically vote in primary elections to select their party's candidate, and then they vote again in general elections for several dozen offices ranging from coroners to judges to members of Congress. In addition, in many U.S. states voters also participate regularly in numerous referendums or initiatives. In contrast, in most other democracies there are no primary elections and the number of elective offices are far fewer. Most national elections in other countries allow their voters choices on only one public office—the member of parliament. Voting still remains the most important political act—and often the only one—in other democracies.

Voting in elections for public officials is often an important political act even in authoritarian regimes. Elections in such regimes rarely offer the voter more than one choice. The political leadership nonetheless expends large amounts of energy to mobilize voters. Elections are occasions for the authoritarian leadership to seek public shows of approval for their regime. The elections legitimize their rule even if there is no choice. The attention to elections was especially great in communist systems where the communist party devoted large amounts of time and energy to the election campaign, viewing it as an opportunity to let the people know what the party had done for them. The overwhelming majorities for the communist party candidates legitimized the regime. China has begun experimenting with competitive elections in local elections. All candidates are approved by the Chinese Communist party, but the existence of multiple candidates seems to produce greater links between citizen attitudes and those of their local leaders.[6]

In developing countries, elections are often periods of great political tension when voters are offered choices between two or more parties. In many developing countries there are no elections. This is true of nearly all military regimes and of many other authoritarian regimes. In other developing countries, elections are held but offer voters no choice other than to vote or abstain. Where voting does involve competition, that competition often is centered on religious cleavages (as in India) or on ethnic divisions (as in Nigeria). Where such themes dominate the campaign, elections are divisive and often violent. Simply to organize an election is a problem in countries where the polling places are far-spread, difficult to monitor except by those committed to the regime, and often lack even electricity to facilitate the counting after the polls have closed. Electoral fraud is often a problem. In Mexico, for example, until the late 1990s elections were almost always followed by protests that the long-term ruling party, the PRI, had stolen the election by corruption or distorting the vote count. The widespread use of international poll monitors starting in the 1990s has allowed impartial judgments on the validity and honesty of many states.

In democracies, citizens go to the poll with the expectation that their actions will affect who governs and the policies that will be adopted. Early research on voting suggested that voters made their election choices based more on inherited partisan ties, social class, or ethnic identification than on a reasoned assessment of which candidate's positions were closest to their own.[7] More recently, there is evidence of growing voter sophistication.[8] Most voters can place themselves within broad political camps based on ideology or self-placement on Left-Right issues. They show less blind party loyalty than in the past and more frequently shift from party to party in different elections.[9] Awareness of issues is higher, and voters appear more likely to vote on issues rather than predetermined partisanship than was the case in the past. This is especially true when the issues cut across traditional party divisions, issues such as immigration, membership in the European Union, and social issues such as women's rights. The growing sophistication of voters in advanced democracies and their willingness to vote on issues rather than partisan commitments or personalities are hopeful signs for improving the linkages between voters and their representatives.

Electoral Systems

There are several ways of structuring the voting process, and the choice of one system over another affects the election outcome.[10] The simplest and most straightforward electoral system is to divide a country into districts with roughly equal population and elect a single representative to serve in the legislature from each of these districts. Whichever candidate draws the most votes is elected, whether or not the candidate receives a majority of the vote. It is known as the single-member-district *plurality electoral system*. In an analogy to a horse race where the horse that crosses the finish line first, even by a nose, is the winner, this electoral arrangement is sometimes referred to as the "first past the post" system. This is the electoral system in use in the United States and Canada. It is also used by many other democratic and nondemocratic regimes.

The advantage of the plurality system is that it is simple and readily understood by the voter. It usually produces clear legislative majorities by exaggerating the strength of the larger parties. Some see this as producing majorities that assist in providing stable parliamentary governments. For example, with only 43 percent of the vote in 1997, the British Labour party ended up with 63 percent of the seats in the House of Commons. In most cases, the plurality system contributes to a two-party system and a dialogue between government and opposition. The elected deputies are closely tied to relatively small districts and see themselves as representing their constituents. The plurality system discourages minor and extremist parties, which are rarely able to get enough votes to win legislative seats under this electoral system.

However, the plurality system is inequitable and distorts the will of the people. For example, if you have a country with four parties competing for a parliamentary seat and party A takes 30 percent, party B takes 28 percent, party C takes 25 percent, and party D takes 17 percent, party A wins the seat even though its candidate received fewer votes than those cast for his or her opponents. When this is repeated in many districts, the result is that important parties cannot win fair representation in the legislature. Again, Britain provides an example: In 1997, the Liberal Democrats took 17 percent of the vote but elected only 7 percent of the seats. Even smaller parties that still represent significant political viewpoints win no seats or do not even contest the elections because they know the plurality electoral system condemns them to defeat.

A more equitable and accurate representation in parliament is assured by using a system of *proportional representation* (PR). Under this electoral arrangement, the seats in the legislature are divided into large, multimember districts. Each party nominates a rank-ordered list of candidates, one for each seat in the district. The vote tends to be more party-oriented than personalized, as the party's list becomes the basis for selecting which candidates will actually sit in parliament. When the votes are tabulated, seats are assigned in proportion to the party's strength in the polls. The top five candidates listed by the party are elected if that party's vote entitles it to five seats in parliament. While specific rules differ from country to country, in principle PR assigns 20 percent of the parliamentary seats to a party if it wins 20 percent of the vote, 35 percent of the seats to the party with 35 percent of the vote, 5 percent of the seats to the party with 5 percent of the vote, and so on. The idea is to make the legislature reflect as accurately as possible the division of political views in the electorate.

Table 4.2 illustrates the effects of electoral systems on representation. In Japan, proportional representation ensured a good reflection in the parliament of all political viewpoints. It did so at the cost of leaving no party with a working majority in the Diet. The result was four different prime ministers in the next eighteen months. In Britain, a single-member-district plurality system essentially disenfranchised the 17 percent of voters who supported the Liberal Democrats. It gave a solid parliamentary majority to the Conservatives who had the most votes but far from a majority of the voters.

The chief advantage of PR is the fairness of representation. It ensures an accurate reflection in the parliament of the political attitudes and views held by the country's population. All views are reflected in parliament in close approximation to their frequency in the electorate. Political parties—and strong parties are a key factor in all democracies—are strengthened because of the party leaders' ability to rank candidates and therefore ensure election of those loyal to the party's principles or leadership. Parties can better balance their tickets by putting women and ethnic minorities on their lists.[11] For example, women are generally better represented in parliaments elected under PR than under plurality systems.

TABLE 4.2   Alternative Electoral Systems and Their Legislative Outcomes

Proportional Representation: Japan, 1993 House of Representatives*

	Percentage of Vote	Percentage of Seats
Liberal Democrats	36.6%	43.6%
Socialist party	15.4	13.7
Shinseito	10.1	10.8
Komeito	8.1	10.0
Japan New party	8.1	10.0
Communist party	7.7	2.9
Democratic Socialists	3.5	2.9
Sagikake	2.6	2.5
Other parties	7.8	3.6

Plurality System: Britain, 1997 House of Commons

	Percentage of Vote	Percentage of Seats
Conservatives	30.7%	25.3%
Labour	43.2	63.4
Liberal Democrats	16.8	7.0
Others	9.3	4.3

*Japan's Diet passed laws in 1995 and 2000 that brought a plurality system to 60 percent of the districts, with the remaining 40 percent of seats still elected through proportional representation.

One disadvantage of proportional representation is that the districts are so large that links between legislators and constituents are more difficult to maintain than when a single legislator represents a relatively concise district. Another problem, faced by Japan and also by Italy, is that the politics of drawing up party lists resulted in extreme factionalization of the larger parties and opened up the parties to corruption.

A more important disadvantage is the effect of PR in permitting the presence of so many parties in parliament that it is difficult to obtain and maintain a governmental majority. Under PR, electoral rules often allow all parties, even those with as few as 1 or 2 percent of the vote, to sit in parliament with the result that parliamentary governments are usually supported by a coalition rather than a single party. That coalition may be unstable and break down, forcing the resignation of the prime minister under the parliamentary system. The classic case of this in recent years has been in Italy, where PR brought over a dozen parties into parliament and where the government needed five parties to have a majority. Some of these parties with as few as 3 or 4 percent of the vote were able to control the government's agenda because they were needed for the coalition to have a parliamentary majority. In such circumstances, the voters lose the ability to hold elected officials accountable for their actions and inactions. The formation of a government and the setting of its agenda depend upon parliamentary wheeling and dealing behind closed doors rather than upon the outcome of a popular election. It should be emphasized that there are countries where PR is used and works well without fragmenting parties or undermining governmental stability. Indeed, PR is the most common form of electoral rules in advanced industrial democracies. It works well in the Scandinavian countries, Belgium, Holland, and Germany.[12]

In recent years, several countries have experimented with mixing the plurality and proportional systems as a way of achieving balance between stability and fair representation. Russia elects half the members of its parliament (Duma) in single-member districts with a plurality vote and the other half based on PR party lists. New Zealand, Japan, and Italy recently revised their former pure PR systems to provide for the election of most of the deputies in single-member districts. In the cases of Japan and Italy, the goals were to address broader political and constitutional problems: governmental instability and excessive party pluralism in Italy; political corruption and party decay in both Japan and Italy. Representation of smaller parties is provided by retaining proportional representation as a means of selecting a minority of the seats. In both Japan and Italy, it is too early to determine the effects of the new electoral rules. The problems of party proliferation and pluralism have emerged in Russia under its system of mixed PR and plurality, complicating the tasks of forming durable governments. But manipulation of the electoral system usually has only marginal effects on the overall political system or even on the party system.

There are other electoral systems in addition to the plurality and PR systems. The French use a two-ballot system that is based on single-member districts. If no candidate receives an outright majority on the first ballot, a second ballot is held a week later with only a simple plurality required for election on that second ballot. Australia has a single transferable vote system with second preferences used when no candidate obtains an absolute majority. There are several variations on this two-ballot system and many other forms of organizing the electoral system. Electoral systems are important political features, but more often they reflect a country's underlying political and social realities rather than shape them.

Changing the electoral rules has emerged in recent years as an approach to more fundamental political problems. There are two problems with this: First, there is only limited evidence that electoral arrangements produce the troubled party system or institutional stability that electoral reforms are usually designed to correct. Much research suggests that the electoral laws are there because they reflect rather than determine the underlying political forms.[13] Second, changes in electoral laws are far from disinterested. When the electoral law changes, it is usually to benefit the political chances of parties making the change. Those in power often manipulate the rules to enhance their electoral prospects.[14] Such manipulations can lead to public alienation when people believe that the rules are designed to thwart the public's will.

Above all, the public's perception of fairness of the electoral system is crucial. Where people feel that the electoral rules are unfair—as many do in Britain's plurality system—or produce alienation from the political system as a result of instability or corruption—as in Italy's and Japan's systems of proportional representation—the result is to strike at the essence of democratic legitimacy. Representative democracy stands on free elections, and if citizens perceive that the elections are not fair, the whole process can be undermined.

Referendums

In the United States, we frequently have referendums where state governments seek voter endorsement of major policy changes. In addition, Americans vote on measures put on the ballot by citizen initiatives at the state and local levels. There has never been a national level referendum or initiative in the United States. In other countries, citizen initiatives are rare, but governments occasionally seek voters' opinions on issues of national importance through referendums.[15] France, for example, voted in 2000 on a referendum to reduce the length of the president's term of office from seven to five years. Switzerland makes extensive use of the initiative and referendum. Canada has used referendums both at the provincial and federal levels to seek solutions to the issue of French Canadian separatism. In the last fifteen years, Italy has had several multiple-issue referendums as a means of getting around the bottleneck of its fragmented parliament. Britain has had only one national referendum—in 1974 on membership in the European Union—but there have been a number of regional referendums: in Northern Ireland, Scotland, Wales, and the London area. Referendums are beginning to be seen by British governments as a way of evading divisive issues. For example, governments have discussed using the referendum to resolve the question of joining the European currency—the euro. Often, referendums are used to approve entirely new constitutional arrangements or to shape new constitutions, as has been the case in postcommunist Russia. In nondemocratic systems, referendums may be used as ways of giving democratic credentials to an otherwise autocratic regime. It is this plebescitarian function of referendums that makes advocates of democracy uneasy about the consultation of the voters through referendums on any but the most important issues.

The referendum is a way of introducing a bit of direct democracy into our representative democracies. New technologies, the web especially, often seem to offer potential for expanding direct democracy.[16] Critics, however, contend that referendums can easily be distorted and turned into plebiscites or votes of endorsement on the government's policies or personnel. Plebiscites are linked with a long tradition of use by authoritarian leaders to legitimize their rule. Other problems include the specific wording of proposals and the danger of demagogic campaigning. In the several advanced democracies that have experimented with referendums, turnout has declined with use. In the most recent referendum in France, for example, only 30 percent turned out to vote on reducing the length of the president's term of office. There is a sense in France, Italy, Switzerland, and elsewhere that elected officials ought to be making these decisions rather than submitting them to the vagaries of direct democracy.

WOMEN IN POLITICS

Among the most important groups taking an increasing role in politics are women. This is true in virtually all types of regimes, but the impact of women is especially important in advanced democracies. Women are playing much more active political roles; they are running for office and winning seats in national politics; they have headed governments in Britain, France, Norway, India, and elsewhere; they are bringing issues of concern to women to the forefront of the political agenda in most Western democracies and, more slowly, to developing countries.[17]

Women did not receive full political rights until after World War I (for the United States, Canada, Britain, Germany, and a few others) or even after World War II (for France, Italy, Japan, and others). In addition, even after winning the right to vote, they were still encumbered by social laws and traditions that kept them to secondary roles in politics. They were often less educated and less likely to be exposed to a variety of influences in the workplace than were their husbands. As a result, there were clear gender differences in political activities until the 1970s. In general, women voted less frequently, were less likely to engage in any other kind of political action, and held more conservative or traditional views than did men. It was accurate to speak of a sharp gender gap in politics.

As women have overcome the legal inequities that they faced as recently as the 1960s, and as they have acquired better education and had more opportunities to leave the home, these gender differences in political activities have declined. This is particularly notable in election turnout. Electoral turnout among women is now at the same rate or higher than men. There is sometimes a "gender gap" in voting, but it is one where women vote more frequently than men for candidates perceived to have greater interest in issues that affect women such as education, health care, and equal rights. However, in many countries there remains greater reluctance among women to vote for parties that are perceived as extremist (both on the Right and the Left) or for candidates who challenge mainline positions or images. Women are also less likely to engage in protest politics than are men.

Since the 1980s, there have been important increases in the number of women serving in elected offices. The increases were especially notable in local and regional politics. As more women choose political careers or avocations, we can expect that tendency to continue and to bring greater equity in the representation of women at the national level. Already the proportion of women in national parliaments everywhere has increased; women figure more regularly and more prominently in national governments. There still remain important inequalities that are due more to continuation of old patterns of political socialization than to formal barriers to women in politics. There often appear to be double standards at work, with women held to a different standard than men. For example, as Kim Campbell was about to be named Canadian prime minister, she was accused of being "ambitious." She responded:

> A man is forceful; a woman is pushy. A man stands his ground; a woman is a complaining bitch.[18]

Campbell caught well a continuing attitudinal barrier still limiting women in politics—and in other social and professional contexts. As attitudes change, these informal barriers will also disappear. Gender now has little effect on voting behavior. In most industrial democracies, voting studies indicate that both men and women are ready to vote for women candidates as willingly as they vote for men candidates.

Women's movements have become important in many democracies. They have emerged out of peace, student, and environmental movements to advocate women's rights and issues. They have mobilized women to become involved in politics, and they have brought to the fore women's issues such as abortion, equal employment, and child care. However, many of these women's movements have aligned themselves with radical Left political groups that leave them politically isolated. Their presence on the political scene, however, has stimulated mainline parties to pay greater attention to women's concerns and to give them more prominent political roles.

There are important differences among democratic countries in the degree of success for women's movements in bringing more women into leading political roles. Tables 4.3 and 4.4 illustrate these differences in several countries. Women

TABLE 4.3   Women in National Parliaments and Governments in Selected Countries

Country	Percentage of Women in Principal Legislative Body	Rank among 176 Countries	Percentage of Women in National Cabinet
Brazil	5.7%	86	n.a.
Britain	18.4	30	22.7%
Canada	19.9	27	21.4
China	21.8	23	n.a.
Denmark	37.4	2	38.1
Finland	36.5	3	37.5
France	10.9	57	35.7
Germany	30.9	7	31.3
India	9.0	68	n.a.
Italy	11.1	56	14.3
Japan	7.3	79	0
Mexico	n.a.	n.a.	n.a.
The Netherlands	36.0	5	26.7
Nigeria	3.4	99	0
Norway	36.4	4	47.4
Sweden	42.7	1	50.0
Russia	7.7	76	n.a.
United States	12.9	48	25.0

Source: For parliament: Interparliamentary Union as of September 2000. Web site: ipu.org. For cabinets: Alan Siaroff, "Women's Representation in Legislatures and Cabinets in Industrial Democracies," *International Political Science Review* 21 (April 2000): 200.

TABLE 4.4   Women Political Leaders

Countries with Women Prime Ministers since 1970

*Bangladesh	Mongolia
Britain	*New Zealand
Bulgaria	Nicaragua
Burundi	Norway
Canada	Pakistan
Central African Republic	Poland
Dominica	Portugal
France	Rwanda
Guyana	Sri Lanka
Haiti	Turkey
Iceland	Yugoslavia
Israel	
Lithuania	

Countries with Women Presidents since 1970

Argentina	Ireland
Bolivia	*Latvia
Burundi	Liberia
China	Malta
Ecuador	Mongolia
*Finland	Nicaragua
Germany (German Democratic Republic)	*Panama
Guinea Bissau	Philippines
Guyana	San Marino
Haiti	*Sri Lanka
Iceland	Switzerland

*Women held these posts at the end of 2000.

Source: Roberto Ortiz de la Zárate Arce, "Zárate's Political Collection." Web site: http://www.terra.es/personal2/monolith/00women3conf.htm

have been most effective in penetrating legislative bodies and governments in Scandinavia. As Table 4.4 indicates, in a growing number of countries, citizens appear willing to have women as their chief executives. This is true in a wide variety of political and cultural settings.

In the developing world, women generally still face traditional barriers to their full participation in society and politics. In much of Latin America, machismo—or the forceful assertion of maleness—keeps women in secondary social and political roles. Islamic religious tenets likewise restrict the social role of women, and fundamentalist Moslems campaign to keep women in traditional roles. In many other traditional cultures, women find customs and values that inhibit or prevent them from playing significant political roles. It is interesting to note in Table 4.4 that despite Islam's reputed treatment of women as inferiors, there

have been several women political leaders in countries with large Moslem populations such as Bangladesh, Pakistan, and Turkey. In India, in spite of the precedent
of Prime Minister Indira Gandhi, women are usually regarded as having fewer
legal and political rights than men. On the other hand, there are several cultures,
notably in southern Nigeria, where women have long played important economic
roles in the marketplaces and have used those positions to gain political influence.

In spite of such problems, even in developing countries women are playing
increasingly active parts in the political lives of their countries. There are often
sharp disparities between the growing political activities of women in the modernized and urban centers compared with the retention of traditional roles in remote
or rural regions. Although there are often women's movements in developing political systems, they are generally tackling more basic problems—gaining equal legal
status and protecting women from traditional practices such as the Indian tradition
of burning wives on the funeral pyres of their husbands—rather than seeking
greater political roles for women.

Full political equality for women means more than simply bringing women
into the existing political institutions. Many expect that the presence of more
women in public office will bring new issues to the fore and give new emphasis to
other issues or that women will govern with a different style. But it is not at all
clear that those things will happen. There is debate over whether women have a
specific set of issues that differ from men or, if they do have such different agendas, that the women who come to power will act on them. In countries where
women have emerged as top leaders or grown in numbers in the legislative bodies, there is often no change in political styles or agendas. There are two ways of
interpreting such experience. The first is that these women were simply interested
in power and in using it fully to achieve their political and ideological goals. Certainly this would explain the performance of Britain's Margaret Thatcher and
India's Indira Gandhi. Neither woman accepted nor advocated a special women's
agenda in politics, but both were very adept in accumulating and using political
power for their purposes. They simply did not seek policies that are features of the
contemporary feminist movement. An alternative explanation is that women politicians and leaders are socialized into and act within "gendered institutions" that
limit their contributions to the usual patterns of politics and policies. In short, even
as women increase their presence and prominence in politics, some argue that they
face obstacles of institutions and practices that are dominated by male biases and
principles.

Increased involvement of women in public office may contribute to greater
legitimacy of the political system. It is anomalous that democracies seem to leave
out of active political roles half of their population. In most countries, both men
and women would like to see women having a greater role in politics. Polls show
that citizens believe women will be a positive influence on the political process.
(See Table 4.5.)

Clearly, this is an area of political life that is changing. Women are increasingly present in the political lives of all types of countries. But it is still not at all

TABLE 4.5 Voters' Perceptions of the Effect of More Women Public Office Holders

Question: "Do you think that this country would be governed better or worse if more women were in political office?"

Country	"Better"	"Worse"	"No Difference"	"Don't Know"
Britain	51%	11%	28%	10%
Canada	50	9	32	9
China	30	14	37	19
France	59	20	15	5
Germany	51	15	26	7
India	50	30	15	5
Japan	44	14	28	14
Mexico	39	13	33	15
United States	57	17	19	7

Source: Gallup Poll, August 1996.

clear that their participation will produce fundamental political change. Some predict that the growing power of women will bring new emphasis to issues that are presumably of direct concern to women: resistance to militarism, reproductive rights, education, health care, equal political roles, and greater roles for women in economic and development issues.[19] Others see women as more likely to follow the examples of Thatcher and Gandhi with political agendas and styles little different from those of the men who have dominated political life until now.

POLITICAL PARTICIPATION AND POLITICAL STABILITY

There is a disagreement among political scientists about how much political participation is desirable and good.[20] "Government of the people" seems to be a nice slogan, but many question how much the people should be involved. The conservative viewpoint stresses the dangers of excessive participation. Under most circumstances, people have other priorities than political involvement and it is only when things are already going badly that mass participation occurs. Then participation is likely to exceed the ability of the regime to respond to it and channel it, and thus it further complicates the resolution of the crisis. This argument is also known as the elitist view of participation since it contends that those who participate under normal circumstances are more likely to hold democratic values than are those who are less interested and mobilized only by some crisis or demagogue.

On the other hand, there are those who argue that only full participation can ensure long-term political stability. Their challenge to the elitist view is based first on democratic ideals and then on practical politics. Those favoring mass participation see that as essential to fulfill the democratic promise. They argue that failure to promote full participation inevitably benefits those who already enjoy the most advantages in society: the wealthy and well-educated. Limits on participation are usually likely to constrain consideration of views by those already dissatisfied. Their inability to express this discontent only exacerbates their political unhappiness. Only when the views of all citizens are freely expressed and considered can the political system be assured of stability.

The argument will go on with persuasive cases on both sides. What seems agreed upon by all is that deliberate efforts to prevent political participation by groups who want to take part is likely to lead citizens to view their system as illegitimate. Too limited participation brings alienation, protest, and then revolt. This process was well illustrated by the fall of communist regimes in Russia and Eastern Europe. By the time communist reformers were able to introduce *glasnost,* or an opening of the system, it was too late. By then the population wanted not reform of the existing system but an entirely new regime. The resulting explosion of new participation poses a challenge to the new regimes still trying to build themselves while facing unparalleled mass participation.

In established Western democracies, the problem is not excessive participation but declining public confidence and lessened public involvement in the political process. Many worry about the dangers of democracy when government must do without the people.[21] While citizens in advanced democracies generally have favorable general impressions of democracy at work in their countries, they are increasingly critical of current political parties, leaders, and institutions that implement democracy. Opinion polls in most advanced democracies find that trust in elected officials to carry out the will of the people rather than their own narrow interests has declined from two decades ago. Political parties have lost members, and fewer citizens are willing even to identify with them as their supporters. Public forums on major issues or campaign debates are poorly attended and, if televised, draw low ratings. Voter turnout has declined in virtually all countries to post-World War II lows. (See Table 4.6.)

While there is little debate about the reality of declining citizen involvement and trust in the political scene, there is little agreement over the causes and consequences of these trends. For some, the trends in political participation are part of a general decline in social trust and involvement in activities beyond the home and family. Others see the rise in political cynicism as the result of multiple, well-publicized scandals involving nearly all mainstream political parties and their leaders. Some give a positive spin to these apparently disturbing trends: They indicate broad satisfaction with the existing system and a sense that there is no need for alternatives to present policies and politics. Two observers of American politics captured this viewpoint:

> Lack of participation can signify relative satisfaction with things as they are. . . .
> [W]hen confronted by matters that they feel are personally relevant, Americans do become politically active. But when nothing particular concerns them, voters are content to remain quiet, occupying themselves with more pleasurable and more edifying nonpolitical activities, while letting the politicians do the dirty work of negotiating with various interest groups.[22]

TABLE 4.6   Decline in Voting Turnout—Mid-1970s to Most Recent National
Parliamentary Election

Country	Election Turnout, Mid-1970 Election		Election Turnout, Most Recent Election		Difference
Britain	77.9%	(March 1974)	59.2%	(2001)	−18.2%
Canada[1]	71.0	(1974)	61.2	(2000)	−9.8
China	*no competitive national elections*				
France	70.6	(1973)	59.9	(1997)	−10.7
Germany[1]	83.8	(1976)	83.0	(1998)	−0.8
India[1]	60.5	(1977)	59.7	(1999)	−0.8
Japan[1]	73.6	(1976)	59.8	(1996)	−14.4
Mexico[1,2]	64.1	(1976)	60.0	(2000)	−4.1
Nigeria[1,2]	35.3	(1979)	52.3	(1999)	+17.0
Russia[1,2]	none		60.5	(1999)	
United States[1,2]	53.5	(1976)	47.2	(1996)	−6.3

Notes: Except as noted, turnout figures reflect voters as a percentage of the voting age population (VAP). Countries marked with a superscript [1] use data on *registered* voters for both election periods. All elections are for parliamentary elections except for presidential elections in those countries marked with a superscript [2].

Source: International Institute for Democracy and Electoral Assistance (IDEA). Web site: http://www.idea.int

Those who see little cause for alarm in figures on declining confidence and political participation also point to the low levels of voter support for antisystem parties in advanced democracies. The surge of support for far Right parties in some European countries is a worry, but the phenomenon occurs in only a few countries and seems to have causes beyond disaffection with democracy in these countries.

It is easy for pundits and scholars to exaggerate the dangers of shifting patterns of participation and lower public confidence in democratic institutions. Concern about the trend of increased cynicism and nonparticipation by the people who are supposed to make democracy is widespread. In some cases, it has led to institutional and political party changes to respond to the challenges. We are likely to see further efforts to renew public confidence in democratic institutions. Such reforms are needed and will be welcomed. Nevertheless, I would share the view expressed by Pippa Norris in the conclusion to her volume on the rise of critical citizens: "the sky is not falling down for democracy."[23]

CONCLUSION

Each political system, whether democratic or authoritarian, faces challenges of responding to the actions and wishes of their citizens as they engage in politics. These challenges will grow in the next decades because more people are gaining the education that allows them to participate effectively. In addition, new technologies associated with the emerging "information superhighways," such as interactive video and electronic communications, offer greater opportunities for citizens to make their views known. The task of government everywhere will be to facilitate, channel, organize, and, most important, respond to that potential for new political participation.

In the meantime, individual citizens play important political roles in a variety of settings. However, the more visible and still more effective political actors are usually the interest groups and political parties that organize large numbers of citizens for collective action. We turn now to look at the role of parties and interest groups.

NOTES

1. Pippa Norris, ed., *Critical Citizens: Global Support for Democratic Government* (Oxford, England: Oxford University Press, 1999).

2. Susan J. Pharr, Robert D. Putnam, and Russell J. Dalton, "Trouble in the Advanced Democracies? A Quarter-Century of Declining Confidence," *Journal of Democracy* 11 (April 2000): 5–25. See also Susan J. Pharr and Robert D. Putnam, *Disaffected Democracies: What's Troubling the Trilateral Countries?* (Princeton, NJ: Princeton University Press, 2000).

3. For discussions of factors influencing participation, see Sidney Verba, Norman Nie, and Jae-on Kim, *Participation and Political Equality: A Seven-Nation Study* (Cambridge, MA: Harvard University Press, 1978), Samuel H. Barnes, Max Kaase, and others, *Political Action: Mass Participation in Five Western Democracies* (Beverly Hills, CA: Sage, 1979), and Alan Marsh, *Political Action in Europe and the U.S.A.* (London: Macmillan, 1990).

4. The best description of these different modes of participation is found in Barnes, Kaase, et al., *Political Action.* See also Richard Topf, "Beyond Electoral Participation," in Hans-Dieter Klingemann and Dieter Fuchs, eds., *Citizens and the State* (Oxford, England: Oxford University Press, 1995), and M. Kent Jennings and Jan van Deth, eds., *Continuities in Political Action* (Berlin: de Gruyter, 1990).

5. Sidney Verba, Kay Schlozman, and Henry Brady, *Voice and Equality: Civic Volunteerism in American Politics* (Cambridge, MA: Harvard University Press, 1995).

6. Melanie Manin, "The Electoral Connection in the Chinese Countryside," *American Political Science Review* 90 (December 1996): 736–48.

7. Angus Campbell et al., *The American Voter* (New York: Wiley, 1960), David Butler and Donald Stokes, *Political Change in Britain* (New York: St. Martin's, 1969), and Michael Margolis, *Viable Democracy* (New York: St. Martin's, 1979).

8. Russell J. Dalton, *Citizen Politics: Public Opinion and Political Parties in Advanced Western Democracies* (Chatham, NY: Chatham House, 1996), pp. 220–39.

9. Russell J. Dalton, Scott C. Flanagan, and Paul Allen Beck, eds., *Electoral Change in Advanced Industrial Democracies: Realignment or Dealignment?* (Princeton, NJ: Princeton University Press, 1984).

10. Arend Lijphart, ed., *Electoral Systems and Party Systems* (Oxford, England: Oxford University Press, 1994).

11. Wilma Rule and Joseph F. Zimmerman, eds., *Electoral Systems in Comparative Perspective: Their Impact on Women and Minorities* (Westport, CT: Greenwood Press, 1994).

12. In Germany, PR determines the final composition of parliament but half the seats are elected under a plurality system. The voters cast two votes: one for an individual candidate in their district, the second for a party list. The results of the vote on the party list determines the overall party composition of the Bundestag. Each party with at least 5 percent of the vote ends up with a percentage of seats that corresponds to the percentage that party receives on the second or PR part of the ballot.

13. See G. Bingham Powell Jr., *Contemporary Democracies: Participation, Stability, and Violence* (Cambridge, MA: Harvard University Press, 1982).

14. See the classic study of this effect in France: Peter Campbell, *French Electoral Systems and Elections Since 1789* (Hamdon, CT: Archon Books, 1965).

15. David Butler and Austin Ranney, eds., *Referendums Around the World: The Growing Use of Direct Elections* (Washington: American Enterprise Institute, 1994), and Ian Budge, *The New Challenge of Direct Democracy* (Cambridge, England: Polity Press, 1997).

16. For an interesting look at the internet's potential in governing, see "Survey: Government and the Internet," *The Economist*, 24 June 2000.

17. Barbara J. Nelson and Najma Chowdhury, eds., *Women and Politics Worldwide* (New Haven, CT: Yale University Press, 1994).

18. *Boston Sunday Globe*, 20 June 1993.

19. See Nelson and Chowdhury, eds., *Women and Politics Worldwide*.

20. A typical explanation of concerns about too much participation can be found in Samuel P. Huntington and Joan M. Nelson, *No Easy Choice: Political Participation in Developing Countries* (Cambridge, MA: Harvard University Press, 1976). G. Bingham Powell Jr. challenges this viewpoint by using empirical data from twenty-nine contemporary democracies and concludes that less not more participation is likely to produce instability. See Powell, *Contemporary Democracies*.

21. See Norris, *Critical Citizens*, Pharr and Putnam, eds., *Disaffected Democracies*, and Pharr, Putnam, and Dalton, "Trouble in Advanced Democracies."

22. John A. Hall and Charles Lindholm, *Is America Breaking Apart?* (Princeton, NJ: Princeton University Press, 1999).

23. Norris, *Critical Citizens*, p. 270.

Chapter 5

Political Parties

Without parties there can be no organized and coherent politics. When politics lacks coherence, there can be no accountable democracy.

E. E. Schattschneider
Party Government (1942)

As I illustrated in Chapter 4, individual participation other than voting is not widespread in most political systems. Individuals who are not interested enough in politics to become sufficiently well informed to make independent decisions and engage in individual political acts often find political parties useful devices for simplifying their political decision making. They join or identify with a political party that seems closest to their views or interests. They rely on that party to guide them in deciding their positions on specific issues and as a means of collectively expressing their viewpoints. Political parties then serve as devices for organizing and focusing political participation. They can also effectively link the general public with the political process to the extent that they crystallize and organize popular demands and seek to introduce these demands into the policy-making process. Since parties become the agents by which most individuals act in politics, they serve as the primary link between the isolated individual and the political system.

In democratic states, there is usually more than one political party. We refer to the *party system* as these multiple parties compete to seek office and to dominate the government. The notion of the state's party system includes the number of parties; how they interact with each other; how close or polarized they are on issues, personalities, and ideas about the purpose and means of the state; and the attachments between the various parties and socioeconomic and cultural cleavages in their country.

Political parties are found in most countries, but they vary sharply in style, form, and purpose from one type of regime to another. There are some countries where parties are not present, either because they have been banned outright or because they have dwindled away as regimes have ignored them. Wherever parties are present, however, they are central to the linkage of people and politics.

PARTIES IN ADVANCED DEMOCRACIES

An early classic treatment of political parties identified clearly the vital role of political parties in modern, representative democracy. The political party is the

> great intermediary which links social forms and ideologies to official governmental institutions and relates them to political action within the larger political community.[1]

This role of parties in linking individuals and groups of citizens to the political process makes parties of vital importance to the operation of modern democracies.[2] Yet the very nature of competitive electoral politics often works in ways that hinder the party's ability to perform this linkage responsibility.

In the democratic setting, political parties center their activities on elections. Their central task is to contest and win these elections. Their health and success is evaluated primarily by their ability to gain votes and win elections. The other tasks they perform of setting issues, recruiting and training political leaders, and participating in the policy-making process are nearly always contingent upon electoral success. Parties in Western democracies generally select their tactics, issues, leaders, and coalition strategies based on calculations of how these choices will affect their electoral prospects rather than on notions of linking people with politics. With the exception of a few very minor parties, such as the Socialist Workers party or Communist party in the United States, who continue as tiny organizations on the irrelevant margins of politics, parties that fail to succeed in electoral competition fall into decline and disappear.

Ideological "Families"

In the United States the political notion of Left and Right has always been a difficult one because both the Republican and Democratic parties have been centrist or "middle-of-the-road" parties. They both represent broad coalitions of conservatives and liberals (in the American sense of those terms). U.S. parties are sometimes criticized as lacking in differences; they are, according to the old saw, no more different than "Tweedledee" and "Tweedledum." Over the past decade, there has been a growing polarization between these parties, and issues have emerged that have opened sharper distinctions between the parties than in most of our history: abortion, welfare programs, the place of Christian values in American society, affirmative action, law and order. Even now, however, the traditional meaning of Left and Right is vague in the United States, with liberals labeling as "reactionary" those positions they reject and conservatives scorning as "liberal" policies that they oppose.

In other democratic countries, the notions of Left and Right have had more clear-cut meaning. The Left championed parliamentary democracy, civil liberties, a limit on the influence of the Church in politics, a strong role for the state in economic matters, and economic and political equality. The Right placed more emphasis on the need for a strong and authoritative state than it did on individual rights, recognized a political and social role for the Church and its values, opposed state economic intervention, and placed little emphasis on the importance of equality. The distinctions between Left and Right and points in between were solidified by the growth and definition of well-developed ideologies such as communism, social democracy, liberalism, and fascism. These ideologies offered reasoned world views of how society is or ought to be structured. The clarity of these Left-Right differences long characterized democratic politics in Europe and other parts of the world, but not the United States.

In the United States, parties avoided formal ideologies but developed a pragmatism that defined both the means and ends of society. Pragmatism reflects a commitment to few ideals other than to solve problems on their merits rather than to seek guidance in an ideology. This approach to problems was supposedly free from any dogma, except the dogma that flexibility and pragmatism should prevail. Yet pragmatism was in effect as ideological as communism or liberalism, in spite of its advocates' denials. It allowed polarization of parties as well as did the old ideologies.

In the second half of the twentieth century, pragmatism spread to parties around the world and contributed to the demise of old notions of Left and Right. Three related developments have weakened the utility of the Left-Right distinction in European and other democracies.

First, many of the issues underlying the notions of both Left and Right no longer have much practical meaning in advanced industrial democracies. The issues of the state's role in the economy, the place of religion in politics, appropriate foreign policies, and the nature of representative democracy no longer separate major parties in most democratic countries. A broad political, social, and economic consensus is firmly in place in most Western democracies. Second, new issues have emerged that do not fit into traditional Left-Right divisions: political decentralization, the nature of sovereignty, immigration and naturalization, law and order, and environmental protection. Divisions over these issues cut across traditional Left-Right categories, and these are the issues that are most likely to be paramount in the coming decades. Finally, as ideologies have become less important both in the minds of the general public and in the rhetoric and programs of parties, much of the traditional meaning of Left and Right has been lost. A good illustration of this can be seen in press discussions of the political developments in former communist countries. Those who oppose democratic and free enterprise reforms are labeled as "right-wing" or "conservative" even though they are usually hard-line communists who for decades have been placed on the far left of the political spectrum.

While the old ideological issues have lost relevance, they remain powerful cues to voters on the underlying values and priorities of modern parties. As a result, Left-Right divisions that have their roots in the nineteenth century still affect voting decisions in the twenty-first century. But the parties are increasingly alike in the acceptance of the neoliberal agenda of the last two decades. For example, in Britain, it is hard to find differences between Tony Blair's new Labour party and the Conservatives. New political and social cleavages on the environment, sovereignty (participation in the European Union for European countries and globalization for all states), urban decline and law enforcement, women's rights, and immigration are of growing interest and importance among voters. But they are rarely incorporated into party programs—beyond very broad and noncommittal statements—because they divide parties within themselves as much or more than they separate different parties. There is a tendency for "leftist" parties to become advocates of new values such as environmental protection, greater tolerance toward immigrants, respect for the rights of those accused of criminal acts, and greater equality for women.[3] New parties championing the new issues, such as environmental parties, have emerged in some countries but have not enjoyed general success. Parties opposing these new values have been more successful, at least in a few countries where extreme Right parties have emerged as powerful electoral challengers to the mainstream Center-Right.

This is a time of transition when the usual definitions of Left and Right are no longer relevant to real politics. New anchors for these traditional labels are only slowly developing, in part because they cut across existing parties and in part because they reflect new controversies that existing parties prefer to avoid.

Party Organization in Advanced Democracies

After the Second World War, a French political scientist, Maurice Duverger, wrote an influential study of political parties.[4] He distinguished among parties on the basis of their organization: *cadre* parties based on small circles of followers around those holding public office; *mass* parties with large memberships drawn from broad social categories; and *devotee* parties of totally committed militants ready to use all their time and talents in the service of an ideological cause. Duverger expected the mass party—with its large numbers of active members, solid basis in specific social cleavage, and clear commitment to a set of doctrines or ideology—would prevail in competitive democracies.

At the beginning of a new century, class-based, mass parties are rare in advanced democracies. Party politicians discovered that it is far more efficient in terms of organizational costs and electoral outcome to cultivate loose coalitions of voters who identify with a party and who come together from all parts of society at election time. To appeal only to a single social group or to those with a particular set of doctrines limits the electoral success of the party. As a result, parties seek broad coalitions around vague, issue-related promises rather than specific doctrines. The emergence of these catchall parties began after the Second World

War;[5] by the end of the century, the catchall party was virtually universal in advanced democracies.

The decline in the meanings of Left and Right and the predominance of a means-driven pragmatic dogma deprived political parties in advanced democracies of some key resources. Links between parties and society through social class or religion have weakened, leaving many parties without a solid core of supporters on whom they can rely. Without visions of a desirable future, it is harder for parties to recruit and retain members. Policy making on the merits of each individual issue and through compromise and accommodation requires patience and negotiating skills, not purpose or zeal. Resulting policies look the same whether they have been enacted by left-wing or right-wing parties. With all parties embracing pragmatism, there should be little wonder why citizens are less committed to political parties and less involved in politics than in the past.

Even with these important changes, parties in most democracies tend to be much better organized than American political parties. They have ranks of card-carrying members and structures that go from the grass-roots level to the national level, with regular meetings even when elections are not imminent. Their members in parliament generally vote together as blocs in contrast to the frequent pattern of cross-party coalition building that occurs in the U.S. Congress. They usually appear more coherent in issue positions than do the varied individuals who claim to be Democrats or Republicans. There is, however, a distinct trend toward the weakening of the party organizations in most democratic countries.[6]

Current trends in party organization in advanced democracies both respond to lessened citizen involvement and further the separation between parties and citizens. Parties are becoming little more than labels that candidates for public office may use as they seek election. The parties' democratic function of linking citizens with government has been replaced in today's "service-oriented" parties by professional vote-getting machines. Party bureaucracies have grown in size even as their grass-roots membership has declined. More important, party bureaucracies have changed in nature from part-time notables and dedicated party activists to the well-educated, career professionals skilled in survey research, organizational management, and public relations. In the new century, trends toward the use of party and candidate web sites, e-mail, and automated telephone calls portend yet further growth in the need for expert and technical support. Party organizations persist now to assist like-minded candidates in winning elections. They provide experts in analyzing public opinion to conduct research on issues and positions that catch people's attention and support. They offer public relations staff to assist in media campaigns and direct candidates toward professional campaign managers. Modern parties are becoming more and more "client-serving" organizations to assist candidates for public office.

The trend toward "parties of service" began in the United States[7] but it is now spreading to nearly all political party systems in large advanced democracies. In Britain, Tony Blair's wildly successful election campaign in 1997 was not based on the Labour party's organization but rather on Blair's personal campaign team, which effectively took over the party, determined the party platform less on the concerns of the party rank and file than on the dictates of focus groups, and set campaign strategies. French presidential election campaigns of the major party candidates are conducted beyond the traditional party structures through heavy reliance on professional campaign managers. In a like manner, the 2000 election for the Canadian House of Commons reflected the professionalization of election campaigning.

The mainstream parties today are sometimes seen as "cartel parties" because in most democracies they benefit from direct and campaign subsidies, free access to the media, and funds to support research on public issues.[8] As the major parties alternate in government, they collude with each other and with government to protect their privileged access to public office and to the benefits available from the state. State subsidies are particularly important as parties have shifted from labor-intensive mass-membership parties to capital-intensive parties relying on professionals and specialists. Indeed, the costs of modern parties and campaigns are so great that even those parties receiving generous state subsidies—such as the Japanese Liberal Democrats, the German Christian Democrats, and the French Socialists and Gaullists—have resorted to illegal contributions that have led to scandals when such illicit contributions are uncovered. These scandals confirm citizens' disrespect for parties and politicians.

The major challenge for Western democratic parties at the start of the century is maintenance of some degree of commitment and loyalty within the electorate. Citizens join parties less frequently than they did in the past; those who do join are less active than in the past. The intensity of voters' partisan commitments is also down nearly everywhere. In most democratic countries, political parties are viewed with suspicion by the citizenry. When respondents are asked how much trust they have in public institutions (such as the courts, legislatures, executives, and the media), political parties invariably end up with the lowest scores. They are seen as self-serving, unrepresentative, and often corrupt; their leaders are seen as unattractive and unqualified for public office.

Parties and Government in Advanced Democracies

Political parties are often seen as playing a key role in establishing governments and providing citizens a link with these governments. *Party government* is a way of organizing representative democracy to assist voters with varying levels of political interest and awareness in exercising democratic control.[9] Ideally, under party government, political parties offer the electorate clear programs of what they will do once elected. The winning party then has a public mandate for its action. The winning party selects all key government figures and then works to accomplish its electoral pledges. It is assured of legislative success by the presence of a cohesive and disciplined party majority in the legislature to enact the government's proposals. A loyal civil service ensures that the new laws are implemented in accordance with the government's intent. Voters, then, at the next election can hold the government responsible for its actions and policies; if the voters like the policies, they can reelect the governing party; if they disapprove of the policies, they can throw out the government and bring in a new party committed to a new program.

This notion of party government is particularly appealing because it facilitates maintaining clear lines of responsibility and accountability in representative democracies. The governing party is accountable for its actions and inactions. Even those who have only marginal interests in politics can make rational electoral choices by their alignment with a party and its policies.

The model party government, however, is the exception rather than the rule. Party programs are not usually as clearly stated as expected under the party government model. Even when a winning party has a relatively clear program, it is not always accurate to view its election victory as a "mandate" for the party's program. Most democratic governments are made up of coalitions of two or more parties, and their policies are not any one of their programs but a shifting compromise among their several programs. In many instances, the composition of the governing coalition is not decided until after the elections and then as a result of behind-the-scenes negotiations among party leaders over who gets which ministry. The legislature is rarely as disciplined, the bureaucracy rarely as compliant as expected by the party government model. As a result, real democratic governments rarely meet the requirements for democratic accountability as posited in the party government model. Nevertheless, in a general sense parties are still the best means for linking citizens with the state and permitting some citizen control over politics in contemporary democracies.

Parties and Democracy

In 1993, Italian democracy was shaken by the growing public revulsion about its political parties. The parties were factitious and unable to govern. Italian parties already bore the blame for Italy's governmental instability as their divisions and indiscipline had produced over fifty governments since 1946, most of which lasted only a few months. Then, in 1993, on a daily basis, one after another party leader faced accusations of financial and political corruption; many faced the additional charge of collaboration with the Mafia. By early 1993, nearly a third of the members of parliament had already been named as facing possible legal action for their malfeasance in office. No longer was the Italian party system blamed only for government instability; it now faced the additional accusation of undermining the very regime. The parties' crises had produced a near crisis of the regime.

As Italy prepared for new elections in 2001, virtually none of the parties that had contested elections in 1992 and dominated Italian politics since 1945 was still a major contender. Christian Democracy, which had headed nearly all governments since 1945, had disappeared. The Socialist party was gone too. The Communist party had split, and both fragments had new names and a different agenda from ten years earlier. New parties, such as the Democratic Party of the Left (with links to the old Communist party), Forza Italia, the National Alliance (based on the neofascist party of the past), and the Northern League were leading contenders for election victory. Italy was not alone in experiencing major reshaping of the political party system. Japan and Canada also underwent major changes in their party systems with new parties emerging, old ones disappearing, and new patterns of interaction among those that survived or entered the political fray.

When we look at the contribution of the party system to democracy, our concerns include the number of parties, their interaction with each other, and their relationship to the public. The number of parties is among the most examined elements of party systems. There has been a tendency to regard the near two-party systems of the United States and Britain as models for the ideal democracy. These two-party systems (and others like them) are seen as supporting stable government by providing voters with a choice between two parties, one of which will have a comfortable legislative majority to enact its program. On the other hand, multiparty systems, especially those in countries using proportional representation, end up with parliamentary majorities composed of two or more parties. Such coalition governments are often difficult to organize after an election. For example, after the 1992 elections in Italy, it took over ten weeks to patch together a coalition government. In the meantime, a caretaker government tried to tend the country's affairs. Once formed, such multiparty coalitions are often shaky and fail when faced with difficult decisions. Japan, for example, went through nine prime ministers during the 1990s.

Many thus associate multiparty systems with chronic governmental instability. That instability paralyzes public action and discredits democracy in the eyes of the citizenry. In extreme cases, it leads to the death of democracy. The classic cases of multiparty anarchy are contemporary Italy, the Weimar German Republic (1919–1933), and the French Third (1873–1940) and Fourth (1944–1958) Republics. While the Italian regime continues to stumble along for the time being, the other examples produced Hitler in Germany, the fascist Vichy government in 1940 France, and a military revolt in 1958 France.

But the link between large numbers of parties and governmental instability is not accurate. In fact, there are a number of successful democracies that have thrived for decades with orderly multiparty systems: Canada, Germany, Japan, the Scandinavian countries, Holland, and many others. Empirical evidence of the weak link between multiparty systems and political instability was provided by a cross-national study of twenty-nine democracies. This comprehensive study covering several decades of democratic experience in a variety of forms found that the number of parties had little correlation with political stability.[10]

Of greater concern in the party system's effect on stability is the question of how polarized the parties are.[11] Polarization refers to the emotional and political distances between parties in a country. This distance may reflect the bitterness of rivalries between parties that are close together ideologically but carry long memories of all-out, no-holds-barred competition with each other. Colombia offered such an example in the 1950s and early 1960s when two parties whose ideological stances were close so strongly clashed over symbols and power that the result was a costly civil war. More typically, polarization is caused by the ideological differences separating the parties in a multiparty system. During the 1970s and into the early 1980s, for example, the French party system was polarized by intense ideological differences between the moderate conservative coalition and a union of the Left with strong attachments to Marxist ideology. With the two camps representing entirely different visions of how society should be organized, the parties were polarized and viewed each other as enemies rather than rivals. On the other hand, in the United States polarization is unusual because ideological differences between the parties are small and there are traditions of "bipartisanship" and of friendships among politicians that cross party lines. The heightened partisan conflict in the United States since 1994 is unusual and runs counter to the trend of depolarization of parties systems in most other industrial democracies. At most times, polarization is low in U.S. party politics, but the recent increase in partisan fighting is by no means unusual.

The general decline of ideologies has helped reduce polarization in most Western democracies. Countries that once had strongly polarized parties have seen their ideological differences dwindle. For example, the French party system is now dominated by parties whose views of society are very similar to one another. It is unlikely and undesirable that partisan conflicts will disappear. Those conflicts offer different approaches to solving a state's challenges and are important in aiding voters to convey their preferences into the policy-making process. But there is clearly a trend toward less polarization in both ideological and emotional senses among parties in most advanced industrial democracies. Indeed, even in France the transition in 1995 from a socialist president to a conservative one proceeded amicably and smoothly. This depolarization contributes to greater stability in the party system and the overall political system.

Of greatest concern today is the ability of democratic parties to maintain the linkages between citizen and state that were paramount to representative democracy during the twentieth century. In part, this comes from public repugnance with the ineffectiveness and sometimes the corruption of the established parties. This can be resolved by the reform of these parties or the rise of new parties to replace them. Canada and Japan seem to be experiencing both kinds of responses to their parties' failures, with major parties trying to reform and new parties emerging as important political actors. Elsewhere, parties are looking for new leaders or new ideas to regain public confidence in them.

The other change is more difficult to respond to because it reflects in party politics some fundamental socioeconomic changes that seem enduring. Old socioeconomic cleavages on which the established parties were based are declining in importance. Better-educated citizens mean voters who are more attuned to issues and less likely to vote on the basis of party identification alone. As parties have responded by basing themselves on loose electoral coalitions, the new party-citizen relationship poses some challenges to contemporary parties. The principal problem is *partisan dealignment,* or the loosening of citizen ties to political parties.[12] Because parties do not present clear views and are not anchored in durable social cleavages, citizen attachment to the parties is not intense. Citizens *identify* with a party but do not join it; their partisan support reflects a mild and often transient preference rather than a close association. In most countries this alignment appears to be declining.

Citizens are now more willing to shift their vote if another party offers an attractive candidate or champions a single issue about which the voter is very concerned.[13] The result is that parties no longer mean much in the voters' eyes. This in turn produces greater electoral volatility (or shifts in support) and sharp swings in election results from one election to another. Electoral volatility is well illustrated in the case of France. Since 1978, the electoral majority has switched from Left to Right in nearly every national election, even in those elections that were only a few months apart. Such volatility endangers continuity of government action and reveals the presence of a group of swing voters with little loyalty to either political camp.

The presence of such unattached voters might provide a ready audience for new parties. Indeed, several countries have seen the emergence of new parties that have become important actors in national politics. Environmental parties have become important in Germany, France, and elsewhere. Extreme Right parties have exploited public mistrust of immigrants to develop strong political showings in France, Germany, and several other West European countries. Separatist parties have emerged in Canada, Britain, Spain, and Belgium to champion the demands of ethnic groups for political autonomy.

Changes in party organization and seemingly perpetual political scandals raise questions about the ability of political parties to continue the linkage function ascribed to them by most theories of representative democracy. Can the professional, service-oriented organizations that now characterize most parties provide the linkage between state and society that we have counted on parties to provide? These parties no longer need mass memberships, and they can count almost automatically on a mass electorate while doing little more than finding the lowest common denominator on major policies. Can parties linked to the state remain mediators between the state and its citizens? Some see today's cartel parties as less effective in linking people to the state and more adept at brokering between the state and powerful interest groups.[14] There is little doubt that "parties with access to state resources and power have a clear advantage in maintaining their own positions and in denying such power to others."[15] Should parties lead according to sets of political ideals or should they follow the directions indicated by the latest opinion polls or the hunches of campaign strategists?

At the start of the new century, political parties in most democracies seem to be in crisis. Without the traditional anchors in meaningful socioeconomic divisions and lacking the ideological guidelines of the past, they often appear to be adrift with no sense of direction or purpose. The public's declining attachment to traditional parties and its hostility toward these organizations and their leaders raise doubts about the ability of parties to serve as effective links between the voter and the polity. The new parties are forcing established parties to greater efforts in forging stronger links with the electorate. If the older parties fail to do so, many of them may be replaced by their new challengers. Despite the possibilities of new technologies in expanding the use of direct democracy, parties remain needed to link people and their state. As Schattschneider pointed out 60 years ago: "It should be flatly stated that the political parties created democracy and that modern democracy is unthinkable save in terms of parties."[16]

POLITICAL PARTIES AND DEMOCRATIZATION

Schattschneider's declaration holds true at the start of the twenty-first century. As a result, one of the great concerns of those hoping to see the current wave of democratizations succeed pay close attention to the establishment and institutionalization of political parties. The emergence of party systems and their ability to acquire a sense of permanency are the keys to moving from the process of democratization to the reality of democracy. It is difficult to make general statements about party building because that process is so much affected by the historical and political background of each specific country. In this section, I will talk about parties and democratization in three countries with different sets of needs: Russia, where democratic party building involved moving from totalitarian rule by a single party; Nigeria, where military leaders set up a new party system as they turned power back to civilians; and Mexico, where a dominant party grudgingly allowed more party competition that brought greater democracy to a state ruled by the same party for eighty years.

Political Party Building in Russia

At the end of the 1980s the dominant Communist party of the Soviet Union (CPSU) faced its first real competition in seventy years. Its dominance had approached totalitarian rule as it not only held a political monopoly control but also sought total control over the economy, society, education, and virtually all aspects of its citizens' lives. There were regular elections to the legislative body, the Supreme Soviet, but nearly always there was only one candidate in each district. This changed in 1989 when party leader Mikhail Gorbachev decided to allow multiple candidates, albeit all screened by the CPSU. The results of the 1989 legislative elections gave broad evidence of the insistence of many Soviet citizens that it was time for a change. But the real changes did not occur until the 1991 presidential election. Candidates ran more as individuals than party representatives. Indeed, all candidates were present or past members of the Communist party. Boris Yeltsin came to be seen as the candidate of reform although he claimed no partisan attachment; Nikolai Ryzhov was the Communist party candidate; and Vladimir Zhirinovsky built on Russian nationalist sentiments in his Liberal Democratic party. Yeltsin won handily with almost 60 percent of the valid votes. In August 1991, clashes between Yeltsin and the legislature, still dominated by Communists, precipitated a Communist attempt to overthrow Yeltsin. By the end of that year, the Soviet Union had dissolved, and fifteen new and independent republics replaced the highly centralized Union of Soviet Socialist Republics.

Since 1991, there have been three presidential elections and three elections to the Russian State Duma.[17] The CPSU's successes in monopolizing politics and society left a vast political void when it was finally overthrown in 1991. The result has been a very slow process of party building. Presidential elections have been dominated by personalities rather than parties. It is in the State Duma elections that we need to look for signs of an emerging party system. After the 1999 Duma elections, we can draw the following conclusions about the evolving Russian party system.

First, the party system is highly fragmented. No party can hope to win a majority of Duma seats on its own. Table 5.1 illustrates the large number of parties competing in these elections. Votes are also spread widely among various parties and independents. No party has ever won even 25 percent of the total vote. Second, the parties' ideological positions are vague and often shift. As shown in Table

TABLE **5.1**   Political Parties in Russia's State Duma Elections, 1993–1999

	1993	1995	1999
Parties Receiving 5+ Percent in the Election (based on votes on the proportional representation lists)			
Communist party	12.4%	22.3%	24.3%
Russia's Choice	15.5		
Liberal Democrats	22.9	11.2	6.0
Agrarian party	8.0		
Yabloko	7.9	6.9	5.9
Women of Russia	8.1		
Party of Russian Unity and Concord	6.8		
Democratic Party of Russia	5.5		
Our Home Is Russia		10.1	
Unity			23.3
Fatherland-All Russia			13.3
Union of Right Forces			8.5
Other Parties Receiving Seats (based on election in single member districts)	*Number of Parties (number of seats)*		
Specific parties	4 (8 seats)	18 (64 seats)	7 (9 seats)
Independents	(141 seats)	(78 seats)	(113 seats)
Parties on the Ballot but Not Electing any Representatives	*Number of Parties*		
	5	21	13
Total Number of Parties Competing in the Elections	13	43	26

Sources: For 1993 and 1995: Stephen White, Richard Rose, and Ian McAlister, *How Russia Votes* (Chatham, NJ: Chatham House, 1997), pp. 123, 224. For 1999, Russia Votes website, http://russiavotes.org.

5.2, Russian parties can be grouped into four broad categories: (1) those favoring liberal (in the European sense of liberalism) reform, (2) those willing to accept some reforms, (3) the Communists, and (4) the Russian nationalists, the latter being two anti-democratic parties that opposed reform under Yeltsin but have been supportive of President Putin. Indeed, under Putin no Duma party has emerged as a clear opposition, perhaps because of Putin's very high standings in public opinion polls.

Third, party alignments are still very shallow. You will note in Table 5.1 that the major parties have come and gone, and those that have remained have often changed their names. The transient nature of party identity can also be seen in the acts of individuals. In the short time between the Duma elections at the end of 1999 and the convening of its first session in January 2000, over 100 deputies had changed their party alignment. There is, in addition, substantial evidence that the voters are highly volatile. There are two votes on each ballot: one for a district representative and the other for a party list. Voters often select different parties for these two votes. And they frequently change their vote from one election to the next. This reflects a fourth problem in the emerging Russian party system: parties have not established clear political, social, or economic bases of support in society. Other than a linkage between older Russians and the Communist party, parties cannot look to certain blocs of voters for reliable support. Finally, many party leaders have been tainted by corruption and scandals that undermine not only their personal stature but also the credibility of the overall party system. Corruption

TABLE 5.2   Groupings of Parties after the 1999 State Duma Elections in Russia

Favorable to Reform (usually pro-government)

Our Home Is Russia
Women of Russia
Yabloko
Minor parties

Moderate Reformers (pro-government)

*Unity
Fatherland-All Russia
*Union of Right Forces

Opposed to Liberal Democratic Reforms

Communists
  Communist Party
  Agrarian Party
Nationalists
  Zhironovsky Bloc/Liberal Democrats

* Endorsed by Vladimir Putin before 1999 election.

among party leaders can be found in advanced democracies, but there, parties can draw on long traditions of public service to counter the misdeeds of current leaders. That is not the case in Russia. In Europe and the United States, scandals weaken public confidence in parties and institutions; in Russia such profiteering by public leaders undermines democracy.

While noting these shortcomings, it is important to remember that the Russian party system is only ten years old. It is trying to establish itself in a hostile setting where parties other than the ruling Communists were forbidden. The weaknesses in the party system reflect the reliance of the parties on individual personalities rather than structured party organizations. Despite this party personalism, those leaders who have the ability to attract broad support have failed to do so. Boris Yeltsin, for example, dominated Russian politics for over eight years, but he failed to use his personal appeal to organize a political party to support him. Nor did he endorse any party in Duma elections. Vladimir Putin did align himself with two parties in the 1999 Duma elections, but he has yet to develop the broad base of support that Yeltsin enjoyed at the height of his power that might be used in party-building.

These problems, coupled with the scandals and corruption that have tainted many prominent party leaders, certainly indicate the challenges of developing a Russian party system that can support modern democracy. However, as two Canadian political scientists note: "If some of these conditions are alleviated, the groundwork is laid for the creation of a viable and reasonably stable party system in Russia."[18]

Mexico: Opening Up the Party System

For nearly seventy years, a single party dominated Mexican politics: the Institutionalized Revolutionary Party (PRI). It claims to embody the spirit and legacy of the Revolution–a series of battles among would-be dictators, peasant and Indian heroes, middle-class politicians seeking modern government, and even bandits. The Revolution took place between 1910 and 1917 but final consolidation of its political gains took another dozen years. By 1929, a party was created to perpetuate the goals and achievements of the Revolution, a party that eventually assumed the name of the Institutionalized Revolutionary Party (PRI) and dominated Mexican politics for the next seven decades. It blended socialist thought with attacks on the Catholic Church, the United States, and other enemies of the Revolution. It carried out a massive redistribution of land and some nationalizations of key industries, notably Mexico's petroleum industry. But it has also had presidents who have followed traditional neoliberal (pro-market economics) policies. Sometimes swinging from one president on the Left to the next president on the Right, the PRI has not had a consistent ideology other than trying to hold onto power.

The PRI has an unusual structure in that it has brought together various sectors of society into a single political formation. This allows the party to reach out to peasants, workers, the military, and middle-class interests. Each sector has an associated interest group that brought large numbers of followers into the party. The sectors negotiated with each other over nominations to key public offices. The negotiations to select the party's presidential candidate were especially important. The PRI candidate was certain to be elected, and the president then controlled other key nominations and played an important, often decisive role in nominating his successor. For decades, the PRI faced no serious political competition and so its sector organization was a way of exercising control over society and mobilizing it for the party leadership's goals. For example, land reform turned most arable land over to the peasants in small plots. The peasants were entitled to farm that land in perpetuity, but they could not sell it or use it as security for bank loans. Banks run by the party's National Confederation of Peasants (CNC) alone were allowed to advance money to the peasants to fund the purchase of seed and fertilizer at the beginning of the new growing season. To get these loans, the peasants had to join the CNC and pledge their support to the PRI. Reformers who tried to found alternative trade unions or peasant groups either were co-opted or they disappeared. The PRI and its associated groups were an effective force in dominating Mexican politics and society. The negatives were the absence of competitive elections, abuses of civil liberties, party control of the media, and massive corruption that diverted public funds to personal accounts of the PRI elite.

In 1939, a right-wing opposition party emerged, the National Action Party (PAN). The PAN seeks to represent the upper-middle class and business interests; it is more tolerant toward the Church and the United States.[19] As pressures to appear democratic grew after World War II, the PAN was tolerated by PRI. Its presence and competition justified the PRI's claims that Mexico was democratic even though the PRI candidates always won. Eventually, the PRI government established token quotas for PAN representation (and for a minor party to the PRI's left) in the Senate and House of Representatives. However, it was a tolerated minority, not one really free to compete. When the PRI faced defeats in key elections, such as gubernatorial elections, the PRI would falsify the election results to ensure the victory of its own candidates. During the 1980s, pressures for genuine democracy grew in Mexico as the new wave of democratizations swept around the globe. It was increasingly difficult to disguise vote fraud. In 1989, the PAN won a governor's seat for the first time and went on to win three others in the next few years.

Meanwhile, several prominent PRI leaders defected and joined other leftists in creating a new left-wing party. It ran under one name in the 1988 presidential elections and soon after became the Party of the Democratic Revolution (PRD). Leadership of this party was assumed by Cuauhtémoc Cárdenas, son of the great PRI revolutionary who was Mexico's president from 1934 to 1940. The famous name, economic decline, and scandals involving top-level PRI figures gave the left-wing party a boost in the 1988 presidential election. Cárdenas won 31 percent of the vote, more than any prior opposition candidate, and this despite widespread accusations of ballot-box stuffing by the PRI. Cárdenas ran again in the 1994 presidential election, but his support was almost half what he had won in 1988. He recovered his public appeal and went on to win the 1997 race for governor of Mexico City. His governorship was marked by a number of errors that raised questions about his ability to govern. These questions and a recognition by public opinion that the best chance to defeat the PRI would come from the PAN led to the PRD's poor showing in the 2000 presidential election.

International and domestic pressures for further democratization forced the PRI to abandon prior political practices. Election fraud declined, and when it occurred at state or local levels, the PRI's national leadership sometimes pressured their zealous grass-roots leaders to play the game more honestly. Another result of the democratization process was the introduction of primary elections to select presidential candidates. In the past, nomination of PRI's presidential candidate was the right of a small and privileged group of top PRI leaders. After experimenting with primary elections as a means of selecting candidates at the state level, the PRI introduced primary elections for its candidate in the 2000 presidential race. The national government also took unusual steps to ensure that the 2000 election would be free from electoral fraud.

The PRI had recognized that democratic reforms were essential, but it failed to grasp broader social and economic changes in Mexican society. As a result, the 2000 elections mark a turning point in Mexican political history.[20] The opening of the Mexican party system culminated in 2000 with the election of the PAN presidential candidate, the end to seventy years of PRI political domination, and the emergence of the PAN as the largest single party in the Mexican Congress. (See Tables 5.3 and 5.4.) The collapse of the PRI political machine bodes well for the flourishing of democracy in Mexico. The PRI needs the chastening of an experience in opposition. If the presidency of Vincente Fox is successful and the PRI is

TABLE 5.3   Election Results in Mexico: Percentage of Vote in Elections for the Chamber of Deputies

Party	1976	1979	1982	1985	1988	1991	1994	1997	2000
PRI	80.1%	69.7%	69.3%	65.0%	50.4%	61.4%	50.3%	39.1%	36.9%
PAN	8.5	10.8	17.5	15.5	17.1	17.7	25.8	26.6	38.2
PRD					10.5	12.7	17.2	25.7	18.7
Others	5.5	14.1	13.0	14.9	21.1	5.6	4.9	8.6	3.8

TABLE 5.4   Election Results in Mexico: Percentage of Vote in Presidential Elections

Party	1970	1976	1982	1988	1994	2000
PRI	80.4%	85.4%	69.2%	48.7%	48.8%	36.1%
PAN	13.9	(no candidate)	15.7	16.8	25.9	42.5
PRD				31.1	16.6	16.6
Others	1.4	1.2	9.4	3.4	8.8	2.6

able to pull together after its 2000 defeats, we may be seeing the emergence of a new, competitive, and democratic party system in Mexico.

Generals Breaking and Making Parties: Nigeria

Since independence in 1960, Nigeria has gone through four different political party systems. All but the first have been the creations of Nigeria's military governments as they prepared to return power to civilian hands.

The first party system (1960–1965) emerged out of the three movements that brought the end of colonial rule in Nigeria. These parties represented the three major ethnic groups: the Northern People's Congress based on the Hausa Fulani in the north; the Action Group representing the Yoruba in the southwest; and the National Congress of Nigerian Citizens, which despite its "national" claim was based on the Ibos in southeast Nigeria. The first election involving these parties occurred in 1959 to provide the newly independent state with its parliament. The results of the election reflected the ethnic support of each of these parties; none was very successful in attracting support from beyond its ethnic group. By the next elections in 1964, the parties' ethnic nature was solidified. With Nigerians "voting for their own kind," parties could hope to increase their vote only by increasing the turnout of their own people. To achieve maximum turnout, party leaders played on the fears of their ethnic group of what would happen if the other parties won. It was easy to do this with ethnic conflict on the increase and election violence already high. The threats of what the others would do—up to and including genocide—greatly increased ethnic tensions. Follow-up elections in 1965 only added to the trend of ethnic confrontation and violence. There were also allegations of massive electoral fraud. Shortly after the 1965 elections, Nigeria's First Republic and the party system fell as the military seized power. Parties were abolished and many party leaders were arrested.

Twelve years later, after a brutal ethnic civil war and long authoritarian rule by a series of military dictators, the military began to prepare to return political power to civilians. The military regime oversaw the reemergence of parties and preparations for elections in 1979. Everyone was eager to avoid the renewal of ethnic parties and tensions, and the military attempted to avoid this by requiring parties to have top leaders from two or more ethnic groups in the party organizations and among its top candidates. The National Electoral Committee monitored the campaign to prevent ethnic appeals and demagoguery. Despite the fact that the parties mirrored those of the First Republic and included the same principal leaders as before, ethnic politics was limited. Elections went well in 1979 and brought the election of a northern politician, Shehu Shagari. Over the next few years, Shagari was successful in building a party with national appeal that reached across ethnic and regional lines. But Shagari was less successful in controlling corruption of political leaders, and the next elections, in 1993, were plagued with fraud. Shortly after the elections, the military stepped in, dissolved the Second Republic, and established a new military regime. Again, among the military's first moves were the abolition of all parties and the arrest of many of their leaders.

Nearly a decade passed under military rule before the generals decided to hand power back to civilians. In preparation, the military government established a commission to approve new parties and to ensure that these parties did not include anyone who had been active in parties during the First and Second Republics. Thirteen "pre-parties" emerged but none was approved. The military government then created by fiat two parties: the National Republican party that was supposed to be just right of center and the Social Democratic party on the left. The Left-Right distinction had little meaning in Nigerian politics. People soon came to see the National Republicans as a northern, Muslim party and the Social Democrats as southern and Christian. The new party system collapsed in its first real test: presidential elections in 1993. Although the military had originally approved both parties' candidates, the country's leader, General Babingida, decided as the election was taking place that one of the candidates, Social Democrat Moshod Abiola, was ineligible. Last minute efforts to cancel the election failed. Then, as the votes were being tabulated and the count showed Abiola in the lead, General Babingida annulled the election, dissolved the parties, and arrested Abiola and many other party leaders. Military rule soon asserted itself in its harshest form ever in Nigeria under the leadership of General Sani Abacha.

Faced with widespread dissent and a growing prodemocracy movement that could not be repressed by violence, Abacha moved toward restoration of civilian rule. In 1996, he established five new parties and began preparations for new presidential elections. The parties excluded known politicians and representatives from the democracy movement. Their nature became clear when all five parties announced in 1998 that they would nominate Sani Abacha as their joint presidential candidate. This was averted when Abacha died suddenly, two months later, reportedly of a heart attack.

His replacement, General Abdulsalami Abubakar, pledged a return to civilian rule within a year. The first step involved creation of yet another party system with minimal interference from the military.[21] Three parties emerged: the People's Democratic party (PDP); the Alliance for Democracy party (AD), with roots in the Yoruba community and the prodemocracy group; and the All People's party (APP) with a base in the north. The PDP nominated Olesegun Obasanjo, a former military ruler who had been jailed by Abacha. The AD and APP joined in support of Olu Fase, a Yoruba from the AD. The parties presented few policy differences. Their campaigns sought to build on ethnic, regional, and personal loyalties. In early 1999, Obasanjo easily won the presidential election (See Table 5.5) and in July 1999 took over the helm of the Nigerian Third Repubic, its first civilian and democratic government in fifteen years.

The success of the new party system—and the Nigerian Third Republic—depends on the ability of these parties to establish themselves as representatives of socioeconomic and issue differences. They will need to do so while resisting attachments to ethnic communities in the ways most earlier Nigerian parties have done. The new Nigerian parties will also need to attract able politicians who will be less vulnerable to the corruption that undermined earlier party systems and

TABLE 5.5   Election Results in Nigeria, 1998 and 1999

Legislative Elections, 1998		
Party	Percentage of Seats in National Assembly	Percentage of Seats in Senate
PDP	57.2%	54.1%
APP	20.6	26.6
AD	18.9	18.3

Presidential Elections, 1999		
Candidate	Party	Percentage of Vote
Olesegun Obasanjo	PDP	62.8%
Olu Falae	AD and APP	37.2

democratic government. The parties and their followers will also need to break with the violent style of party politics of the past. These challenges will need to be met while the new democratic regime faces growing pressures from a weak economy and rising ethnic and religious tensions.

Political Party Institutionalization

These three case studies illustrate the challenges of building new party systems as democratization occurs. These three countries have made important starts in that process of party building. Whether they succeed or fail in this, however, will take years, even decades, to demonstrate. To be successful, the new party systems in Russia, Mexico, and Nigeria must become established institutions on which citizens can rely for consistent behavior and positions in the political process.

Party institutionalization involves several steps. First, the parties need to acquire a political or social base that they can represent and speak for, and in which they can expect to find electoral and other support. This gives the party a sense of purpose beyond satisfying its leaders' personal ambitions to hold public office. It gives the voters a set of constant and reliable reference points as they try to make decisions at the polls. To establish such a base is difficult when the social cleavages that traditionally define Left and Right have little relevance in society. Nigeria illustrates the dangers of unrest and violence that can occur when parties align themselves along ethnic or religious divisions. Most of the parties in new democracies have had their origins in the need to compete in elections rather than in representing societal differences. The electoral function is very important but not enough. A party that is successful in implanting itself into its society and polity is more likely to be able to fulfill the function of linking people with politics as we expect parties to do in representative democracies. As parties make these attachments, voter volatility (change from one election to the next) will decrease and political predictability and stability will increase.

A second part of institutionalization involves the ability of a party to move beyond being the political machine for a single person. Many of the new Russian parties are little more than vehicles for the ambitions of a single person; Nigeria's PDP benefitted from the popularity of its presidential candidate, Olesegun Obasanjo. Such parties have difficulty developing other leaders within their ranks to replace the dominant personality when he or she leaves politics. There are examples of successful parties in advanced democracies that began as personality-based parties, notably the French Gaullist party that was founded as a means of supporting Charles de Gaulle. But there are more examples of personality parties that have faltered when their leaders have been defeated or retired. Institutionalization requires parties to be able to recruit alternative current leaders and leaders for the next generation.

Third, parties need to acquire durability. They need to continue to compete in successive elections under the same title and banner. In Table 5.1, you can see the significant changes in the parties competing in Russian elections within a single decade. Such durability usually requires the establishment of an effective party organization that can keep the party going between elections. Continuity requires identifying and defending a set of positions that will give a party identity and purpose over time.

Finally, institutionalization requires flexibility and adaptability in the face of changing social and political needs. Mexico's PRI claims in its name to be "institutionalized" and for decades this claim could not be challenged. But now the proof of its institutionalization will be tested over the next few years as the PRI adjusts or fails to adjust to its opposition role and to the political and social changes that led to its electoral defeat. Parties that are unable to respond to change are unlikely to succeed in linking people with the political process.

Nearly everyone recognizes the importance of political parties in the process of democratization. Yet the process of developing a stable party system is not well understood. Most of all, it takes time and good luck. This is one of the main reasons that the new democracies that emerged during the 1990s will require another decade or two to acquire legitimacy and strength.

PARTIES IN THE DEVELOPING SETTING

There are a wide variety of political parties in the developing world. Many of them bear scant resemblance to parties in the democratic setting. Their purposes vary also quite widely. They are so diverse that generalizations are difficult to make. Here we will look at them based on the number of parties present in the developing political system.

Multiparty Democracies

In 1999, India held its fourth parliamentary election in five years. Elections in the world's largest democracy, with a voting age population of 600 million, 5,000 candidates, and 850,000 voting places, are colorful and impressive events.

One candidate sent trained parrots to drop copies of his party's emblem to prospective voters; candidates and voters consult astrologers for campaign advice; wild and domesticated elephants are frequent threats or props at election rallies. One candidate dismissed the threat of an elephant stampede at his rally: "Elephants have strong senses and can distinguish between good and evil. So they will not harm my voters."[22] Voting is spread over the period of a month. The resulting parliament included representatives from 38 parties; it took 25 parties to achieve a tenuous governing majority in the Lok Sabha or House of the People. Even where third world parties face competitive elections, the party style and structure obviously is markedly different from their forms in the West.

Multiparty competition in third world countries is rare. It has been most successful in Latin America, and even there the party rivalry sometimes becomes so intense that it disturbs political order and sometimes becomes violent. Among the eighty or so new countries that have emerged from colonial rule since World War II, peaceful rotation in power between competitive parties has been achieved in less than ten of them. India is one of the few new third world countries to go through such rotations on a regular basis.

Even where the parties are not far apart on their issue positions, they often tend to be polarized from previous political battles. Elections are almost always tense times when the police or military must maintain public order and secure voting places. Competition among the parties diverts energies away from the task of national economic and political development toward struggles by the incumbents to hold on to power. More often than not, the intense competition yields to violence and that becomes a pretext for the military to suppress all parties and establish dictatorships.

In third world countries with multiparty systems, parties are most often based on ethnic or religious cleavages rather than class or political cleavages. Such communal cleavages heighten tensions from the party competition as they are often less open to accommodation or compromise than are parties based on political or social divisions. Nigeria is one example, as I have already noted. It can also be seen in the religion-based parties in India, which challenge the democratic stability that this country has tried to achieve. In their extreme forms, ethnic-based parties can produce such high tensions that they provoke ethnic violence and civil war. It is very difficult to surmount these ethnic divisions in newer countries where people lack a strong sense of identification with the country as a whole and instead identify with their communal group. Other bases for party support—such as class or political ideologies—are poorly developed and are superseded by the ethnic cleavage.

Where ethnicity and religion are less powerful cleavages, party politics in multiparty developing states still may be tumultuous. Personal rivalries, historical divisions, regional tensions, and other sources of conflict, and poorly established norms of democratic conduct often make elections times of instability and discredit the parties involved in them. Rallies and efforts to disrupt the meetings of rival parties bring conflict and violence. Electoral fraud is difficult to avoid where polling places are numerous and spread out, illiteracy makes voting a challenge for many citizens, and the lack of electricity in polling places complicates accurate tabulation of the results. Nevertheless, over the past decade a growing number of developing countries are opening their party system to genuine competition. Mexico is only one of several success stories in building new and competitive party systems under developing political systems.

Single or Dominant Party States

Until the recent era of democratizations, most states had only a single party or one party that clearly dominated its politics. While less common than a decade ago, such one-party systems are still often features of the third world. An example would be the strong party that backed General Suharto's long rule in Indonesia. Mexico's PRI was another example until very recently.

Another variety of one-party rule is the communist pattern. One of V. I. Lenin's contributions to Marxist doctrine was his notion of the political party as the "vanguard of the proletariat" with responsibility to bring communism into place through "a dictatorship of the proletariat." The party became the means of achieving Marxist and Leninist ideological goals and of controlling society according to the wishes of the party's top leadership. In following this model, in communist countries the communist parties in effect had states of their own that they totally dominated. The parties also sought with greater or lesser success to monopolize control over society and the economy.

Party rule under communism was highly centralized and hierarchical. Lenin established a party tenet of "democratic centralism," which had both democratic and centralizing principles at work. The democratic elements were the election of higher-level party officials by the lower levels and the accountability of the party leaders to the membership. The centralizing elements obliged lower levels of the party to accept and implement the decisions made at the top. In practice, the centralizing elements prevailed and democratic centralism became a highly effective means of assuring rule by the party elite.

For decades, the party organization was successful in penetrating and controlling the societies and politics of most communist countries. Vast propaganda efforts took the party elite's views to the general citizenry; the party mobilized millions to participate in party-dominated political forums that shaped public opinion to conform to the leadership's will. The party was charged with selecting the key economic, social, and political leaders at every level in the society from the neighborhood to the nation. It did so by establishing lists of positions (*nomenklatura*) at each level of society that party officials selected or approved. Most importantly, the party's vast and disciplined structure provided a parallel bureaucracy to oversee the actions and loyalty to the party of the state bureaucracy, the police, and the military.

In the end, this vast party bureaucracy helped spell the doom for communism in the Soviet Union and Eastern Europe. Its size was compounded by the retention of political and economic control of virtually all of society at the center. This control was held by a small group of leaders who were in office more because they had acquired seniority than because of their ideas and leadership skills. They were old men more concerned with preserving their privileges and passing them on to their loyal followers than with adjusting their societies to a changed environment. The state's highly centralized decision making ultimately stumbled to a virtual halt as their economies and societies became more complex. Reform was blocked by an ideology that few still believed valid.

There remain only a few communist countries in today's world: China, Cuba, Vietnam, and possibly Laos. They have abandoned their Marxist-Leninist ideology except for periodic, ceremonial reassertions of their loyalty to past heroes. Marxism-Leninism seems to have little relevance to the social and economic realities of the twenty-first century. The remaining ruling parties are less tightly organized and lack the verve that ideological commitment gave them in the past. They are more like traditional one-party dictatorships than Lenin's organizational weapons. They are seen by others and even by the more perceptive of their own members as dinosaurs of the past rather than as ways to the future.

Often the single dominant party is the successor to the independence or revolutionary movement. After independence or revolution, the party continues as the principal agent for mobilizing public support for the new elite. Under the best circumstances, it contributes to maintaining the process of political and social change began by independence or revolution. A good historical illustration is the Kemalist party created after World War I in Turkey to press for Ataturk's program of nationalism, secularism, and modernization. This party dominated Turkish politics from 1923 to 1950 and was an important agent for change, especially in its early years.

One of the chief challenges for dominant or single parties is the need to maintain their vitality when they do not face real competition. The life of a political party is usually centered on elections since few single-party third world states have working legislatures. With little role for the parties in the legislature and elections often far apart, the parties soon lose their vitality.

Most third world countries have a limited pool of able leaders because of the overall low level of education. Party leaders are naturally selected for government offices; others seek the security and prestige of senior civil service positions; still others seek wealth through careers in public or private business. As a result, there are few talented people left over to maintain the party as an organization. Many of these party leaders see the party as a way of making money for themselves. They trade political favors with their friends in government for bribes. Not only does the party's organization suffer but it is also tainted by corruption. In many countries, the party continues to exist formally but it is simply a shadow organization revived periodically for symbolic elections.

It is interesting to note the current waning of the one-party state. Once a prominent feature of the developing and communist worlds, the one-party state has been opened up by the current era of democratization. But this pattern is far from obsolete. When democracies falter, they may once again reappear.

Political Clientelism

I have noted the presence of patron-client links as a frequent feature of party organization in many democratic settings. Political clientelism is even more common in the developing world as a form of party organization and a means of mobilizing support. Under clientelism, political leaders, or "patrons," develop a grass-roots following among the population. These "clients" provide political support in the form of voting, attendance at party rallies, distribution of party literature, or personal assistance to their patron. In many settings, it is not unusual for the clients to be expected to show up for the marriage of their patron's daughter. In exchange for political and personal services, the patron provides material benefits such as government jobs, public contracts, loans, access to education, even food and clothing.

These relationships are highly personalized and based on direct contact between the patrons and their clients. But they are often linked together in vast networks with patrons at the top having a set of clients who in turn are patrons to a lower set of clients, and so on until the top is linked neatly to the grass roots. A typical patron-client network is illustrated in Figure 5.1. They are highly effective means for parties to mobilize and benefit from the direct help of large numbers of citizens. Such relationships also give individuals a sense of political participation and involvement in the party's life. And they can offer material security and the opportunity for advancement to individuals with otherwise modest resources at the grass-roots level.

Patron-client networks have their disadvantages as well. They are hierarchical relationships that are often sensed as demeaning by those at the bottom. They create or perpetuate dependency upon political friends who may lose the influence that enabled them to protect their clients. Patron-client ties are also vulnerable to corruption. The awarding of government contracts on the basis of clientele relations may make political sense, but they often are not wise economic decisions. They waste scarce resources and contribute to bribery and corruption.

Mexico offers a good case study of patron-client relationships. The PRI has used clientelism as an organizational form. There are a number of cliques organized around potential party leaders linking them with interest groups and party followers at all levels. These relationships form the basis of competition within the party for key positions, especially the presidency and governorships. When in office, the

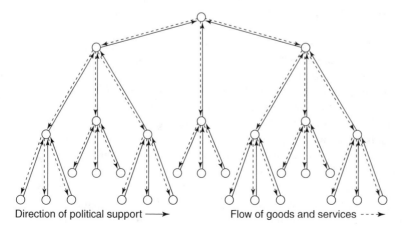

Direction of political support ——▶   Flow of goods and services ----▶

FIGURE 5.1   A Typical Patron-Client Network

president and governors use these networks of supporters to establish links with the grass roots. Government jobs and contracts, government-sponsored loans, access to educational opportunities, and other material benefits are distributed on the basis of such clientelistic ties.

Clientelism is a durable form of political organization. While especially common in developing states, patron-client politics is not restricted to that part of the world. It is also found in advanced democracies such as Japan, Italy, and France. It is reflected in the "pork barrel" politics in the United States, where members of Congress and senators bargain with each other for government investments in their districts or states. In the current era, however, clientelism is increasingly linked with payoffs, illegal campaign contributions, and other financial scandals. The newly vigilant media point to what used to be a common form of political organization as a sign of contemporary political corruption and contribute to the cynicism and disillusionment of citizens in many countries.

Parties and Stability in the Third World

The contribution of parties to political order and stability in third world countries is problematic. As we have seen, multiparty competition, which we value for its democratic potential, may be divisive and destabilizing in third world settings. Single or dominant parties more often than not lose their vigor through corruption and the siphoning off of their most able leaders for other pursuits. The parties often contribute to public disaffection with the regime because of their involvement in graft and corruption.

On the other hand, at their best—as in Ataturk's Turkey or Mexico—parties can become agents for change and for mobilizing the citizens for political action. Indeed, political parties seem an ideal choice for promoting and channeling political action.[23] Their organizations can provide political and material support for regimes interested in social or economic change. Parties are inclusive rather than exclusive in that they seek to involve large numbers of people in politics. They are therefore more likely to promote participation than stifle it. Such an orientation toward citizen involvement by a party helps its political system avoid the accumulation of suppressed grievances that can destroy the regime's legitimacy.

States with strong and effective single or dominant parties can use these organizations to build national pride. For example, the PRI became the symbol and embodiment of all that was good in the Mexican Revolution. A single party can overcome separate ethnic or communal loyalties and create a sense of national identity. Another example of this can be seen in the role of the Congress party in forging a united India in the 1950s and 1960s.

Powerful, well-organized parties can also be counterweights to the political strength of privileged economic powers or the military. Most governments find it difficult to challenge the wishes of the economic forces that keep the economy moving; they are better able to resist such pressures if they have a party that is able to mobilize thousands of members and sympathizers to support reforms not wanted by the economic elite. Similarly, civilian leaders who can count on their party to turn thousands into the streets when the armed forces threaten to intervene are less vulnerable to threats from the military.

Even when parties are little more than vast patron-client systems, they promote links between the state and the citizens. In addition, there is the electoral connection. Parties are oriented toward elections, whether they face competition or not. This electoral concern leads them to promote at least some interest in democracy. In addition, parties are able to give their followers a sense of involvement in a political process that otherwise would be distant and alien.

PARTIES AND POLITICS

Political parties are key political actors wherever they exist. They are vital in developing and maintaining stable political systems. In democratic countries, they are the chief means of linking people and the state; they are what make representative democracy possible. In nondemocratic settings, parties are also important as tools for organizing support for the leaders and their goals. In developing countries, parties can be the means of creating a sense of nation and of developing durable political institutions. They can become the means of introducing greater public control and involvement, even in authoritarian settings.

Though the stability of party structures is a good indication of the overall stability of the political unit, it would be inaccurate to designate the party system as the only causal factor in the establishment and maintenance of political stability: the party system generally reflects social divisions, leadership skills, political norms and attitudes, and other sources of political stability and instability. But the contribution of the party system is highly important. Political decay and disorder frequently occur where political parties falter or disappear, because the political system is no longer able to channel participation or meet the needs of a politically mobilized populace. The failure of parties is thus a prelude to military rule, bureaucratic stagnation, and worse.

CONCLUSION

In all democratic and many authoritarian countries, political parties are the most active and visible forms of political activity. In democracies, they are vital links between the people and their governors. They are the institutions that make representative democracy work. That is why there is so much concern now, when parties appear to be in decline and to have lost public support. In authoritarian settings, they are often the vehicles of political control and even socioeconomic change. As such, political parties warrant extensive study as we seek to understand the political processes around the world.

In many settings, parties play key roles in representing and organizing political feelings and popular demands. But they are not the only important political actors that seek to provide representation of the concerns of society. Nearly everywhere, organized or unorganized interest groups also play a role in this task of representation. We turn now to an examination of interest group politics.

NOTES

1. Sigmund Neumann, ed., *Modern Political Parties* (Chicago: University of Chicago Press, 1965), p. 396.

2. Kay Lawson, ed., *Political Parties and Linkage: A Comparative Perspective* (New Haven, CT: Yale University Press, 1980).

3. Ronald Inglehart, *Modernization and Postmodernization: Cultural, Economic, and Political Change in 43 Societies* (Princeton, NJ: Princeton University Press, 1997), pp. 237–66.

4. Maurice Duverger, *Political Parties: Their Organization and Activity in the Modern State* (New York: Wiley, 1954).

5. Otto Kirchheimer, "The Transformation of Western Political Parties," in Joseph LaPalombara and Myron Weiner, eds., *Political Parties and Political Development* (Princeton, NJ: Princeton University Press, 1966).

6. Richard S. Katz and Peter Mair, eds., *How Parties Organize: Change and Adaptation in Party Organizations in Western Democracies* (London and Thousand Oaks, CA: Sage, 1994).

7. John Aldrich, *Why Parties? The Origin and Transformation of Political Parties in America* (Chicago: University of Chicago Press, 1995).

8. Richard S. Katz and Peter Maier, "Changing Models of Party Organization and Party Democracy," *Party Politics* 1 (January 1995): 40–57.

9. Richard Rose, *The Problem of Party Government* (New York: Free Press, 1974).

10. G. Bingham Powell, *Contemporary Democracies: Participation, Stability, and Violence* (Cambridge, MA: Harvard University Press, 1982).

11. Giovanni Sartori, *Parties and Party Systems: A Framework for Analysis* (Cambridge, England: Cambridge University Press, 1976).

12. Russell Dalton, Scott Flanagan, and Paul Beck, eds. *Electoral Change in Advanced Industrial Democracies* (Princeton, NJ: Princeton University Press, 1984).

13. Ivor Crewe and D. T. Denver, eds., *Electoral Change in Western Democracies* (New York: St. Martin's, 1985).

14. See especially, Katz and Maier, "Changing Models."

15. Paul D. Webb, "Party Organizational Change in Britain: The Iron Law of Centralization," in Katz and Maier, eds., *How Parties Organize,* p. 129.

16. E. E. Schattschneider, *Party Government* (New York: Rinehart, 1942), p. 1.

17. Stephen White, Richard Rose, Ian McAllister, *How Russia Votes* (Chatham, NJ: Chatham House, 1997).

18. Jon H. Pammett and Joan DeBardeleben, "Citizen Orientations to Political Parties in Russia," *Party Politics* 6 (January 2000): 373–84.

19. Robert A. Pastor, "Vicente Fox and the Rise of the PAN," *Journal of Democracy* 11 (October 2000): 25–32.

20. Andreas Schedler, "The Democratic Revelation," *Journal of Democracy* 11 (October 2000): 5–19.

21. Peter M. Lewis, "An End to the Permanent Transition?" *Journal of Democracy* 10 (January 1999): 141–56.

22. *The Christian Science Monitor,* 1 October 1999.

23. Samuel P. Huntington, *Political Order in Changing Societies* (New Haven, CT: Yale University Press, 1968).

Chapter 6

❖❖❖❖❖❖❖❖❖❖❖❖❖

Groups and Politics

When Americans think of pressure groups, they immediately conjure up visions of lobbyists wining, dining, and forking over campaign money to their politicians in exchange for special treatment. They rarely recognize their own neighborhood efforts to protect zoning restrictions or to get a crossing guard for a nearby intersection as a part of group politics. Yet both forms—and many others as well—are part of interest group politics.

The impact of a single person on the political process is not likely to be great. The typical citizen lacks knowledge of the political process and of the most appropriate points to bring pressure to bear in order to shape public policy. For both of these reasons, citizens in all types of political systems often find it useful to band together for political action. In most countries, interest groups play an important role in the political process.

It is not only the presence and activities of formal interest groups that are important for representative democracy. The interaction of citizens in many forms of voluntary associations facilitates the development of a "civil society" that many observers see as essential for democracy. Indeed, when the French journalist Alexis de Tocqueville toured the United States in the 1830s to find the sources of American success in building democracy, he discovered that an important part of the answer came in the "art of association" he found in the presence of so many autonomous, voluntary bodies.[1] From churches and temperance movements to neighborhood associations to political clubs, broad participation by Americans in voluntary associations contributed to the emergence and strength of American democracy. De Tocqueville wrote:

> If men are to remain civilized or to become so, the art of associating together must grow and improve among them in the same ratio in which the equality of conditions is increased.[2]

I will conclude this chapter on groups with a discussion of civil society and its importance in creating and maintaining modern democracies.

TYPES OF INTEREST GROUPS

A group does not have to be organized in order to have political influence. Political decision makers in all types of systems often refer to broad social categories as they set public policy. The French education minister wants to know what students think before setting university policy; the feelings of faithful Hindus are important as Indian policy makers consider social policies; Nigerian politicians try to anticipate the reaction of housewives as they remove price controls on food; Chinese leaders are concerned about the needs of the elderly as they change retirement benefits. These social categories have meaning and impact even if they do not have formally organized interest groups to advocate their concerns. Virtually all political leaders, even the most autocratic, want to know the needs and concerns of various social categories. They want to anticipate reactions of those affected by their decisions if only to be prepared to impose them. They make reference to these informal, unorganized groups as they consider policy options. Hence, even unorganized groups have political impact.

Of course, formally organized groups are more likely to have greater political effect than are unorganized groups. Unless they are members of activist groups, the elderly or women may have to rely on guesses by politicians about their preferences and reactions as policies affecting them are made, whereas the business community has formal organizations skilled in presenting their interests to advocate their cause with even reluctant policymakers. In many third world states and authoritarian regimes where organized groups either do not exist or are dominated by the ruling elite, this awareness of informal groups may be the only or the most effective form of interest group politics.

Occupation-Based Interest Groups

There are a variety of different types of organized interest groups. Among the most important in nearly every country are those groups defending the interests of a particular occupation: trade unions, employers' and business groups, farmers' groups, teachers' associations, doctors' associations, and so on. These groups are usually the best organized and most effective interest groups in any political system. Occupational groups also have a broader set of policy interests that affect them and motivate their political involvement than do most other interest groups.

The centrality of the daily work experience makes it important for individuals to join together in groups to defend their occupation's economic interests. The state's involvement in society and the economy leads groups from the various occupations to devote major attention to government policy making. Government policy makers are also glad to have groups to consult with as they set economic and social policies to help them avoid mistakes and facilitate implementation of the policies.

In virtually every political system two of the major political actors are the trade unions representing employees and the business and employers' associations. These groups have vital interests at stake in public policies dealing with the economy and social benefits. Often their interests clash over these and other policies. Both labor and business insist on their say in the political process over a broad range of economic and social issues. Their influence is not equal. Even leftist governments that we might expect to show special concern for trade union interests usually end up paying greater heed to the business interests.

Trade unions base their strength on numbers and their ability to tell their members how to vote in elections of public officials. Occasionally unions call general strikes asking workers in all parts of the economy to strike in support of a particular political position. Both of these resources have limits. Increasingly as socioeconomic cleavages have lessened in importance, trade union members vote with little regard for directives from their union leaders. General strikes are very difficult to organize and can be used for only the most urgent matters. Even then, few are successful. And it is the workers who pay the price in lost wages during the strike. Politicians know of these weaknesses and consider them as they assess their need to respond to trade union political demands.

As you can see in Table 6.1, the level of unionization varies widely. What is common is a pattern of constant decline in union membership. The table shows that from 1985 to 1995, most trade unions have lost about one-fourth of their membership. Part of the explanation is a shift in economic activities away from heavy industry where unionization was high to more service jobs where unionization is difficult. Another part of the explanation is the "free-rider" phenomenon where non-union members do not pay dues but still benefit from the pay increases and other benefits won by the union membership. This decline in unions is worrisome

TABLE **6.1**   Density of Trade Union Membership and Declining Density
in Selected Countries, 1995

Country	Percentage of Total Workforce Belonging to a Union	Decline in Percentage of Workforce Belonging to a Union, 1985–1995
Britain	32.9%	−27.7%
Canada	37.4	+ 1.8
France	9.0	−37.2
Germany	28.9	−17.6
Italy	44.1	−7.4
Japan	24.0	−16.7
Mexico*	42.8	−22.2
United States	14.2	−21.1

* Figures for Mexico are from 1991.

Source: International Labour Organization news release, 4 November 1997. From ILO website ILO.org.

since the trade unions were the means of integrating blue collar workers into the capitalist and democratic systems. The decline also weakens the hands of union negotiators when dealing with government or management.

Business interests derive their influence from the impact that their actions have on the economy. This is true in democratic and authoritarian regimes, in industrial and developing states. Democratic leaders know that they will have a harder time winning reelection if the economy is weak; authoritarian leaders know that a stagnant or declining economy will decrease their legitimacy and spur the hopes of military and civilian rivals. Politicians thus have a strong interest in seeing the economy thrive and grow. Such economic good times come only when business invests. If business lacks confidence in a government or if it perceives that government will heavily tax its profits, the business community will be less likely to entertain the financial risks of investment.

A good illustration was the experience of the French Socialist government in the early 1980s.[3] The party arrived in power with an orthodox socialist doctrine and immediately nationalized a large number of private firms and banks. It imposed new wealth taxes and new government economic regulations. The business community feared what the government would do next. Confidence in the future fell, private investment lagged, and the economy slipped deeper into recession. It was only three years later, when the Socialist government moderated its stance, that business regained its confidence in the government and the future of its investments. Some French Socialists complained that this was another example of capitalist blackmail against a reform-minded government. But it is less that than rational business calculations by free enterprise. Rarely will business leaders ignore opportunities to make money, but their calculations of how likely they are to make a profit are influenced by how friendly they perceive government to be to business.

Farm groups also are highly influential in politics. Their interests are narrower than business and labor. As a result, farm associations are able to focus their attention on a limited range of policies that have a direct impact on their members. Nearly every country has a high level of government involvement in agriculture with price supports, subsidies, and loan programs that affect the livelihoods of farmers. For these policies to work, government needs the cooperation of the farmers in implementing state policies. Farmers are also seen as a bloc of voters or supporters who must be courted by democratic and nondemocratic politicians even when the rural population is very small. Agriculture is a vital part of all economies, and governments need the cooperation of their farmers to keep this part of the economy strong. Finally, there is a natural sympathy for rural values and hard-working, individualistic farmers that is part of the political culture in many countries. This too helps make farm groups more influential than might be expected by their membership size.

As a result, farm policy is usually set by government in close collaboration with farmers' groups. In many industrialized countries, such as Germany, the political influence of farmers has waned as their numbers have decreased and as agriculture has lost its economic weight. But the political clout of agriculture still remains disproportionate compared to other parts of society. Even in a highly industrialized country such as Japan with only a very few farmers, agricultural interests have dominated the ruling LDP. Many Japanese leaders have wanted to ease Japan's economic relations with other countries by reducing tariffs on farm products but the farm lobby's strength within the LDP has blocked such reform.

In many instances, interest groups from the liberal professions are deeply involved in making what is essentially public policy. For example, lawyers' associations administer the exams that determine who is admitted to the bar; they set and enforce ethical standards for the legal profession. Doctors' associations set curricula for medical training and define new medical specializations. In these cases, the policies that affect the lives of all people in the country are set nearly entirely outside the political framework by these interest groups. In other cases, the groups work hand in hand with public officials to set policy. For example, insurance associations work closely with politicians in drafting the state's insurance code. Construction engineers and contractors set the building codes and standards that are then enforced by local governments.

Advocacy Groups

Another set of powerful interest groups is organized around the defense of rights and benefits for recipients of government services. These are groups representing people who draw upon government for services and want to press for continued or expanded support. They include such groups as veterans' associations, automobile clubs, parent-teacher organizations, associations of retired people, organizations defending the rights of the handicapped and mentally disabled, and airplane owners' associations. Generally, they are based on those receiving economic benefits provided by the government. They are often well organized and successful in pursuing their narrow objectives of additional government funding. Veterans' associations, for example, are powerful interest groups in Britain and France that succeed in retaining generous government benefits for the dwindling number of veterans. Automobile associations in Germany keep the government from limiting speed on the autobahns. Ethnic organizations in Nigeria fight successfully for community development funds.

Other groups are less motivated by financial interests and more interested in advocating particular causes. They include organizations based on consumers' rights, families, environmental protection, neighborhood improvement, animal protection, and hunting and sport fishing rights. They are usually less well organized than both the occupational groups and the economic-based advocacy groups. Their weaker structures and lower levels of member commitment tend to limit their political effectiveness. For example, consumer protection groups in Japan have less influence on commercial policies than do manufacturers' associations. However, these cause groups are sometimes able to influence government policy, especially when they face little opposition from other groups. For example, the animal protection lobby is strong in Britain and the hunting and fishing clubs are often listed among the most influential interest groups in France.

Community Action Groups

In many countries there has been an explosion in the number and effectiveness of advocacy groups based on local community issues. These are small, ad hoc, and temporary neighborhood associations that come into existence in response to an immediate and short-term issue. Neighbors will organize to block a zoning change that will allow an industrial development that will decrease their property values; a small group may emerge to demand repairs of a dilapidated school building; a clean government committee may form to challenge corrupt local officials. Such groups are often quite effective because they bring a group of dedicated and often militant citizens together and focus their political action on a single and narrow issue. Their opposition is usually based on broader community interests and it is not as mobilized as those people who see their interests as vitally affected by the issue. Sometimes the purpose is to block government action: this is the "not-in-my-backyard" (NIMBY) phenomenon. Other times the goal is to seek government action on behalf of a particular community. Virtually all political systems, open democratic states and autocratic ones as well, experience this type of local group action.

Occasionally, these local groups may evolve into much larger political movements. This is what happened in Japan during the 1980s when the protests of local inhabitants against the new Tokyo airport at Narita escalated into a major protest movement challenging all types of government action and inaction. However, this is exceptional. Ordinarily, the small neighborhood action groups disappear as the issue that mobilized them is resolved. They lack the kind of organization that would allow them to move from one issue to another or to a broader set of interests.

BASES OF INTEREST GROUP POLITICAL STRENGTH

It is always difficult to assess the impact of interest groups on public policy. Occasionally we can find a specific issue where the influence of a group is evident. One of the best examples of this is the effectiveness of the National Rifle Association in blocking gun control legislation in the United States in spite of broad public support for such controls. In most other matters it is more difficult to assess the impact of groups. Even when a policy decision clearly coincides with an interest group's position, it may be so because government independently shared the same view as the group rather than because of the group's power. But there are some factors that contribute to group strength and weakness.

Autonomy from the State

A key factor in the strength of interest groups is their autonomy from the state. To exercise influence on public policy, groups need to be able to independently formulate their own position and then choose the means and times for trying to affect the government's decision process. An illustration of the lack of autonomy comes from China and the former communist regimes of the USSR and Eastern Europe. Under communism, organized interest groups were dominated by the Communist party; they were agents to extend the party's influence beyond its own membership to shape the views of the group's members. Interest groups became little more than "transmission belts" that conveyed to farmers, workers, women, or students the views of the party elite. The transmission of views from the groups' members to the party elite was always possible but in fact quite limited. Group leaders were usually selected by the party; the groups' policy statements always mirrored the party elite's views. Occasionally, party leaders who had risen to party leadership from the mass organizations were turned to by their comrades in leadership positions for their interpretations of their groups' views. But the lack of group autonomy severely limited the ability of interest groups to affect public policy.

At the other extreme are the interest groups in many Western industrial democracies. These groups jealously guard their independence from government. Leaders are selected by the groups themselves with only rare instances of government influence on these leadership choices. Indeed, in the few cases where leadership choices appear to be influenced by government it is indirect and designed to strengthen the group with relationship to the government. Thus, when the French Socialists returned to power in 1997, the principal employers' group selected a new leader—one presumed to be better able to take a tough stand against the new government. In nearly all cases, democratic groups are careful to maintain a distance even from "friendly" governments. They recognize that a government must seek a broad consensus, and the "friendly" groups want to maintain their distance from the government in order to press hard for their own positions and to criticize the government's policies.

These autonomous groups compete with each other and with government for influence over state policies. Working from outside the formal governmental structures, rival groups try to press their ideas on policy makers using a wide range of tactics from public relations campaigns to protest demonstrations. Groups that felt that their interests were not adequately heard in policy-making circles were free to organize and enter the political fray. This pattern of multiple, autonomous interests that pressure government from outside the formal policy-making is referred to as *interest group pluralism*. It accurately characterizes much of the pattern of interest group politics and relationships with the state in most advanced industrial democracies.

In between these two extreme patterns of transmission belts and pluralism is *corporatism*. Under the corporatist model of interest group politics, there are fewer groups than under pluralism, usually one for each interest sector such as labor, management, farmers, and so on. The group's monopoly over its sector is officially approved by the state and sometimes protected by the state. These officially sanctioned groups become the privileged interlocutors with government. They become direct participants in policy decision making as members of corporative bodies that bring them together with each other and with government officials.

There are two forms of corporatism: state corporatism and societal corporatism.[4] Under *state corporatism,* the state is dominant. Interest groups are brought into the official decision-making process. Presumably decision-making processes are open, but in fact they are dominated by the state. The groups are then used to legitimate the state's decisions and to win compliance with the state's policies among their members. Usually, membership in these groups is mandatory among the affected people. Groups that emerge to challenge these officially approved groups may be suppressed by the state. This pattern of interest group–state relationships has been common among the authoritarian regimes in Latin America and on the Iberian peninsula prior to the establishment of democracy in the late 1970s.[5]

The experience of Mexico from 1950 to 1975 comes close to this model of state corporatism. The governing PRI party had official sectors in its organization that corresponded to farm, labor, and business interests. (See Figure 6.1.) Membership in one of these official interest groups associated with a sector of the PRI conferred automatic party membership. These PRI-dominated interest groups were involved officially in making policy. But in fact these groups lacked autonomy. They simply endorsed the president's decisions and defended them among the members of their groups. The state used its coercive powers to force rival groups to merge with the approved groups. When a group refused to do so, it risked violent repression by the police or army.

Societal corporatism, or *neocorporatism,* involves a similar kind of relationship but one that is not dominated by the state. To the contrary, it is the autonomy of the state that is drawn into question. The state becomes little more than the legitimat-

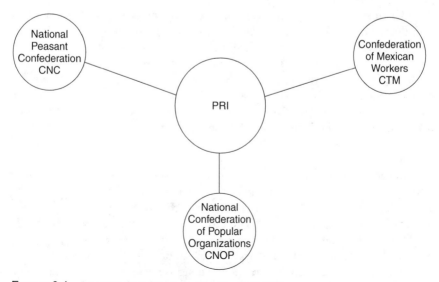

FIGURE 6.1   Interest Groups Linked to Mexico's PRI

ing body for decisions reached by the interaction of these official interest group monopolies. Unlike the situation under pluralism where groups use a wide range of tactics, societal corporatism brings groups together in state committees, boards, or councils where they meet together to set official policy.

Many observers detected a trend toward societal corporatism in many West European democracies during the 1970s. Neocorporatism appeared strongest in the smaller democracies in Scandinavia, the Low Countries, and Austria. Germany, too, was seen as advanced on the road to societal corporatism. However, the corporatist pattern of interest group–state interaction was largely restricted to only a few policy areas where neocorporatism seemed most highly developed. It was most evident in those states where governments had tried to introduce "incomes" policies: policies that set wages and controlled prices. For such policies to succeed, they needed the intimate cooperation of the affected labor and management groups. Other policy areas continued to be characterized by more pluralist patterns.[6]

By the 1980s, even this mixed neocorporatism was on the ebb. In some countries, such as Germany, the labor unions pulled out of the corporatist relationship; in others, such as Sweden, it was business that pulled out; in still others, such as Britain, it was the government that ended its special partnership with both kinds of groups. The ease with which these various partners ended their privileged relationship with each other demonstrates that even as they entered these relationships they did so while protecting their own autonomy from each other and from the state. There are still some policy sectors where neocorporatism remains a good description of the relationship between the state and groups. With the possible exception of agriculture, most of these policy sectors are very narrow and involve highly technical government decisions. It is chiefly a pluralist pattern that characterizes the broad picture of interest group–state relations in most democracies.

In summary, the autonomy of interest groups is a vital determinant of the effectiveness of the groups in defending the viewpoints of their members. They can do so only when they are free from state interference. Where they lose their autonomy, they can become agencies by which the state manipulates and controls society.

Strength of the State

Another key factor in the influence of interest groups is the strength of the state. The strength of the state is not always easy to measure. In general, it refers to the autonomy of the state from social groups such as business, labor, or agriculture and its ability to make decisions without excessive interference from these or other outside groups. This does not mean that groups do not pressure strong states but rather that the state is able to remain aloof from these pressures to make its own decisions. A strong state is also one with the capacity to enforce its decisions on reluctant groups or sectors of the population. The strength of a state has little to do with its democratic or nondemocratic character. There are both strong and weak democracies and both strong and weak authoritarian regimes. Strength of the state refers more to the effectiveness of the political elite in carrying through policy ideas than to how this elite is selected. What makes for a strong state, then, is not its economic resources, military prowess, or size. What counts is the ability of its political elite–elected or nonelected–to impose its views on public policy decisions and then to succeed in implementing those decisions.

Britain is often pointed to as an example of a strong state. Its political system is highly centralized in the executive of the national government in London. A handful of key officials from the cabinet and the senior civil service make decisions on virtually any desired policy with impact throughout the country. Access by groups is limited by this centralization and concentration of political power; it does little good for groups to lobby members of Parliament because MPs vote strictly along party lines. The government is able to remain aloof from group pressures when it wishes to or to involve groups on its own terms. The civil service is noted for its impartiality and obedience to the politicians' decisions.

In contrast, the United States is often viewed as a weak state. Its federal structure greatly decentralizes policy making, allowing interest groups many points at which they can seek to influence policy. The national government is fragmented by the separation of powers so that groups can seek influence in the executive branch, two houses of Congress, and ultimately even in the courts. Policy making is slowed by the need to build broad coalitions across these various branches of government and across the two major parties in Congress. This slowness and the difficulties of building coalitions leaves policy making open to short-term shifts in public opinion. Members of Congress vote as they please and can therefore be influenced by group lobbying. Finally, the implementation of policy by the civil service is often open to manipulation at all levels. The result is a highly penetrable and incoherent policy-making process open to many different social forces. Hence, it is seen as a weak state.

In the developing world, a variety of factors make most states "weak" in these terms.[7] Inexperienced political elites are often so preoccupied with the struggle to stay in office that they have little time to seek to master the decision-making process. Communication of political decisions may be difficult because of underdeveloped transportation, telephone, telegraph, or television networks. The elites may also face pressures from international sources that abridge their autonomy. Bureaucracies are often underdeveloped and ill disciplined. Corruption may make a state policy unenforceable. The developing state may lack the police or military power to coerce recalcitrant groups into accepting the centrally made decision. In such settings of weak government, organized groups may well be able to usurp state power at least as it pertains to regulating them or making decisions that affect them. The business community is usually among the most effective groups in such settings. Its impact on the country's economy, its ties to international finance, and sometimes its control by multinational corporations give the business community a powerful organizational base to confront a weak state. In India, for example, political leaders aimed at creating a socialist economy through a series of centrally imposed five-year plans. However, the influence of private enterprise was strong enough to block the achievement of a state-dominated economy and to shape the economic planning to meet the interests of the business community.

Organizational Strength of Interest Groups

Clearly, another important factor influencing group power is the organizational strength of interest groups. If the group is not well organized it will matter little how weak the state may be; it will not be able to use this advantage to see its wishes prevail. This is quite often the case in developing countries where weak states face organizationally weak groups. In democratic states—both strong and weak ones—organizational strength goes a long way in explaining the differential success of various groups in seeing government heed their interests.

Organizational strength is determined not only by numbers of members but also by how many of the represented sector of society are members of the group. This is often referred to as the density of membership. For example, the political influence of trade unions depends not only on their size but also on how many potential workers join the unions. Union membership is more easily measured than other kinds of interest group membership. For example, employers associations and farmers' groups are always very tight-lipped about their membership: They claim to represent the entire social category. But membership nevertheless does have an impact on their power. As a result, small businesses, which are less densely organized, usually are less influential than are the more densely organized large business firms.

Another aspect of organizational strength is the coherence of the group. Groups that are highly unified in their positions on a small number of issues about which they care a lot are more likely to be influential than are groups with members who have varying views on a broader range of issues that they hold with only moderate conviction. In Japan, for example, the owners of pachinko slot machines are highly unified and hence very powerful over government policies affecting their interests. On the other hand, in France, for example, parents' groups have less influence on educational policies than do educators because the parents' groups are more diverse than are the teachers' unions.

A related resource is the ability of the group to persuade government that their views represent the views of the people they claim to represent. Sometimes there will be a gap between the interest of the members and the group; even the perception of such a gap weakens that group's strength. For example, in Japan, government feels free to ignore the positions of women's groups because they are not seen as representative of women in general.

Of course, financial resources are also important. A group can do more if its coffers are full. Money seems especially important in the United States, where campaign contributions are an important way for groups to catch the attention of legislators. Money is important elsewhere, but group leaders cite it as a key resource less than they do membership or coherence.[8]

A final organizational resource is the strengths and skills of the group's leaders. Groups with inept leaders are likely to be ineffective even when these groups have other organizational strengths. Because of this, the effectiveness of a group often changes as it changes leaders. Leadership effectiveness includes not only the organizational skill of the leaders but also their friendships and contacts with government leaders. This usually works to the advantage of business interests because political leaders are often former classmates or fellow club members of the people who end up as the entrepreneurial elite. This is especially true in smaller countries where the economic and political elites emerge from the same schools. Even in a middle-sized country like France, this effect can be seen in the large numbers of government officials and economic leaders who have been trained alongside each other in the elite *grandes écoles*.

All of these organizational factors are important elements of interest group power. But there is no way of toting up these various elements and deciding precisely which groups are powerful and which are not. These organizational features do help in understanding why an environmental group is less powerful than a trade union. But they do not always tell us which environmental group will be most successful in getting government to accept its position. Perhaps as important as these organizational resources are situational ones. Generally those groups that are most influential are those viewed by government as friends that play the game well and fairly. Groups that can convey the impression that their interests are the same as the interests of government and the general public are much more likely to be effective than are groups perceived to be pursuing narrow, special interests.

THE SHARED POWERS OF GROUPS AND GOVERNMENTS

Perhaps the most important factor in interest group strength is the fact that groups often possess key powers that the state needs to be effective in drafting and enforcing its policies. As the state meddles more frequently in society and the economy, interest groups come to hold two key resources that all governments need to regulate society: information and acquiescence. By offering these resources to the state, groups can ensure that their interests are heard and considered as the state makes its social and economic decisions.

Often interest groups have information that governments need to make wise and effective policies. When issues regarding public health are under consideration, governments frequently find that the best sources for information on the medical aspects are the doctors' associations; school reorganization may require information that only principals' associations can provide; bank regulations need facts that bankers' organizations alone can offer. The information may be highly technical, relating to the expertise that those in the profession are most likely to possess. It may be facts regarding the needs and likely reactions of the professionals to a pending policy decision.

Of course, groups will shape the information they provide government in order to best suit the needs of their clientele or members. In exchange for that valuable information, governments will promise to consider the group's opinions as well. In many cases, governments are even willing to grant access to the decision-making process to those groups that have essential information to offer. For example, the British government has always granted the British Medical Association a strong voice in the administration and reforms of the state-run National Health Service. The government recognized that the BMA had information it needed to make the system work and to respond to changes in medical needs.

The second resource that groups have is their ability to help in winning voluntary acquiescence in new policies. In an age when governments of all types intervene more deeply and directly into people's lives, governments become increasingly dependent upon the public's voluntary compliance with their policies. Even in authoritarian systems, the political elite cannot coerce compliance with social and economic regulations over the long term. Of course, the need for voluntary acquiescence to the law is especially important in democratic states; it is also essential in authoritarian regimes. Widespread disobedience or neglect of government policies can result in the state's loss of legitimacy.

Groups can offer help in winning public acquiescence to state policies in two ways. First, they can assist the government in explaining and advocating the policies to those they seek to represent. For example, acceptance of a new system of agricultural subsidies in India is promoted when farm groups take part in selling the new policies to farmers. Secondly, the groups can assist in legitimizing the state's policy. Advocacy by the Indian farmers' own organizations adds to the legitimacy of the state's subsidy policy. Of course, policies seen as legitimate are more likely to be accepted by those affected even if the policies cause them inconveniences.

It is easier to show this principle at work by looking at an authoritarian system. Thus, in the USSR, party leaders had to abandon a major educational reform when it met with noncompliance from the educators' groups.[9] But this same principle is at work in all settings. For example, German governments have long wanted to impose speed limits on the autobahn to promote driver safety, conserve scarce petroleum, and protect forests from the pollution emitted by speeding vehicles. But no government has actually set speed controls because of the powerful opposition of automotive clubs and the threat of noncompliance by German drivers.

Here again, groups can exchange their ability to help build acquiescence to a new policy for a say in the decision. They are more likely to legitimize policies when the decision making has involved their consultation. Most governments take the initiative in consulting affected groups and sometimes involving them directly in the decision process in order to preempt the danger of their later opposition to the policy. Even when the decision does not reflect a group's view, the fact that it was consulted before the decision was made makes it more difficult for the group to question its legitimacy or to orchestrate noncompliance.

The involvement of groups in the decisions that touch their clienteles in many ways seems laudable. Most of us would think it normal and desirable for governments to consult with those who are going to be most directly affected by a policy. This participation makes government policies legitimate not only for them but for all citizens who see such involvement by the affected as appropriate.

The involvement of groups provides for the representation of interests, or *functional representation,* as a supplement to the representation of individuals. In effect, geographically based representation through the usual electoral districts and voting may not provide adequate or fair representation to specific interests. The voice of a minority ethnic group may be lost if its people are distributed evenly in a number of districts that always elect candidates from the majority ethnic community. Similarly, the mix of interests in electoral districts may mean that the concerns of merchants are neglected because the industrial workers and employers always make up the electoral majority. Functional representation would base representation on interests rather than geographic areas. Some democracies—such as France, Germany, and Italy—try to accomplish this through the creation of "social and economic councils" made up of representatives from employer associations, trade union representatives, consumer advocates, and other social groups. They advise parliament on economic matters, but they usually are able to do little more than issue advisory opinions that lack power over the policy process.

Functional representation may be a useful supplement to individual representation, but it is not a good replacement for it in the democratic context. When affected groups make laws, they reflect the concerns of their clienteles but tend to ignore the interests of those not included and the general interest of the entire society. In addition, there are always concerns about how well the group leaders reflect their members' views and interests. The leaders usually have interests of their own through which they interpret the views of their followers. As leaders from a variety of groups meet together over time to negotiate public policy, they acquire shared values that may make their perspectives resemble each other's more than those of their members.

NEW SOCIAL MOVEMENTS

Over the past thirty years, many democratic countries have experienced the emergence of a new form of interest group activity.[10] The "new social movements" are organizations around some of the great social issues of our era: women's rights, environmental protection, minority rights, civil liberties, peace, and globalization. To these movements should be added some groups that have similar styles and structures that come from the opposite end of the political spectrum: antitax movements and anti-immigration groups. For the most part, these new social movements have emerged to champion issues that have been neglected by political parties and government. They also are often new and more dynamic organizations that have challenged older and stodgier groups advocating the same cause. Thus, there have long been women's movements in many countries, but they have lacked the political clout that new feminist movements have gained in recent years. Similarly, more militant ecological groups have taken up causes with new vigor that older conservation societies had earlier defined.

The new social movements share certain characteristics even though they have different objectives. They are usually poorly organized. This is purposeful since many of these movements express disdain for the conservative nature of all formal organizations. They prefer spontaneity, which makes the movements exciting but also unpredictable. The German Greens, for example, always include a protest demonstration as part of the agenda for their conferences. The delegates pack up and travel often hundreds of miles to demonstrate on-site against some environmental risk. New social movements generally prefer the tactics of direct action in boycotts, protests, or demonstrations rather than working through the "established channels." They believe those channels to be ineffective and potentially corrosive to the spirit and goals of their movements.

Many of the new social movements have serious reservations about the ability of representative democracies to ever accomplish what they think must be done. As a result, the movements often appear to be antiregime and even antidemocratic. This makes it less likely that the established parties and groups will want to cooperate with them in seeking their goals. Often the movement takes stands so extreme that they are unattractive even to those who support some of their goals. For example, Japanese women's movements have adopted radical feminist stances that are unappealing even to the many women who believe in the need for greater women's rights but reject sweeping social and political changes.

The new social movements have had great impact on politics in Western democracies. Some democrats have been alarmed by their extremism, tactics, and antiregime orientations and have seen them as dangers to Western representative democracy. However, these groups have brought to the forefront of politics important issues that needed to be faced. They have compelled the more traditional groups and parties to review and often revise their agendas and priorities, if only to undermine the appeal of the new movements.

THE CIVIL SOCIETY

As we conclude this chapter on groups, let's return to de Tocqueville's arguments on the importance of volunteer associations in creating a climate for successful democracy. Such associations may become buffers between families and their governments. They open the way for citizen involvement in a wide range of civic activities and prepare citizens for broader participation in political actions. Participation in groups and associations builds citizens' trust in each other. It creates a "civil society" that is supportive of democracy. Indeed, many scholars of democratization insist that building successful, durable democracies requires the presence of a civil society.

Civil society is people's activity in social actions beyond the economy and the state in associations that are not linked to the state. The associations may or may not have political agendas. In any case, their interests go beyond trying to influence government. The range of activities that make a civil society includes participation in churches, cultural and artistic associations, book groups, educational organizations such as Parent-Teachers Associations, card clubs, sports and recreational clubs, women's clubs, environmental and nature groups, charitable organizations, neighborhood or historical preservationist associations, veterans' groups, and so on. These groups are all nongovernmental and often nonprofit. One scholar noted that the political role of civil society

> is not just to aggregate, represent, and articulate interests, but also to create citizens, to shape consciousness, and to help define what is public and political. Civic actors build "social capital," serve as intermediaries between the state and private citizens, and sometimes exercise authority in specific issue areas (such as education, development, and resource management).[11]

Authoritarian regimes have generally limited autonomous associations because they fear that such assemblies might become centers of opposition to their rule. The former communist regimes were effective in eliminating, but not entirely removing, associations that they did not control. Dictators often used arrests and violence to limit voluntary organizations. As a result, many of the countries currently going through democratization lack the social capital (trust in others, tolerance of the ideas of others, instinct to participate, and the voluntary associations themselves) to assist in building democracy. And there is the rub: The social capital needed to build democracy is hard to create. Established patterns of interaction and association perpetuate themselves into the present and the future. A recent study of southern Italy discovered that the levels of involvement in social groups and government were about the same as they were seventy years earlier.[12]

How to build social capital where it does not exist or is weak is a difficult challenge. Granting basic liberties including the right to assemble and freedom of speech are important steps. In some places governments have provided subsidies to help associations maintain themselves. Certainly another force at work in promoting civil society is the influence of the international communication revolution. People in one country may seek to emulate the actions of those in other countries. The free movement of ideas in the age of the World Wide Web, e-mail, and satellite communications makes it difficult for authoritarian regimes to control the thinking and actions of their subjects. Some believe that the establishment of modern democratic institutions will itself foster the development of civil society. One author notes:

> . . . even limited civic democratization efforts may lay the groundwork for future transitions, and increasing transnational diffusion may allow some societies to overcome objective restraints.[13]

The achievement of a civil society does not mean successful democracy. Some countries with considerable social capital remain undemocratic. Other successful democracies work well enough with weak civil societies. In a celebrated article, "Bowling Alone," Robert D. Putnam claims that voluntary associations in the United States are dying as a result of social changes that promote hyperindividualism.[14] He worries about the consequences for American democracy if we lose these sources of social capital. Putnam's claims are controversial both in regard to the reality of a decline in voluntary associations and to the consequences of such a decline on the polity.[15]

In the meantime, most observers watch hopefully for the emergence of civil society in the form of healthy and autonomous interest groups and in the development of the art of association. Both these sets of groups have important political roles. Both contribute to the social capital needed both to support fledgling democracies and to buttress older democracies in times of stress.

CONCLUSION

The American student who sees in other countries little visible lobbying like that seen in the United States and concludes that interest group politics there is less important than here would be mistaken. In all kinds of political settings, organized and informal groups are important political actors. In many cases, they serve as essential vehicles that allow individual citizens sharing common concerns to have a meaningful impact on the policies that govern their lives. Indeed, the free play of groups in politics is essential to the presence of both pluralism and civil society that we now see as important in building and maintaining modern liberal democracy.

NOTES

1. William A. Galston, "Civil Society and the 'Art of Association,'" *Journal of Democracy* 11 (January 2000): 64–70.

2. Alexis de Tocqueville, *Democracy in America,* trans. by Henry Reeve, revised by Francis Bowen, and edited by Phillips Bradley (New York: Vintage Classics, 1990), vol. II p. 110.

3. Howard Machin and Vincent Wright, eds., *Economic Policy and Policy-Making Under the Mitterrand Presidency, 1981–1984* (London: Frances Pinter, 1985).

4. Philippe C. Schimitter and Gerhard Lehmbruch, eds., *Trends Toward Corporatist Intermediation* (Beverly Hills, CA: Sage, 1979).

5. Howard J. Wiarda, *Corporatism and National Development in Latin America* (Boulder, CO: Westview Press, 1982) and *Corporatism and Development: The Portuguese Experience* (Amherst: University of Massachusetts Press, 1977).

6. See, for example, Clive S. Thomas, ed., *First World Interest Groups: A Comparative Approach* (Greenwood, CT: Greenwood Press, 1993).

7. Joel S. Midgal, *Strong Societies and Weak States: State-Society Relations and State Capabilities in the Third World* (Princeton, NJ: Princeton University Press, 1988).

8. Frank L. Wilson, *French Interest-Group Politics* (Cambridge, England: Cambridge University Press, 1987).

9. Gordon F. Skilling and Franklyn Griffiths, eds., *Interest Groups in Soviet Politics* (Princeton, NJ: Princeton University Press, 1971).

10. Russell J. Dalton and Manfred Kuechler, eds., *Challenging the Political Order: New Social and Political Movements in Western Democracies* (New York: Oxford University Press, 1990).

11. Alison Brysk, "Democratizing Civil Society in Latin America," *Journal of Democracy* 11 (July 2000): 153.

12. Robert Putnam with Robert Leonardi and Rafaella Nanetti, *Making Democracy Work: Civic Traditions in Modern Italy* (Princeton, NJ: Princeton University Press).

13. Brysk, "Democratizing Civil Society," p. 164.

14. Robert D. Putnam, "Bowling Alone," *Journal of Democracy* 6 (January 1995): 65–78.

15. On this debate, see Theda Skocpol and Morris P. Fiorina, eds., *Civic Engagement and American Democracy* (Washington, DC: Brookings Institution, 1999), and Robert K. Fullinwider, ed., *Civil Society, Democracy, and Civic Renewal* (Lanham, MD: Rowman & Littlefield, 1999). For Putnam's response to his critics, see Robert D. Putnam, *Bowling Alone: The Collapse and Revival of the American Community* (New York: Simon & Schuster, 2000).

Chapter 7

❖❖❖❖❖❖❖❖❖❖❖❖❖❖

Political Elites

At the peak of every political system is a relatively small handful of individuals who are far more involved in politics than ordinary citizens. They are the ones who dominate the political processes and make politics and government a full-time career. This small group of leaders is usually referred to as the *political elite*. It is small because in every political system the number of people who are very interested and very active in politics is limited. The political elite is the most influential of this small group of interested and involved citizens.

The term *elite* often carries a pejorative connotation of a small band of willful individuals who monopolize power and use it for their own advantage. In this textbook, I use the term *elite* in a nonpejorative sense to refer simply to those few people who are more active in the political process, who hold office or aspire to hold office, and who consistently are involved in shaping national political decision making. This elite may or may not have the negative characteristics that are often associated with the term: a small group who conspire to monopolize political power and use it for their own benefit. The members of the political elite may or may not conspire to monopolize power; they may or may not represent only their own interests and use their power to improve their social and economic positions; they may or may not attempt to exclude others from political processes. All of these are empirical issues that must be resolved by looking at specific elites rather than attributing these characteristics to political leaders simply because they are fewer than the total population.

The political elite is made up of three components: the politicians; opinion leaders and influence wielders; and the senior civil servants. In the democratic setting it is relatively easy to identify the politicians: those who seek or hold elective and appointed office and those who help them in political campaigns. It is less clear in third world countries where traditional village, clan, or religious leaders, civil servants, and military figures may be the dominant political leaders. Opinion leaders include interest group leaders, their political negotiators, and lobbyists; journalists and media people; and other influential figures whose ideas and views shape the political values and preferences of others. The third component of the political elite is the senior civil service. Often very influential, the civil servants will be discussed in Chapter 10. In many countries, the military plays such an important part in politics that it is a separate and even dominant political elite. Chapter 8 deals with the military's political role. In this chapter, I will focus on the top national politicians whose activities are most likely to affect the lives of large numbers.

RECRUITMENT OF POLITICAL ELITES

Among the key concerns in examining political elites are the questions of how elites are selected, by whom they are selected, and how they are trained for public duties. As might be expected, the answers to these questions vary widely even when we look at countries of the same general type, and the differences between democratic regimes and authoritarian ones are even greater.

A key concern is whether the political elite is selected on the basis of *ascription* or *achievement*.[1] Some individuals emerge as political leaders simply by virtue of who they are. They are leaders because they are sons or daughters of kings or queens, religious leaders, or the oldest men in the community. This is the ascriptive mode of political recruitment. For example, Elizabeth II became monarch of the United Kingdom because she was the eldest child of the ruling Windsor dynasty. Other leaders base their entry into the political elite on their own individual achievements or skills. The skills may be technical, but they may also be in money making or interpersonal relations or leadership. This is the pattern of achievement-based recruitment.

Ascriptive patterns of recruitment are characteristic of more traditional societies. Village elders, religious leaders, large estate owners, chiefs, and kings become political leaders with impact over the lives of others because of birth or age rather than what they have personally achieved. In more developed political systems, individuals obtain political leadership because of their own achievements rather than their innate qualities. However, even in highly developed political systems it is not uncommon for ascription to play a role in gaining political leadership. For example, there are often political families where successive generations become highly involved in politics. Children learn to be political leaders by observing their politically active parents and by using family friends to ease their way into leadership positions. The Kennedys and Bushes are good examples in the United States; in India, Prime Minister Jawaharlal Nehru was succeeded by his daughter, Indira Gandhi; and the position of mayor of Lyons, one of the largest and most important cities in France, passed from father to son for over fifty years. Marriage is often an ascriptive path to political leadership. Under the highly developed and modern communist political systems in China and the Soviet Union, despite communism's claims to provide equal opportunities for women, the few women who reached the top political elite were usually wives of leading politicians, such as Mao Zedong's wife. Inherited wealth sometimes becomes a pathway to political leadership. Indeed, the British House of Lords until 2000 drew most of its members from hereditary peerages.

Sometimes there is the assumption that as polities develop and become more modern, they will shift the basis of their political recruitment from ascription to achievement. In general, there is such a trend, but ascription often proves to be very durable. For example, in Nigeria the traditional elites of village, clan, and communal group chiefs or elders are often found in the newly emerging achievement-based political elite. Even when they do not become involved directly, they still play key political roles behind more "modern" leaders whom they have backed. But the phenomenon of durable ascriptive patterns of recruitment exists even in very highly developed Western democracies. In France, for example, the traditional local "notables"–public school teachers, parish priests, pharmacists and doctors, and notaries–still have important political roles in many small towns and villages. And the support of such notables is often crucial as national politicians seek to build local political bases.

There are many ways in which people reach the top levels of politics in democratic states. The differences reflect historical patterns as well as the formal political institutions. There are some emerging commonalities in advanced democracies, however.[2] Successful candidates for political leadership tend to be experienced politicians rather than outsiders or amateurs. They are skilled in raising substantial amounts of financial contributions, even in countries where the state subsidizes much of the cost of elections. Leaders everywhere need to be telegenic and have appealing personalities. For example, the British Conservative party leader, William Hague, found himself at a distinct disadvantage because he lacked the dash and glamor of the Labour Prime Minister Tony Blair.

In most democratic countries, there is greater emphasis on involving the public or at least the party's rank-and-file members in the process of selecting candidates and party leaders. The United States has one of the most open political recruitment processes: Aspiring public officials need only to declare themselves candidates and seek a party's nomination in the primary elections. Of course, money, well-connected friends, and name familiarity are useful in succeeding in the process. But the primary system of nominating candidates for elective office allows individuals from a wide range of backgrounds to seek entrance into the political elite. Nominations for the major political parties are thus made by the voters, not the parties, and the result is a variety of backgrounds for American politicians: businesspeople, entertainers, sports figures, television personalities, neighborhood leaders, and so on, even when they have little political experience and no party membership. It also means that inexperienced people end up in top leadership positions. In addition, candidates not at all representative of their parties sometimes end up on the ballots for general elections. For example, a few years ago, the Republican candidate for governor of Louisiana was a member of the Ku Klux Klan.

Embarrassed party leaders were unwilling to endorse or support the candidate foisted on them by the primary election process.

The only other major country to experiment with primary elections as a means of nominating candidates for major political office has been Mexico. The PRI introduced the use of the primary to select presidential candidates in 1999 although not all other parties used that process. The PRI hoped to demonstrate its commitment to democracy and to break the traditional elite's hold over the party. It worked also as a means of reinvigorating an older party faced with new challenges and calls for its democratization. But it did not work well enough for the PRI to fend off its defeat in the 2000 presidential election by PAN's Vicente Fox.

In nearly all other democracies, parties control nominations for elected offices. The selection may be made at the local level or by the national party organization, but the national party usually has absolute control over the use of its name by candidates running in elections. It is the party that names its own candidates and it gives the privilege (or, in some cases, duty) of running for public office. Candidates cannot use the party's name without the approval of the party they claim to represent. Such control leads to more coherent parties and greater discipline. Rebellious elected officials may find that they are not renominated by their party, and without the nomination of a major party most candidacies are doomed to fail in countries such as Britain, Canada, Germany, France, and nearly all other Western democracies.

In most democratic states, politics becomes a full-time career for those engaged in national politics. Aspiring politicians serve apprenticeships in local politics and internal party offices before running for national offices. In Britain, for example, it is unusual for individuals to be selected for top leadership positions before they have served ten years or so in the House of Commons. During this period, politicians learn how the system operates, develop political alliances and friendships, and become ingrained with the party's expectations on doctrine and democratic procedures. In France, many leading politicians emerge from a similar recruitment process, but local politics is also an important avenue to national political careers. Still other French leaders enter national politics directly from senior civil service positions—something that is explicitly barred in Britain. Occasionally, political novices are able to take very senior positions in France. For example, Georges Pompidou was named prime minister before he had ever run for elected office. But this openness to "outsiders" is rare in democratic politics outside the United States. In Germany, the path to national leadership usually lies through years of success in state politics and party leadership positions. In Japan, the patron-client pattern plays an important role in selecting and training future political elites.

In China and other current and former communist states, the top political elites were individuals who had made careers in the party. They emerged from China's party cadre and the Soviet Union's apparatchiki—the full-time, professional party employees. They advanced through the party ranks as paid employees with little other professional activity beyond service to the party. Often the most successful aspiring politicians were those who won the support of powerful patrons or sponsors already in positions of power. Once at the highest level, the party's Central Committee, access to the very top positions in the ruling Politburo and Party Secretariat was determined by personal links, skills, and age or tenure.

In other authoritarian systems, three pathways to political leadership have been common. In many of these countries, there are well-articulated patron-client systems that recruit and train future political elites. Would-be politicians tie themselves and their futures to promising political leaders. By providing these leaders with assistance in reaching high political positions, they hope to be rewarded with ever greater opportunities as their patron succeeds. A second pathway is through the civil service. Able civil servants often are selected to serve as ministers in areas within their expertise; some of them can use this entrance into public office as a means to develop full-time political careers. The overlap of senior civil servants with the ruling party or elite facilitates and encourages such political recruitment. A third route to top political positions in many countries is through the military. This will be explored more fully in Chapter 8, but here it is important to note that in many societies, military careers are major avenues of political recruitment. Indeed, traditions of repeated military coups sometimes make this the primary source of new political leaders.

WHO GETS RECRUITED?

When political scientists examine elites, one of their major concerns is with the socioeconomic characteristics of the political leaders compared with the general socioeconomic composition of the population as a whole. Who gets recruited? The answer is almost always the same whatever the type of political system and however well developed or traditional it is:[3] Those who attain political leadership are from the middle and upper classes; people from the working class or the least-advantaged parts of the population rarely make it to the political elite. The political leaders are more prosperous than the rest of the population; few poor people enter the ranks of the elite, and if they do so they usually soon become well-to-do. The political elite is better educated than others. It is disproportionately drawn from the dominant religious, ethnic, and communal grouping. The elite is always overwhelmingly more male than the general adult population. In short, the political leadership is never a representative elite that mirrors the general citizenry. It is an elite that in every way resembles the already privileged more than it does the typical citizen and even less resembles the disadvantaged.

Even when leftist parties or groups are in power, the elite is unrepresentative of the disadvantaged whose interests the Left promises to defend. In the Soviet Union and Eastern Europe the hypocrisy of a "workers' party" that was mainly concerned with accumulating benefits for its leaders ultimately contributed to the fall of communism. In Western democratic countries, the leadership of left-of-center parties differs from that of the conservative parties: Left-wing parties usually draw leaders from an education and trade union elite, while conservative parties bring in leaders from business and high society. But the overall nature of both elites is still unlike the nonelite population: Both Left and Right elites are better educated, more prosperous, more male, and more frequently from the dominant cultural groups than the general population.

This poses a dilemma for all countries, and it is an especially important problem in democratic countries. If the elite that dominates politics is unrepresentative of and unlike the typical citizen, can it govern on behalf of the general population? This is a very controversial question that has no easy answer. For some, the very fact that the elite is unrepresentative disqualifies it from being able to understand and support the interests of the less advantaged parts of society. Even if the elite draws in individuals from less advantaged backgrounds, membership in the elite by itself gives these people values and perspectives different from those of people who remain in more modest situations. The gap between the nature of the elite and the mass population produces cynicism about any kind of political system when all elites—those of both Left and Right—inevitably perpetuate the dominance of the better-off.

Others contend that the problems of political elitism are linked to the economic system.[4] Where property is privately owned, monopoly capitalist interests always dominate the state; government inevitably reflects only the will of the ruling capitalist elite. The result is a ruling elite based on economic structures.[5] Such radical critics believe that if capitalist economic structures were replaced by a socialist society, elitism would disappear in a state free of hierarchy and privilege. Even though actual experiences in earlier socialist countries—such as the Soviet Union and Eastern Europe—were discouraging, these radical critics believe that a more genuine socialism in the future will bring an end to political elitism.

Still others are less concerned with the gap between the background of the political elite and the general population. They see the issue of elitism as based on two questionable assumptions: (1) that the political elite always rules in its own best interests; and (2) that the best political representation of a particular class or group is always made by people who come from that part of the society. Neither of these assumptions is supported by empirical evidence. In nearly every country, there are many examples where the political elite has backed policies that were not in its own interests or in the interests of the most advantaged strata of society. For example, the extensive social welfare programs in France, Germany, and Italy were all put in place by conservative governments more aligned with middle and upper classes than with the popular classes most helped by the social programs. Some critics of capitalism assert that social welfare programs and other state measures to ease the worst features of economic cycles are not evidence of the absence of the economic elite's dominance but rather token concessions allowed by employers because they see them as good for business or as means of perpetuating their control. Such criticism is difficult to rebut simply because the critics can explain any apparent lack of elite rule by simply changing the definition of the elite's interests to include virtually any conceivable policy. Most observers, however, see little evidence of a genuine ruling elite based on economic power in the social and economic policies pursued by most industrialized democracies.

Nor is it at all clear that individuals from disadvantaged groups are more likely to advocate those interests once in political power. Indeed, "self-made" people who rise from adverse conditions to political power often are convinced that if they can make it on their own so can others if they will only try. Indeed, many of the most successful reformers in Western democracies come from privileged backgrounds and press for changes because of a sense of public duty coming out of those privileges. A similar result can be seen in the attitude of ethnic minorities once they achieve power.

Those who feel that democracy can work even when there are few and unrepresentative people in government point to the heterogeneity or pluralist nature of political elites.[6] Within the political elite, there are many rivalries and differences that prevent domination by any single set of political or economic viewpoints. These differences among political leaders reflect partisan differences in democratic settings, but they also include the varying importance that elements of the political leadership attach to specific issues or interests. Such differences in the political elite exist even in authoritarian systems. Critics of the elitist views of society see elites as pluralistic also because separate elites exist in most industrial democracies and many authoritarian systems for politics, economics, religion, and society. The various elites compete with each other for influence over politics and prevent the emergence of a single, unified ruling elite.

ELITE STYLES

It is far easier to obtain data on the socioeconomic backgrounds of political elites than it is to develop similar data on how they exercise their power. But that information is essential to evaluate the disinterestedness of elites. The assumptions about what unrepresentative elites do or do not do with their power are unsupported. It is much more important to look at the style and products of elitism.

Legitimacy

In Chapter 1, I discussed the concept of legitimacy and the importance of legitimacy in the survival of a regime. The same is true of the political elite: A key quality of elites is the extent to which they are regarded as the rightful or legitimate people to exercise political power. Coercion is an inefficient and ineffective means of maintaining a political elite in power. Even elites in authoritarian regimes seek and profit from a public sense that they are the appropriate and legitimate leaders who deserve the obedience of the population. Elites that are seen by their publics as illegitimate are unlikely to endure very long.

As we saw in Chapter 1, legitimacy of regimes may have its roots in tradition, charisma, or accepted rational/legal processes. But another important element in maintaining the legitimacy is the elite's capability of achieving the expected aims of government: economic growth, maintenance of the general welfare and security of the people, political stability, domestic order, and protection against foreign attacks. Political leaders who are unable to meet these universal needs soon become illegitimate. Elites that are perceived as seeking only their own interests and as preoccupied with maintaining their powers rather than using them for broader public goals lose their legitimacy. When an elite loses legitimacy, the public's sense that the leaders are self-seeking and self-defensive becomes even stronger. Illegitimate elites survive for long times only with difficulty and luck—good luck from their perspectives but bad luck from the viewpoint of the ruled.

Political Style of Leadership

Another element of elite style is the approach of political leaders to getting the ruled to do what they want them to. This obedience does not always come automatically or easily even when the elite is regarded as completely legitimate and the law itself makes sense. Here's an illustration of how dependent governments are upon voluntary compliance with the laws they adopt. In 1979, the city government in Paris announced it would begin enforcing a law requiring the use of headlights when driving after dark. That might seem logical to people everywhere, but Parisians had acquired the habit of driving in the city using only their parking lights during the blackouts of the Second World War. While drivers in other cities had resumed using headlights after the war ended, Parisians felt the streets were bright enough in the "City of Light." The 1979 ordinance was passed in response to the growing numbers of pedestrians who were being hit by cars that they could not see approaching. But the announcement of the new law met with widespread public resistance: Eye doctors claimed that the bright lights would increase the risk of blindness; residents complained that the extra light would disturb their rest; and traditionalists complained that car lights would disturb the beauty of the soft illumination of monuments and landmarks. Enforcement of the new law was difficult with such widespread opposition. In the end, the political leaders opted for a gentle enforcement policy that stressed publicity campaigns and time to bring compliance. As a result, more than twenty years later visitors to Paris will find many drivers still refusing to use their headlights in the city. This example comes from a democratic country where voluntary compliance is especially important. But even authoritarian governments find it inefficient and dangerous to their hold on power to try to rigidly enforce laws that their peoples reject.

Most political elites rely on their legitimacy to gain the public's acceptance of their laws and policies. In part, the legitimacy of a set of leaders makes compliance automatic in most cases. Because laws are proposed by a leadership that is legitimate and enacted in accordance with procedures that are regarded as legitimate, most citizens feel a strong sense of obligation to obey. Individuals are reluctant to challenge such collective decisions, especially when they feel that they have had a say in choosing the leaders or in approving the policy-making process. Leaders are followed and obeyed because they should be obeyed.

Some political elites stress ideological themes to win acceptance of their leadership and policies. Established political beliefs and ideologies can be used to explain and justify specific actions of the elite. Ideological appeals are less frequent in the current era of declining ideologies, but there are still many examples. Margaret Thatcher, for instance, stressed free enterprise liberalism in promoting her programs to privatize the public economic sector. Chinese leaders invoke communist notions of social justice to support actions against profiteering and black marketers.

Elites can also use material rewards to maintain their support. Citizens can be provided with government contracts, educational opportunities, or jobs in exchange for their support of the political leadership. This is very common in settings where patron-client politics are well established as in Japan, Mexico, or Nigeria. Entire regions are wooed by elites with promises of major public works projects such as dams, highways, or airports. Supporters of the elite can also be rewarded with public honors and recognition. In the Soviet Union, for example, workers who exceeded their quotas received local and national recognition; in Britain, citizens are rewarded for their public service by the annual honors list, knighthoods, and other royal recognitions.

Ultimately, and usually as a last resort, political elites control the means to force compliance through their control of the law, police, and military power. Chinese students, for example, reluctantly dropped their democracy campaign because the state used violence and imprisonment to force them to do so. In less dramatic forms, the use of force or the threat to use it brings obedience to laws that people do not like or accept on other grounds. The use of force is inefficient and weakens the legitimacy of a regime and its leaders. But it is the ultimate means that governments alone can use on a broad scale to assure enforcement of the elite's will.

While I have stressed the collective style of elites, the style of individual leaders varies in important ways.[7] Some leaders perceive their responsibilities in broader ways than do others from the same country. Current Russian President Vladimir Putin had more decisiveness in ruling than did his predecessor, Boris Yeltsin. Britain's Tony Blair ruled brusquely in spite of the large parliamentary majority that made such heavy-handedness unnecessary. French Prime Minister Lionel Jospin built consensus on changes even though his policies differed little in basic orientation and success than did his more aloof conservative predecessor. Nigeria's military ruler from 1993–1999 aggravated ethnic, regional, and religious differences to divide his enemies and shore up his rule.

These differences reflect the individual leaders' personalities, but they also are influenced by the times and challenges the leaders face at a given point. Some times force dramatic leadership from individuals who are inclined by their personalities to more modest leadership styles. For example, Chancellor Helmut Kohl, inclined by personality to be a conciliator and passive leader, was compelled to more creative and forceful leadership styles by the spontaneous union of East and West Germany in 1989–1990. On the other hand, some leaders are able to make strong imprints on their societies even in ordinary times by their ability to capture the imagination of their people and to use fully the resources at their disposal. Such leaders are able to bring out the best in their followers as they transform their societies.[8] More frequently, leaders are not up to meeting the challenges of their times.

For example, Indian prime minister P. V. Narasimha Rao struggled ineffectually in dealing with rising religious and ethnic tensions in India during the 1990s.

Leadership styles are very important in understanding the successes and failures of particular sets of leaders to meet the challenges facing them and their countries. They are also important in understanding why people follow their leaders at times and ignore them or overthrow them at others.

The mesh between the cultural values and expectations of a people about their leaders and the performance and style of these leaders is a crucial factor in the ability of elites to obtain and maintain the loyalty of their followers. Margaret Thatcher was Britain's strongest and most successful prime minister of the twentieth century, yet she was ultimately forced out of office by her own supporters. They came to believe that her abrasive style and high-handed ways of dealing with her supporters and rivals conflicted with the British political culture.

Open and Closed Elites

By definition, political elites are small compared with the size of the total population. This reflects the fact that people's interest and willingness to become politically active vary, and only a few even want to be highly involved in national politics. The fact that an elite is small, then, does not make it evil or dangerous. What is of concern is the extent to which political elites are *open* or *closed*.

In some cases, the political elites are relatively closed bodies that are not easily penetrated by outsiders who want to become involved. They may also be closed to influence from individuals and groups outside the elite. Closed elites allow only those they approve to enter the elite. They co-opt aspiring politicians and give them a place in the elite on the condition that these new participants accept the rules and priorities of the existing elite. Such closed elites conspire to maintain their monopoly of political power. They are closed both in the sense of new recruits and with regard to their willingness to heed the concerns of those outside the elite.

Closed elites are characteristic of most if not all authoritarian political systems. For example, leadership positions in Nigerian politics required the approval of the military elite for most of its years as an independent state. Even as Nigeria moved toward civilian democracy in 1999, aspiring politicians and political parties had to have the explicit endorsement of the military regime. Until the mid-1980s, entrance into the Mexican political elite was controlled by the dominant PRI and especially its leader. Groups or individuals who sought to present separate political agendas and who refused co-optation by the party faced arrest or violence. While the Mexican president was limited to a single term, in most cases he selected his successor. With the adoption of primary elections to select presidential candidates and the election in 2000 of the first-ever non-PRI president, Mexico's political elite now appears to be opening up.

Some critics of Western democracy contend that the political elites in North America and Western Europe are also closed.[9] Unlike the ham-fisted techniques of authoritarian elites, the elites in Western democracies are allegedly more subtle. Critics claim there is an inevitable linkage of economic and political elites with the real powerholders among monopoly capitalists who manipulate the formal leaders from behind the scenes. This argument sees little hope for democracy to break away from the economic elite. Even when reform-minded leftists come to power, they are soon compelled to play the capitalist's game. The French Socialist government in the 1980s can be cited as an example. The Socialists came to power in 1981 with a clear commitment to achieve a definitive break with monopoly capitalism, but within three years they had retreated to economic and social policies that differed little from those of their conservative predecessors.[10]

It is difficult to challenge these arguments of elitism, not because there is no evidence to the contrary of open elites, but because the definitions used by elitist theories are vague. I argued earlier in this chapter that advocates of a ruling elite can interpret virtually any state policy as serving the interests of the economic elite and therefore confirming their view of a ruling elite. As a result, you soon reach the tautological position where it is impossible even to imagine a policy that does not correspond with the will of the capitalist ruling elite. The identity and location of the ruling elite also tends to shift. As critics of elitism disprove the existence of a ruling elite at one level, elitists respond that there is another, better-concealed and even more insidious elite behind the one that has been discounted.

Most observers, instead, see the majority of advanced democratic regimes as characterized not by a single ruling elite but by several competing elites. The pluralist nature of democratic societies means that there are numerous sources of independent power, and the groups and individuals with those fragments of power contend with each other over who will occupy key positions in the political elite and over what policies these elites will implement. The elites are open in the sense that outsiders have multiple opportunities to enter the elite. They also have the ability to remain outside of the elite and still exercise influence over those who are in it.

SUCCESSION POLITICS

The year 2000 brought with it a series of changes of political leaders in many parts of the world. Americans watched with awe as a narrow election and ballot-counting irregularities shook what had been over a century of orderly successions from one popularly elected president to the next. After recounts and court appeals, Republican George W. Bush was determined winner in the presidential race with Albert Gore, Jr. Vladimir Putin became only the second person ever elected president of Russia in free elections. In Nigeria, Olesegun Obasanjo was elected president and led the transfer of political power back to civilians for the first time in seventeen years. Vicente Fox, from the opposition National Action party (PAN) became the first person in over seventy-five years who was not a member of the dominant PRI to be elected president of Mexico. In Taiwan, Chen Shui-bian became that country's first opposition candidate to win the presidency. In other countries, elections confirmed the rule of existing leaders. Canada's prime minister, Jean Chrétien, called for early elections, increased his parliamentary majority, and became the first Canadian prime minister to win three successive general elections. In Italy and Japan prime ministers were changed even though there were no elections. And in still other countries, leadership changes accompanied civil unrest and violence. Peru's President Alberto Fujimori was forced to resign due to accusations of abuse of power and corruption. Serbia's Slobodan Milosevic tried to hang on to power after presidential elections resulted in the victory of his rival. In the face of growing public rioting, Milosevic was compelled to step down. Abortive elections brought ethnic conflict and military rule in the Ivory Coast.

All of these events occurred within a few months of each other. Most marked the transfer of political power from one leader to another. Some of these transfers occurred in orderly and democratic fashion in accordance with long-established rules. In the United States such accepted electoral traditions were severely tested. Elsewhere, especially in authoritarian and third world countries, succession developments were unpredictable and fraught with tension and the risk of violence. The ability of a political system to make a transition in leadership in an orderly and predictable manner is a key indicator of its stability and durability.

The process of changing leadership is known as *succession*. It involves three stages: the vacating of power by the old ruler; the selection of a new leader; and the legitimation of the new leader. The departure from power can be predicted in many instances. Leaders in democratic countries serve established terms, and when those terms end, new elections provide opportunities to throw out unwanted leaders. In between, changes can occur in parliamentary systems when prime ministers lose majority support in parliament. Most democratic systems also have arrangements to assure succession when unexpected deaths or resignations leave the leadership position open.

However, in an authoritarian system, there is no automatic end to a ruler's term. Most authoritarian leaders see no fixed term; indeed, some have made themselves "presidents for life." In such cases, the departure of leaders comes from coups d'état (seizures of power by the military or political rivals), revolts, the natural or unnatural death of the leader, and, least often, voluntary retirement. Such unpredictable events may also interrupt the normal process of succession in democratic states and bring new authoritarian systems.

Selection of new leaders in democracies is influenced by electoral results. In some cases, the linkage is direct and clear. In countries where a single party makes up a parliamentary majority, the contending parties usually designate the person who will be prime minister if their party wins. This choice is often made well in advance of the election. For example, Canadians knew in 2000 that Jean Chrétien would be prime minister if the Liberals won again. In countries where multiparty coalitions are needed for the majority, however, the person who will be prime minister may not be known until after negotiations among the parties after the election. No one could predict who would be Italy's prime minister until the parties concluded their negotiations several weeks after the resignation of the outgoing prime minister. In Japan, the selection of Yoshiro Mori came only after prolonged behind-closed-doors negotiations among leaders of his party factions and with leaders from allied parties.

In most cases, however, the citizens know that whichever party gains a majority in parliament will dominate the government and provide the prime minister and other key leaders. Parliamentary systems where the prime minister and cabinet are dependent upon continued support from a majority in parliament provide considerable flexibility. If there is a need for change in the prime minister between elections—because of death, illness, or retirement—the transition is usually simple and direct since the majority in parliament can select a replacement without delays or public elections. In democratic contexts, such changes are legitimate since the top leadership is always endorsed by a majority of the elected parliament even though these leaders are not directly elected to their positions. They serve as agents of a democratically elected parliament.

Changes may also occur as the parliamentary majority shifts its balance. Votes of censure may remove one leader, but a new leader may emerge who is able to reform the government without a new election. This happened in Germany in 1982 when the Social Democrats lost their majority and the Christian Democratic Helmut Kohl was able to forge a new majority in the same Bundestag. In other cases, votes of censure are followed by new elections. This happened in Britain in 1979 when elections after the censure of Edward Callaghan's government brought Margaret Thatcher into office.

While these shifts in leadership in parliamentary systems are varied and seem quite complex, they are approved in the eyes of their citizens because they follow established procedures and precedents. Succession under both normal and special circumstances is followed easily by legitimation because the ultimate decision can be traced to the voters or their elected representatives. Succession occurs in accordance with legitimate and well-established processes that citizens expect to be followed as power changes hands.

The problem of obtaining legitimacy for new authoritarian regimes is much more problematic. Usually, such systems lack accepted patterns of succession that provide the new leaders with instant legitimacy. Often power is so highly personalized in the hands of the current leader that it cannot be readily transferred to the next leader even when the outgoing leader designates which leader should follow.

China may be an exception: The Chinese Communist party's ruling elite of often elderly officials who have served for decades provides for succession. The Chinese public's acceptance of the right of this body to make that selection gives the new leader legitimacy. Early succession crises in China were marked by turmoil as several contenders sought support in the party and army for top leadership. However, the transition from Deng Xiaoping, China's ruler from 1978–1997, was prepared ahead by Deng's gradual transfer of powers to Jiang Zemin. By the time Deng died in 1997, power had already switched to Jiang. At the present, Jiang Zemin seems to be preparing a new generation of leaders. He had barred reelection to party governing bodies of anyone over 70 years old—except himself! Jiang is grooming several leaders to fill key party and government positions over the next couple of years, notably Hu Jintao as party leader and perhaps president. Jiang plans to step down from his public positions but he is expected to stay on as chair of the party's Central Military Commission, a post used by Deng Xiaoping to oversee Chinese policy long after his formal retirement from top party and government positions. How successful this preordained succession will be is open to question. More than ever, clear factions are developing within the party elite over economic policies, expansion of social and political rights, and dealings with the United States and other countries. Whether or not Jiang Zemin will be able to control the likely clashes among these factions from the Central Military Commission will be a key factor in avoiding the tumult of previous Chinese succession crises. But China has a better chance of orderly succession than do most other authoritarian regimes because of the high degree of institutional power held by the party.

Often new leaders come to power as a result of coups or revolts that may give the air of illegitimacy to the new regime, especially when the action has been accompanied by violence. But most coups are relatively bloodless. This was the case with the Nigerian military's most recent seizure of power in 1993. It is always difficult for military leaders to acquire legitimacy, but in Nigeria, and several other recent military regimes, the military often gains public acceptance as they oust corrupt civilian officials or restore civil order to troubled societies.

Successions are often tense times for all types of regimes. Even where there are established procedures and easy legitimation, it takes time for the new leaders to build their team, to learn their new responsibilities, and to become acquainted with the key personnel and power points. Where the procedures are not clear and legitimation is not automatic, succession can be an even more trying time for regimes.

CONCLUSION

While social and economic conditions and the challenges or strengths of a given moment in time are often important, the personalities and choices of individual leaders and groups of leaders shape history. Gorbachev's own interpretation of the Soviet Union's problems in the late 1980s and how to solve them left a firm imprint on the fate of his country and much of Eastern Europe. Thatcher's explanation of Britain's long-term economic malaise and her prescriptions for overcoming it were different from most of her fellow Conservatives and certainly different from Labour leaders. Thatcher's choices affected not only her own country but also many other Western democracies. Leaders do make a difference!

In the democratic setting, and even to a lesser degree in authoritarian ones, there are two competing leadership needs. On the one hand, the leaders need to have enough power to rule effectively in the sense of making and implementing policies needed for the country's well-being and security. On the other hand, power needs to be sufficiently restrained to prevent abuse of power and to protect individual and group rights. It is a delicate and difficult balance that all regimes seek to achieve.

NOTES

1. Talcott Parsons and Edward Shils, "Orientation and Organization of Action," in Talcott Parsons and Edward Shils, ed., *Toward a General Theory of Action* (New York: Harper & Row, 1951).

2. James W. Davis, *Leadership Selection in Six Western Democracies* (Westport, CT: Greenwood Press, 1998).

3. Robert Putnam, *The Comparative Study of Elites* (Englewood Cliffs, NJ: Prentice-Hall, 1976).

4. Ralph Miliband, *The State in Capitalist Society: An Analysis of the Western System of Power* (New York: Basic Books, 1969).

5. C. Wright Mills, *The Ruling Elite* (New York: Oxford University Press, 1956).

6. Robert A. Dahl, *Who Governs?* (New Haven, CT: Yale University Press, 1961).

7. On leadership styles, see Bernard M. Bass, *Handbook of Leadership,* 3rd ed. (New York: Free Press, 1990).

8. James McGregor Burns, *Leadership* (New York: Harper & Row, 1978).

9. Mills, *The Ruling Elite,* and G. William Domhoff, *The Higher Circles: The Governing Class in America* (New York: Vantage Books, 1970).

10. See W. Rand Smith, *The Left's Dirty Job: The Politics of Industrial Restructuring in France and Spain* (Pittsburgh: The University of Pittsburgh Press, 1998).

Chapter 8

The Military and Politics

On November 16, 1993, a delegation of senior military officers headed by General Sani Abacha came to the office of Ernest Shonekan, Head of State and Commander in Chief of Nigeria's Interim National Government, to tell Shonekan that his rule was at an end. There was no resistance from Shonekan or his few supporters. The military already held all the strategic locations: airports, radio and television stations, ministry of defense, and other government offices. Shonekan asked for and received the right to make a television address to the Nigerian people the next day and in his speech he urged support for the new military regime. The Nigerian people scarcely gave notice to this latest of nine military coups in thirty years; in forty years of independence, only nine have been under civilian regimes. And so ended civilian rule in Nigeria only eighty-two days after the previous military dictator had reluctantly turned power over to civilian leaders.

In many developing countries military coups like this one are the principal means of changing political leaders. The military seizes power either for itself or to install leaders it views favorably. So widespread is this pattern that military rule has been the most common form of government in many parts of the world: Africa, Latin America, South Asia, and Southeast Asia. For example, in Latin America, every government except for three experienced at least one and often several military regimes between 1960 and 1985.[1] It is only in the last decade of democratization that we have seen this pattern of military rule challenged by long-lasting civilian governments. Even where the civilians have won power, the tradition of military intervention remains in place. These civilian regimes still often face powerful militaries able to defend their own interests and to stand as alternatives should the civilians falter.

Military intervention in politics is not restricted to the third world. Under communism, the military often had important roles, especially during succession eras when the military became a key power base for aspiring leaders. This was unexpected because Leninism stressed the importance of maintaining close party control over the military. In practice, party control was often difficult to achieve. In China, the People's Liberation Army (PLA) played the major part in the revolution, which was more a traditional war between organized armies than a popular uprising. After the revolution, the PLA had a key political role over the next twenty years. When the Great Proletarian Cultural Revolution destroyed the state and even the party at the end of the 1960s, the PLA ruled the country virtually alone. It was not until the late 1970s that the party and state were able to fully recover the powers lost to the military during the Cultural Revolution. China's military no longer has the power that it once exercised.[2] But it is significant that the chairmanship of the Communist party's Central Military Commission was held by the country's top leader, Deng Xiaoping, for decades and now is held by party leader Jiang Zemin.

Military intervention is less frequent but not unheard of in Western democracies. Greece fell to a military dictatorship in 1967. A revolt by the French military toppled the Fourth French Republic in 1958 and then military leaders tried in 1960 and again in 1961 to overthrow the man they had helped install in office, Charles de Gaulle. There were rumors of planned military coups in Italy during the troubled 1970s. In 1981, the Spanish army seized the parliament building and held the deputies hostage. Facing opposition from democratic politicians and King Juan Carlos, the bloodless coup collapsed after eighteen hours.

This pattern of frequent military intervention exists in many parts of the world despite the widely accepted norm that civilians should rule and the military should obey civilian masters. This has not always been the case. Japan entered the modern era with a long history of rule by military shogun and samurai that provided legitimacy to military leaders who ruled behind the façade of imperial rule. With such a militaristic tradition, it was not surprising that the military gradually acquired all the levers of political power in Japan during World War II. Only after its defeat in the war did the norm of civilian supremacy become established in Japan.

Examples of legitimate military rule as in pre-1945 Japan were rare in the late twentieth century and the early years of the twenty-first century. Military rule now is seen nearly everywhere as a violation of universal cultural values favoring civilian political leaders. These norms are found even in those countries where the military has often ruled. In an era of democratization, it is simply no longer fashionable to be a military despot. One analysis of the military in Latin America suggests that "The tanks that not too long ago roamed the streets have vanished from sight, military uniforms seem passé, and the era of generals appears finally to have been consigned to the archives."[3] With these values so common, military rulers find it difficult to gain legitimacy for their regimes. They see themselves as temporary exceptions justified only until they can arrange the return of new and more appropriate civil leaders.

THE RANGE OF MILITARY POLITICAL ACTION

The ebbing of direct military rule still leaves much room for the military to influence policies in their home countries. Indeed, once ruling militaries are now seeking new ways to remain present in the social and economic lives of their countries.[4]
There is a wide range of political activities used by the military in various countries and eras, ranging from those that are perfectly normal and compatible with
the norm of civilian supremacy to full military control of the state and society.
Table 8.1 summarizes some of these activities, listing them in ascending order of
military political power—the farther down the list the greater the military's role.
Often the military's different kinds of political action are used simultaneously.
Sometimes the progress toward direct intervention is step-by-step; other times the
military moves to that direct action immediately.

The Military under Civilian Rule

There are very few countries with no military forces of any kind. Costa Rica
is one that comes closest to that pattern in the contemporary era. This small Central American state was able to overcome the political patterns of the region and
do away with its military during the 1950s, leaving only a small paramilitary force
within the civilian police. Japan incorporated a constitutional provision barring the
creation of an army in the post-World War II era. It has created a paramilitary
"self-defense" force, but there are legal and political barriers to using this paramilitary body in virtually all circumstances. Germany rearmed, but only after adopt-

TABLE **8.1**   Types of Military Political Action

Civilian Rule
No military
Military as interest group
Ex-military officer in power as civilian
Military with special say in national security
Military-industrial complex

Praetorianism
Military as veto group
Military blackmail
Military as key to civilian power

Military Rule
Seizure of power
Military in power
Military as a revolutionary force
"Nation in arms"

ing a constitutional amendment barring the use of the military in any setting other than a joint NATO operation.

Nearly everywhere else, there are strong military forces that employ an important part of the population and consume a large share of the gross domestic product. (See Table 8.2.) The armed forces exist presumably as a protection against external aggression; in most countries the threat of such aggression is virtually nil. Armies exist because they are seen as a key right of sovereign states. They flourish even in the absence of threats from without because many regimes see military force as important in maintaining order *within* their countries. The armies are needed to prevent political revolts, domestic terrorism, and popular uprisings.

In most Western democracies and many civilian authoritarian regimes, the military confines its political actions to lobbying politicians for its material needs: salaries, benefits, new weapon systems, or additional equipment. It is also not unusual for the military to play an important role in shaping defense and security policies. Such influence-wielding normally is restricted to routine interest group tactics. The military usually benefits from two assets that civil interest groups do not: the sense that they represent the security interests of the nation and, as part of the government, privileged access to policymakers.

In some instances, former military officers become civil political leaders once they leave the armed forces. This is not necessarily a sign of increased military rule. In Western democracies, there are two examples that illustrate this. In the United States, retired General Dwight D. Eisenhower was elected president, but his presidency did not produce any greater influence for the military. Indeed, it was Eisenhower who coined the term *military-industrial complex* to warn about the growing danger of the military in the politics and economics of the country. The other case is a bit more complicated in that General Charles de Gaulle came to

TABLE 8.2   Military Size and Costs for Selected Countries, 1998

Country	Percentage of Gross Domestic Product	Active Troops
Britain	2.7%	635,000
Canada	1.3	61,600
China	1.9	2,840,000
France	2.8	380,800
Germany	1.5	347,100
India	2.1	1,145,000
Japan	1.0	235,600
Mexico	0.6	175,000
Nigeria	0.7	77,000
Russia	3.2	1,240,000
USA	3.2	1,448,000

Sources: Percentage of GDP: Stockholm International Peace Research Institute; active forces: *The World Almanac 2000* (St. Martin's Press, 1999).

power in France as the result of a military revolt. Once in office, however, President de Gaulle defied the military by granting Algeria independence—the very issue that had brought the near coup—and compelled the military into unwanted strategic realignments by pulling France out of the military integration portions of the North Atlantic Treaty Organization (NATO). In the end, de Gaulle's rule forced the military to back out of politics after its brief flirtation with political intervention.

In some basically civilian regimes, the military is able to appropriate for itself basic defense and security policy-making. For example, in both Russia and China, the military hierarchy played the major roles in deciding national security issues. Their power over this part of national policy was symbolized by the fact that the ministers of defense were nearly always senior, active military leaders. This phenomenon is especially common in countries that face or have faced major security threats from abroad as in Israel or India. In many developing countries, especially those with legacies of military rule, the ministry of defense is headed by a senior military officer. Although the regimes are dominated by civilians, such countries often leave defense matters largely in the hands of their military officers if only because the other tasks of government are usually demanding enough for these often fragile regimes.

In many settings, defense expenditures and armament industries become so powerful that they exert an inordinate influence over society and the economy. Most young Americans, for example, are probably unaware that the interstate system of highways was begun as a military program or that many college foreign language teachers got their university degrees with the help of national defense fellowships. As a nation's economy becomes increasingly dependent upon military expenditures, a large block of supporters linking the defense industry and the armed forces develops into a military-industrial complex that lobbies for costly defense programs. While the problem has been especially difficult in the United States—as we have seen in the past few years as efforts have been made to reduce defense spending and to close military bases—it is a problem in many countries where the defense industry has become an important part of the economy: France, Russia, the former Czechoslovakia, Israel, and even Sweden.

Praetorianism

In ancient Rome, the Senate selected an elite body of troops as its guard against foreign attack or threats from victorious imperial armies: the Praetorian Guard. Eventually, the Praetorian Guards gained political power and were able to control even the selection of the emperor by threatening to withhold protection or to act themselves against the Senate. Today, many civil political systems in the developing world are so fragile that they stand in similar fear of their armed forces. *Praetorianism* refers to the condition where the civil authorities face constant threats from powerful military forces who try to shape all kinds of political decisions while remaining formally out of government.[5] Those regimes that are dependent upon their armed forces to protect them against domestic terrorism, civil uprisings, and unrest are particularly vulnerable to praetorianism.

In some versions of praetorianism, the military gains a veto over certain policy decisions, such as law enforcement, education, or racial and ethnic relations. A higher level of military intervention occurs when the armed forces exercise blackmail to ensure that their interests are heeded in broad areas of policy making. It is extortion based on the military's threat to refuse protection for civil authorities from their domestic enemies. This was the case in Nigeria during civil rule under the Second Republic (1979–1983). Even greater intervention brings the military into the position where it is able to determine the top civilian leadership. It may do so by simply providing the key block of support that an aspiring leader must court in order to take office; or the military may make it clear that certain leaders are unacceptable to it; or the military may overthrow a new set of leaders and replace them with another set of more sympathetic civilian leaders. Implicit in all these military controls over the composition of civil political leadership is the generals' threat to directly intervene if their wishes are not respected.

Military Rule

Next come the high levels of military involvement in politics when the military actually rules. In nearly every case, the military comes to power with a short-term perspective: The armed forces will govern only for a short period. Once the immediate economic crisis or threat to public order is overcome, the military proclaims its intention to return power to civilians. In some cases, this actually happens. Military rule lasts only a short period and then civilian leaders–usually handpicked by the military–return to power.

More often, however, the promises of returning power to civilians are forgotten or put off for long periods of time. Political parties, legislatures, and nationally and locally elected officials are proscribed; open politicking by civilians is prohibited. The military settles in for the long term with generals or admirals heading the ministries and other officers in regional and local offices. The military's influence is usually a modest one, rarely reaching beyond the political realm to tamper with the economy or society.

In a few instances, the group of officers seizing power have nationalist or ideological goals to dramatically reshape society and the economy. The Kemalists came to power in the 1920s through a military coup with nationalist goals to bring Turkey into the modern world. In this and other instances of revolutionary military regimes, the military becomes more involved in the country's social and economic lives, reshaping them to fit the ideological or nationalist ideals that motivated the military's intervention. In such cases of revolutionary military regimes, the army attacks traditional social forces such as the church, village elders and chiefs, and small and large business.

An even greater involvement comes when the military takes over control of the schools and uses them primarily for training new soldiers. In these cases, the military supplants virtually all social bodies as well as controlling or eliminating independent political and economic groups. The product is the "nation in arms" of which ancient Sparta is the classic example. Fortunately, there are few contemporary examples of this military state; Paraguay in the 1940s and 1950s when General Alfredo Stroessner ruled under a perpetual state of siege comes closest to this ideal type.

WHEN AND WHY THE MILITARY INTERVENES

There are a variety of reasons that explain why the military is so often a major political actor. Some derive from the internal characteristics of the military itself. Others come from the condition of the civil government that the military seeks to control or topple. Still others come from specific circumstances of a given situation or time.

Internal Characteristics of the Military That Predispose It to Political Intervention

Among the most important factors leading to the military's prominent political position is its monopoly of arms and the means to use violence. When crises strike and there is a need for arms to protect against internal or external threats, the army alone can provide it in many developing countries.

The military is often the only organized and disciplined force capable of exercising governmental power in developing political systems. Despite the wide acceptance of the norm of civilian mastery, in many instances the military acts because there is no other body capable of doing so. The military simply fills a political vacuum produced by the failure of civilians to provide the essential necessities of life and public order.

Military intervention may also be motivated by the collapse of the legitimacy of the civil government. The public may withdraw their feelings of legitimacy about civilian leaders if they are ineffective in responding to the country's needs, if they are perceived as ruling in their own interests, if they are corrupt, or if they are unable to protect the public from disorder and violence. When the civil leaders lose legitimacy, it is much easier for the military, inherently illegitimate, to intervene.

In such cases, the public may well breathe a sigh of relief at the arrival of the military in power and its promises to restore order, honest government, and economic well-being. That welcome may not last long, but it does provide the military with a guise of public acceptance at the delicate beginning of its rule. While the military is rarely seen as legitimate, certain characteristics of the armed forces give them public acceptance. The military views itself as above the partisan and special interest divisions that often plague politics. Often, especially when the civilian leaders are corrupt or stalemated by narrow interests, the armed forces can convince the broader public to perceive them as having the national interest at heart in contrast to squabbling and self-interested politicians. Their discipline and organization are admired in countries where those virtues may be absent from civilian government. People admire the military's patriotism and service to country. Thus, when corruption and lack of effectiveness destroy civilian governments, the army may offer discipline, order, and a reputation (often undeserved) for honesty and modernity. In troubled times, when civilians have failed, these traits give a "moral halo" for the military's intervention that many citizens will accept.[6]

Motives for Intervention

The motives for military intervention are many. They can be summarized in four categories: defense of the military's own interests; defense of the "national interest"; protection of certain class, regional, or ethnic interests; and the desire to promote or stop sweeping political reforms. In some cases, the military decides to intervene in politics and even to overthrow civilian regimes in pursuit of their own interests: higher wages, better equipment, more troops, or better career opportunities for senior officers. The armed forces may be so scornful of civilian efforts to "meddle" in defense issues they believe are their own prerogatives that they intervene in politics.

More frequently, while it may have some of its own interests in mind as well, the military is driven to intervene by a sense of duty to rescue the nation from shortcomings of the civil regime. The military's sense that it perceives more clearly and is duty-bound to protect the "national interest" may bring it to pressure, threaten, or overthrow civilian leaders. The military may see the national interest as endangered by the civilians' inability to solve an economic crisis, to rid the state of internal corruption, or to maintain domestic order. To counter these threats to the nation, the military feels compelled to intervene. Such was the case in Nigeria in 1983 when the military took over amidst accusations that the civilian government was rife with corruption, economic mismanagement, and electoral fraud.

In some cases, the military intervention is not motivated by the national interest but by sectional interests. These sectional interests may be based on ethnicity, religion, social class, or particular ideological views. Two illustrations from Nigeria again can be used to illustrate this motivation. The first military coup occurred in 1966 when southern Christians reacted to a shift of the civilian government toward the Islamic north. An Ibo general, Johnson Aguyi Ironsi, overthrew the First Republic, instituted military rule, and tried to eliminate northern influence from the military and politics. A few months later, Ironsi was assassinated and a northern-based military regime was installed. In turn, it purged southern officers from the military and shifted political balance back to the more populous Islamic north.

Finally, military coups are sometimes motivated by the desire to bring about sweeping programs of social and economic reform. In the early 1920s, Mustafa Kemal led a military revolt against the traditional regime with the purpose of bringing Turkey into the Western world through vast economic, social, and political changes. Thirty years later, Gamal Abdel Nasser led a military revolt to modernize Egypt, although he rejected the Western model in favor of one of his own that he believed was more in keeping with Egyptian values. Similar revolts based on political views motivate counteraction by the military *against* civilian-driven social and economic reforms. Chile offers an example when General Augusto Pinochet led a military coup against what he labeled a radical socialist regime and brought repressive military rule to a country that previously had one of South America's best records of liberal democracy.

The overall economic performance of a country is also important in its vulnerability to military coup. Huntington contends that countries with very low per capita GNPs are especially susceptible to successful military coups; those with per capita GNPs of $1,000 or more do not have successful coups. Those countries with GNPs between $1,000 and $3,000 per capita may have coups but they are not successful; those with GNPs over $3,000 per capita do not have coups.[7]

While I have treated these various categories of motivations separately, the more motives felt by a military at the same time, the more likely that military is to seize power for itself. Most real world coups occur when several motives coincide: The military simultaneously sees its interests as threatened and the national interest in danger, and disagrees with the incumbent government's approach to socioeconomic change. The more motives, the more likely that the level of intervention will move into those types that involve the overthrow of the civilian regime. Pressure or blackmail is not likely to resolve the concerns of the armed forces when there are several reasons for their political malaise.

Triggering of Coups

In a classic treatment of the military in politics, British political scientist Samuel Finer proposed a "calculus of intervention."[8] Successful military intervention into politics at the highest levels depends upon the military having motives for intervening and an opportunity to intervene. Without the right opportunity, the armed forces might remain in the barracks in spite of a high interest motivating political intervention.

Among the specific conditions that might trigger intervention are military defeats or invasion, especially when the armed forces can make a case that the defeat was due to the failure or ineptitude of the civilian leaders. Domestic rioting or a spate of domestic violence may provide the immediate occasion for military intervention. This is particularly the case when the situation is so dangerous that the civil leaders have to call upon the military to save their regime. Sudden economic crises may also be the immediate stimulus for intervention. Succession eras often provide occasions for military intervention. As the new leaders take office, the new regime often requires time to establish its legitimacy. The election process may be widely denounced as rigged or fraudulent. Or the new political leaders may hold socioeconomic or political views unacceptable to the military leadership. For all these reasons, the transition period between sets of leaders is often a propitious moment for military intervention.

Longer-term factors cumulatively create a moment for intervention. Civilian regimes that come to rely on their armies to fight domestic wars or to control long-lasting civil strife are highly vulnerable to military takeover, especially if there is a defeat of the military force or successful attacks on military officers by the rebels. Finally, long-term trends showing the inability of civilians to govern may eventually create a political void. The vacuum may become apparent as a result of a foolish act by the civilian leadership. Then the military cannot resist filling the political space with its own disciplined and structured power.

WHEN THE MILITARY RULES

In most cases, the military takes governmental power with modest objectives to remedy the immediate causes of its intervention. Once the military has seized power, it sets up a political system of its own. As it does so, it becomes more involved in politics and its objectives often expand. In some cases, the military sees its tenure in government as a chance to reform or modernize the state. The record of military regimes in achieving modernization is a mixed one. While military rule is authoritarian, the military's record regarding human rights varies widely.

Before examining these various aspects of military governments, it is important to note that in many situations, the consequences of a military coup are not felt by most of the population. Many people have little contact with government beyond the schools, post office, and tax collectors; those services continue virtually unchanged even as regimes come and go. It is only a few of the most active in politics who may find their lives changed by a military coup. If they were party leaders or activists, they may find themselves barred from political action or perhaps even jailed.

Most military coups are nearly bloodless. Opponents to the military rarely have the arms needed to resist the army; the army is unwilling to add to its problems of establishing legitimacy by killing a lot of citizens. Of course, there are exceptions that do produce much violence and bloodshed. The violence of the 1966 coups in Nigeria contributed to the secession of Biafra and a long civil war. The ouster of Salvadore Allende in Chile was also accompanied by violence, leaving scars that have yet to heal.

Political Forms

In most cases, the military sets up a military council, or junta, to govern the country. This council includes officers who backed the coup and, when needed, representatives from the various branches of the armed forces. In some cases, the leader of the coup takes the title of president; in others, he retains only his military title. However, he is the chief of state and the principal political figure. The military council sometimes becomes a cabinet with its members assuming responsibility for specific ministerial portfolios. Lower-ranked officers assume responsibility for controlling or ruling outright regional and local units. Decision making is usually on an ad hoc basis with few established rules of procedure.[9]

The military council nearly always works in close cooperation with existing nonpolitical elites. The generals often turn local politics over to the traditional leaders with the understanding that they will follow the military's directions as far as major policies and national issues are concerned. Traditional ethnic and religious leaders are left alone on condition that they promote civil order without challenging the generals. The police easily transfer their loyalty from civil to military leaders. Economic interests are usually left unmolested and even protected by the military.

The military usually works in close cooperation with the civil service. Bureaucrats are used to following the directions of other political decision makers. They usually find that military masters allow them a freer hand than do civilians. Military leaders give the bureaucrats many of the high-level government positions formerly held by politicians, including ministerial portfolios. It is a natural and friendly alliance. The military and the bureaucracy share many perspectives and work styles that make them compatible partners for governing developing countries.[10]

The Military and Modernization

There has been a long debate about the ability of the military to promote modernization.[11] Those who see military regimes as able to bring modernization better than civilian regimes point to the interest that all armed forces have in the latest weaponry. Such an interest leads them to be interested in developing the ability to purchase that equipment or to produce it at home. The military also brings organization and discipline to society—something that is useful in modernizing the economy and society. Furthermore, many claim that the military's discipline and Spartan ethics make military men less open to corruption than civilians.

On the other hand, there are strong arguments that suggest the military may not be such a great modernizer. When the military rules, the country's resources are directed disproportionately toward the armed forces in higher wages, better benefits, new weapons, and more soldiers. This diverts funds that might otherwise have been used to promote economic development. Military regimes are notably uninterested in investing in education and agriculture—areas that are important for the social and economic development of most developing countries.[12] The military's vaunted organizational efficiency and style are not easily transferred to the economy. As one observer notes:

> Military officers have learned that there are no easy solutions to the intractable economic, social, and political problems confronting the respective countries, and that sustained involvement in politics has disastrous effects on the coherence, efficiency, and discipline of the army.[13]

In spite of the military's belief in its own ability to stand aloof from graft, officers appear to be as open to corruption as civilians. For example, General Sani Abacha, who ruled Nigeria with an iron fist from 1993 to 1999, managed to divert $6 billion into foreign bank accounts for himself, his family, and cronies.

Whatever the situation with economic growth, there is little dispute about the military's ability to contribute to political development: It doesn't. The very institutions that are most needed for political development—those that promote and organize political participation—are the very ones first suppressed by military rulers.[14] Political parties and elections are barred; other forms of political participation are discouraged or even sanctioned with imprisonment. Instead, the military tends to enlarge the role of the bureaucracy and traditional leaders whose organizations and perspectives are not conducive to political development.

Human Rights under Military Regimes

The record of military regimes in respecting human rights differs widely from country to country and even from government to government in the same country. Nigeria, for example, has a tradition of gentle military rule that leaves many human rights unaffected. Freedom of religion, freedom of the press, free speech, and the right to assemble or strike are usually respected by Nigerian military regimes. There are exceptions: General Gowon's rule during the Biafran War; General Buhari, who jailed thousands of former politicians and civil servants; and the brutal rule of General Sani Abacha from 1993–1999.

On the other hand, other countries lack a humane tradition or end up with military leaders who care little for such a tradition. General Pinochet's rule in Chile during the 1970s and early 1980s was characterized by a very heavy hand controlling strikes, meetings, and the press. This occurred despite a long Chilean history of civil rule and respect for human rights. Likewise, in Argentina the military suppressed most civil rights and enforced that rule with "murder squads" of soldiers and policemen who abducted and assassinated those believed to oppose the regime. Only the church and business establishment were left alone—and then only because they stayed out of politics and supported military rule.

Military regimes are, after all, authoritarian regimes. Inherently illegitimate, they rule by force, although not necessarily with any more force than some repressive civilian regimes. They may be no more harsh than are civilian autocracies, but they are usually no less abusive of basic human rights.

BACK TO THE BARRACKS

Most armed forces seize political power with the goal of solving a few immediate problems. They expect soon to return power to civilians and their troops to their barracks. Officers recognize the problems they have in acquiring legitimacy: They resent the distraction of politics from their primary tasks of national defense, and they worry that closeness to power will bring corruption into their ranks.

Despite their intentions, however, the military usually stays in office longer than its leaders had expected. The allure of power is strong and addictive. Furthermore, the military is not adept at organizing civilians to regain political power. Its disposition and outlook are inherently undemocratic, and officers have shown little skill in teaching democracy to others. As a result, the military spends many years in power. Then it often botches the job of shifting power to civilian hands and has to return to power again. As a result, many developing countries, notably those that have received self-rule since the 1950s, have established traditions of regular periods of military rule. In Nigeria, for example, it is the civilians who seem to rule by exception. Military regimes account for thirty years of Nigeria's forty years of independence.

The Nigerian case is not an unusual one; the road back to civilian rule is twisting and uncertain under nearly all military regimes. Then, when civilians are back in power, the military returns to the barracks but still keeps a close eye on the new civilian regime and stands ready to intervene again if the regime falters or if it ignores the military's interests.

Few countries have succeeded in breaking traditions of military rule. In Japan, that tradition died only because of its military's total and devastating defeat in 1945. Fear that the tradition might revive inspired the U.S. occupation forces to have the Japanese include an antiwar provision and a proscription against raising an army in the new Japanese constitution. While some Japanese and foreign observers occasionally express concern about rising nationalism and militarism, the old tradition does appear to be dead.

Mexico offers an example more relevant to the experience of today's developing countries. Mexico had a long history of military rule and intervention until the 1920s. The military's activism was finally checked by several tactics. First, a strong, mass-based party—the PRI—was organized to give civilian rulers a large number of followers who would turn out in the streets if the party's rule was threatened by the military. Next, the military was given a prominent role in the PRI, but not so large that it could dominate the party. It was one of four party "sectors"; the other three were effective counterweights to the military's influence. Years later, when the military's threat was over, the military sector was eliminated. Above all, the military knew in those early years when it might have been tempted to intervene that such an act would be met with violent resistance and perhaps civil war. Such knowledge meant that the costs of intervention were much higher than they would be where the military would face little resistance. In addition, senior officers were given "silver cannonballs" to get them out of the military and away from politics. Some were retired and given civil service or public sector positions; others were pensioned off to large and sometimes remote ranchos. By early in the 1930s, the once politically active Mexican army was in the barracks for good.

Unfortunately, the Mexican case is an uncommon one. But others that have succeeded in imposing civilian mastery over politically active armed forces have incorporated some of the elements of the Mexican prescription. The key element seems to be the ability of the civilian leaders to create a strong political party that is able to turn mass numbers into the street to support the leadership.[15] The prospect of facing with guns drawn the citizens they are pledged to support is a powerful deterrent to military political intervention. Few military commanders are willing to run the risk of provoking a civil war that they know will weaken the country they serve and protect.

The task of restoring civilian ascendancy over the military is a bit easier as we enter the twenty-first century due to the broad spread of the democratic ethos.

Successful military coups against civilian democracies are unusual except where such civilian regimes have lost their legitimacy in the eyes of their citizens through ineffectiveness or corruption. As a result, very few of the new democracies that have emerged in the past twenty years have reverted to military rule, even where the country had long traditions of military intervention. But fledgling democracies will still find controlling the military a major challenge. Some scholars are working on approaches to limiting military influence in new democracies—and old ones too.[16] Keeping the military in the barracks requires reciprocal efforts both on the part of the military leaders to accept the rule of law and remain above politics and on the part of civilian leaders to respect and properly finance their militaries.[17]

CONCLUSION

This chapter has focused primarily on the developing world because it is there that the military is so often a prominent political actor. As this chapter ends, let me remind you that no country is immune from inappropriate political action and intervention by the military. France, Spain, and Greece have all faced attempted (and in Greece successful) military coups in the past forty years. In the United States we fret about the power of the military-industrial complex, watch the military force civilian leaders to dilute their efforts to provide equal opportunities for homosexual troops, and observe many retired officers and some active ones take partisan positions, as in the 2000 presidential elections. Ultimately, what keeps the military's role minimal is the vigilance of the citizens and their strong commitment to a political culture that holds military rule in opprobrium. Without those cultural norms held dearly, even advanced democracies can fall victim to military intervention.

NOTES

1. Alain Rouquie, *The Military and the State in Latin America* (Berkeley: University of California Press, 1987).

2. Alastair I. Johnston, "Changing Party-Army Relations in China," *Asian Survey* 42 (October 1984).

3. Consuelo Cruz and Rut Diamant, "The New Military Autonomy in Latin America," *Journal of Democracy* 9 (October 1998): 115.

4. Ibid., pp. 116–126.

5. Amos Perlmutter, "The Praetorian State and the Praetorian Army: Toward a Taxonomy of Civil-Military Relations in Developing Politics," *Comparative Politics* 1 (April 1969): 382–404.

6. S. E. Finer, *The Man on Horseback,* 2nd ed. (Boulder, CO: Westview, 1988).

7. Samuel P. Huntington, "Reforming Civil-Military Relations," in Larry Diamond and Marc F. Plattner, eds., *Civil-Military Relations and Democracy* (Baltimore: The Johns Hopkins University Press, 1996), p. 9.

8. Finer, *The Man on Horseback.*

9. Christopher Clapham and G. Philip, eds., *The Political Dilemmas of Military Regimes* (London: Croom Helm, 1984).

10. Edward Feit, *The Armed Bureaucrats* (Boston: Houghton, Mifflin, 1973).

11. For a summary of some major arguments on both sides of the debate, see Henry Bienen, ed., *The Military and Modernization* (Chicago: Aldine-Atherton, 1971).

12. Eric A. Nordlinger, *Soldiers in Politics: Military Coups and Governments* (Englewood Cliffs, NJ: Prentice-Hall, 1976).

13. Huntington, "Reforming Civil-Military Relations."

14. Samuel P. Huntington, *Political Order in Changing Societies* (New Haven, CT: Yale University Press, 1968).

15. Huntington, *Political Order in Changing Societies.*

16. See, for example, Richard H. Kohn "How Democracies Control the Military," *Journal of Democracy* 8 (October 1997): 140–153.

17. Joseph S. Nye, Jr., "Epilogue: The Liberal Tradition," in Larry Diamond and Marc F. Plattner, eds., *Civil-Military Relations and Democracy* (Baltimore: The Johns Hopkins University Press, 1996).

PART III

GOVERNMENT DECISION MAKING

We now come to the study of what often seems to be the heart of politics: the formal institutions of government and how they interact with political actors such as parties and groups to formulate and apply public policy. We have seen that there is far more to understanding politics than simply reading a country's constitution. But we must not forget that the constitutions do count even in authoritarian countries. It is important to understand what institutions are in place and how they are supposed to function. Of course, constitutions are difficult to interpret and are often subject to informal changes in response to experiences and new circumstances. They do help to answer the basic question of how political power is shared between people and governments, among various branches and institutions of government, and between the central, regional, and local levels of government.

Actual policy- and decision-making processes do not always coincide with the formal constitution and its institutions. Often, important actors not mentioned in the constitution or not even formally part of the government become involved in policy making. The same is true of policy implementation. In theory, it is easy to claim that policy is made by politicians and applied by civil servants. But in fact the relationship is much more complex. Nongovernmental organizations are often involved in both the decision making and the implementation; bureaucrats often make policy and politicians almost always influence the implementation of policies. This dynamic and complicated process of decision making and policy implementation forms the heart of politics in all countries.

Chapter 9

Political Frameworks

A political system is an accident. It is an accumulation of habits, customs, prejudices, and principles that have survived a long process of trial and error and of ceaseless response to changing circumstances. If the system works well on the whole, it is a lucky accident—the luckiest, indeed, that can befall a society . . .

Edward C. Banfield[1]

We are in an era of building new political institutions. The large number of new states and new democracies that have emerged over the last two decades have been seeking new political frameworks to organize their political systems. By "political framework," I refer to the basic political institutions such as executives, legislatures, courts, government agencies, and relationships between different levels of government that interact to make public policies and govern a society. In most countries, these institutions are the most visible signs of politics. They dominate the news reports of government actions. The institutions occupy magnificent old palaces or new architectural wonders that may be bullet-pocked from historical or recent struggles over the role and survival of these institutions.

In the epigram, Edward Banfield, one of the top interpreters of American politics, correctly points to the gradual emergence of political institutions and the "luck" involved in their success. New states and those undergoing dramatic political and social turmoil may lack any regularized pattern of government decision making. Such ad-hoc regimes are often necessary for interim or crisis periods. Over time, however, most political systems develop institutionalized patterns of decision making. In the long run, the need for efficiency, effectiveness, and predictability leads authoritarian as well as democratic leaders to establish regular patterns of government and institutions to make and carry out policy decisions. As countries seek new political institutions that will be conducive to successful democracies and established democracies look for ways to strengthen their own institutions, it is important to understand the basic institutional patterns, their strengths and weaknesses, and how they affect democratic government for good or ill. That is the purpose of this chapter.

CONSTITUTIONS AND CONSTITUTIONALISM

For Americans, the U.S. Constitution is among the most powerful and revered political symbols. This 220-year-old document stands not only as a definition of how government should proceed but also as a link with a glorious past and a long tradition of democracy. The mere thought of significantly changing this document stirs fears that such "tampering" might well destroy the democracy that the Constitution has provided. In contrast, during the life of the United States Constitution, France has gone through over a dozen formal and informal constitutions. At one point, the French constitution changed so often that a joke circulated that book stores declined to carry copies of the latest constitution on the grounds that it was a periodical best handled by newspaper kiosks. Even now, the French show little of the reverence for their constitution that Americans evince for theirs.

Whether revered or simply accepted, most countries have some form of constitution that identifies the key political institutions, defines their powers, and establishes relationships among them in setting and executing public policy. Not all constitutions are formal documents.[2] The British refer to their "constitution," and it clearly establishes procedures for policy making even though there is no written constitution. Instead, the British constitution is a combination of historical documents, laws, unwritten traditions, and practices that have established rules on where political power is located and how it should be exercised.

Of course, there are often gaps between the formal constitutional framework and the reality of the political process. For example, the United States Constitution says nothing about political parties, presidential cabinets, judicial review, or congressional committees in spite of the importance that these institutions play in the policy process. Few Americans are concerned about such gaps between the formal and the real because they see the overall pattern of political power as conforming to the broad principles of the Constitution. Similar gaps are not unusual in other countries. Again, to use France as an example, the president there usually plays a far more important role than the arbiter role that is found in the constitution of the Fifth Republic.

In authoritarian settings, it is common for there to be constitutions that are entirely neglected. For example, in China a constitution adopted in 1982 is observed more in the breach of its principles than in its observance. The constitution places power in the hands of the National People's Congress. But this parliamentary body rarely meets, and real power is exercised by the top leadership of the Chinese Communist party acting in the party's Politburo or its Standing Committee.

Similarly, in Nigeria the military leadership there exercised power for over a decade without any regard for the country's constitution. Constitutions, where they exist in nondemocratic settings, exist less to structure politics than to provide a democratic façade for the elite's rule.

Constitutionalism, however, implies that established rules and procedures direct policy making and place effective limits on the exercise of power. The existence of a constitution is no assurance that constitutionalism prevails; constitutionalism requires the observance of the restraints the formal rules place on the use of political power.[3] It means that there are normal and effective means to challenge government actions that violate the constitution. Such challenges may be through the courts, public opinion, or elections, but they must have some ability to compel political elites to confine their actions to those in harmony with the constitution.

Constitutions typically cover three kinds of issues. First, constitutions enunciate the basic rights and freedoms that individuals may have to protect them from the actions of their government and fellow citizens. Second, constitutions identify the key political institutions—executives, legislatures, and courts—and define how political power is divided among them. This involves a horizontal separation of powers. Third, constitutions also establish a vertical division of power by determining how power is allocated between different levels of government—national, regional, and local. In the United States, the horizontal division of power among various national-level political institutions is determined by the constitutional notions of "separation of powers." The vertical division of power is set by the sections dealing with the rights of states and federal principles. But these American solutions are not the only ways to deal with the issues of allocating power horizontally among national institutions and vertically among national, regional, and local layers of government.

HORIZONTAL SEPARATION OF POWERS

Americans are familiar with the notion of dividing power among different branches of government. Under the U.S. Constitution three branches of government—the executive, legislature, and courts—share power. These theoretically equal branches of government provide checks and balances that are intended to prevent the abuse of power. Other countries, even democratic ones, are less concerned with the American preoccupation with dividing power. They have few reservations about the concentration of power in a single, all-powerful branch of government: the legislature. The result of these two differing perspectives and traditions has produced two distinctive patterns of organizing political power: presidential and parliamentary governments.[4]

Presidential and Parliamentary Patterns of Government

Unlike the U.S. Constitution's careful delineation of powers between the executive, legislature, and judiciary, the parliamentary system of government is based on the key principle of the absolute supremacy of parliament. As the only popularly elected set of national political leaders, parliament stands as the embodiment of popular sovereignty and the voice of the people. It delegates some of its power to a *government* comprised of a prime minister and cabinet of ministers to conduct the executive functions. Figure 9.1 illustrates the basic institutions and their relationships in parliamentary and presidential systems. In the former, the government constitutes the functioning executive with the prime minister serving as chief executive. It is the government that sets policy and determines state actions.

In addition to the prime minister, parliamentary systems have another executive, a monarch or emperor (as in Britain and Japan) or president (as in Germany and India), who fills the largely ceremonial tasks of chief of state. When the chief of state is a president rather than a hereditary monarch, the president is usually elected by the vote of members of parliament. In some cases, presidents or monarchs may have some political influence, but in general, they are figureheads who stand as symbols of the state rather than key political actors.

In most cases, the prime minister and other members of the government are selected from among the members of parliament and continue to hold their seats and to vote in parliament even as they fill government leadership positions. Since the government is a creation of parliament, it can serve only so long as it retains the confidence of a majority in parliament. As a result, its mandate is uncertain and lasts only so long as it retains majority support in parliament.

There are several ways in which the government gauges its level of support in parliament. The first and most obvious is its success in getting its legislation through parliament. However, the consequences of failure to get government proposals enacted is more serious than in presidential systems. Losses on key votes are signs of the loss of parliament's confidence in the government. In many cases, governments that frequently lose key votes feel obliged to acknowledge the loss of

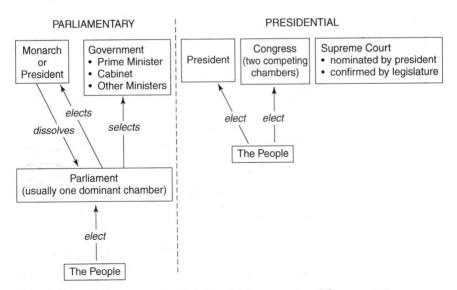

FIGURE 9.1   Parliamentary and Presidential Frameworks of Government

their parliamentary majority and resign. For example, the defeat in parliament of a major political reform in Japan in early 1994 weakened the government of Prime Minister Morihiro Hosokawa and threatened its existence.

In addition to this sensing of parliamentary confidence through success in parliamentary votes, there are two formal procedures that can test a government's support. The government may take the initiative and call for a *vote of confidence* in parliament. If it loses that confidence vote, in most cases the government must resign. The other procedure is a *vote of censure,* where the government's opponents take the initiative and introduce a motion censuring the government. If the censure motion is adopted, the government in most cases must resign. The resignation of the government under any of these considerations is a normal part of the parliamentary system. If you read in a newspaper about the "fall" or "overthrow" of a democratic government, this is what is usually meant. The democratic structures remain in place; democratic procedures have simply brought a change in government.

For all these reasons, the government remains technically at the mercy of the parliamentary majority. Party discipline and cohesive majorities usually ensure the tenure of the government, but the government always faces the danger of losing its support. Another device used by parliament in many places is "interpellation," or the practice of regular questioning of the prime minister and other cabinet ministers. Usually, a time is set apart each week for questions from the floor of parliament that must be answered by the government. These questions are often pointed and are designed to draw attention to the government's failures or weaknesses. The resulting dialogue can damage a government's standing in parliament and with the public. Prime minister question time in Britain occurs once a week and is a lively and important part of parliamentary life.[5]

In the preceding paragraphs, I have qualified my statements with words such as "in most cases" or "generally." That is because the detailed procedures for votes of confidence and censure and governments' reactions to other parliamentary defeats vary considerably by law and by practice from one country to another. However, the general principle of parliamentary systems is that the government can stay in office only so long as it retains the confidence of a majority in parliament.

A government that loses that majority is not without its defenses. There are often special rules that make censure procedures difficult. For example, in Germany the Bundestag can force a government out of office only by electing a new chancellor. In France a censure motion requires fifty sponsors, and once they have introduced one censure they cannot sign for another during the same legislative session. In most countries, a government that is defeated in parliament may simply resign and let parliament find a new government that has its confidence. But the defeated government may also direct the chief of state to dissolve parliament and call new elections. The threat of new elections is much greater for ordinary members of parliament than for the members of the government because the government ministers are usually senior politicians who are consistently reelected in safe districts. In contrast, those who are not in government positions are usually younger politicians who face difficult elections in marginal districts. As a result, unhappy deputies, especially those from the government's party or coalition, are disinclined to vote against the government and precipitate elections that may cost them their seat in parliament.

While in office a parliamentary government does not have to struggle as do American presidents to gain legislative approval of its proposals. With a disciplined parliamentary majority, the government is virtually certain to get a positive vote in support for its legislative proposals. The government introduces its own legislation directly to the parliament. It usually controls the legislative calendar and agenda. In most parliamentary systems, the only bills that have a chance of enactment are those endorsed by the government, and most legislation introduced by the government is adopted. The situation, of course, is much different in the American presidential system. The president there must find sympathetic congresspeople to introduce his bills, and he usually must compromise on the content of the bill to gain such congressional sponsors. The legislative agenda cannot be controlled by the president. Most legislation that is adopted is the product of protracted negotiation within and between the two houses of Congress and between Congress and the president.

The executive in parliamentary systems is usually collective in that executive powers are exercised by a cabinet of government ministers.[6] Prime ministers are "first among equals," but they must have the support of the other ministers. These ministers are powerful political leaders who hold positions because they represent important interests and viewpoints within the party. Prime ministers are loath to ignore their advice over the long term since cabinet revolts often lead to the replacement of the prime minister. Government decisions are usually taken in weekly cabinet meetings after a full discussion by the ministers of policy and action proposals. Prime ministers have gained considerable stature and power in the last fifty years, but they still must maintain the support of their fellow ministers. In contrast, in the American presidential system, the presidents make the key decisions based on consultations with their inner circle of advisors. Their cabinets meet only occasionally and then usually for ceremonial reasons. Rarely does a president ask the cabinet to collectively reach a policy decision. While cabinet members usually are consulted on matters under their direction, they are not "equals" with the president and his top advisors.

A final distinction between presidents and prime ministers is in their pathway to power. Prime ministers nearly always emerge from long careers in parliament. In Britain, for example, the prime minister is always a member of the House of Commons and on average has served over fifteen years as a member of Parliament. Prime ministers are experienced insiders well-versed in party politics and legislative procedures. In contrast, the American presidential system is open to contenders with a wide variety of backgrounds. Indeed, American voters often seem to prefer voting for outsiders rather than for those with long experience in Washington. Since 1953, the U.S. presidents have included a retired army general, state governors, and a former actor. Only Lyndon B. Johnson and Gerald R. Ford had long legislative careers before becoming president, and both of them acceded to the presidency as vice presidents.

There are both advantages and disadvantages associated with the long apprenticeship of prime ministers in parliament. On the positive side, they are well-experienced politicians who know how the system works. They are dedicated to parliament and their parties and have proved their reliability in decades of service. Their leadership goes beyond personal ambitions and is based upon long-term involvement and commitment to party and parliament. On the negative side, the long service in parliament prior to assuming top leadership may result in the recruitment of mediocre leaders. They are "insiders" who are tied to existing policies and political party gamesmanship. The party leaders who become prime ministers have not been selected by national elections, since, like all other M.P.s, they are elected in individual districts. In addition, they usually serve in safe districts where election skills are not necessary. As a result, prime ministers often lack the ability to mobilize the general population. Those traits that make them effective party leaders are not always the same ones that attract voters. In many cases, their long parliamentary apprenticeships make prime ministers less likely to innovate or to bring new approaches to political problems. Their skills in putting together a coalition of party factions may compromise their ability to change or initiate new actions.

The presidential system has the advantage of being able to attract worthy candidates from a far wider range of alternatives since legislative service is not required. This makes it more likely that the presidents will come to office without commitments to past approaches and may be more open to innovation than prime ministers. They may be better able to capture the imagination and win the support of the public. Their popular, nationwide election allows them to speak with more authority than prime ministers who are elected in one local constituency and who owe their leadership position to their parliamentary colleagues. There are disadvantages, too. Presidents often come to office without the extensive national political experience needed to succeed in the complicated labyrinth of national politics. They must spend months or even years learning the political ways and the key people. They also do not have the same attachment to party and fellow officeholders that prime ministers do. In the United States, they have succeeded because of their own personal political machines and have more commitment and loyalty to them than to their own political parties and their party's congressional leaders. A good illustration was Richard M. Nixon's prolonged struggle to stay in power against threatened impeachment. This two-year battle weakened the presidency and the Republican party. Personal ambitions based on the American presidential election system called for such a struggle, whereas in the parliamentary system the leader would have felt greater obligation to spare his party and fellow party members the embarrassment of such a bitter conflict.

Table 9.1 provides a summary comparison of executive powers under the parliamentary and presidential systems. They represent entirely different approaches to the organization of politics. Most constitutions are based on one of these two formulas for politics.

TABLE 9.1   A Comparison of Executive Powers

	Presidential Systems	Parliamentary Systems
Mandate		
Source	Popular	Parliamentary
Duration	Fixed Term	Variable
Legislative leadership	Weak	Strong
Executive leadership	Exclusive	Collective
Recruitment path	Open	Parliamentary

Mixed Presidential-Parliamentary Systems

There are a few countries where their constitutions try to blend features of the presidential and parliamentary systems. But such mixtures pose important problems because they start from such different bases of power: the parliamentary system, which finds sovereignty residing in parliament, and the presidential system, which divides sovereignty among two or three separate branches of government.

The French Fifth Republic has such a mixed presidential-parliamentary system. France divides executive powers between a powerful popularly elected president and a prime minister selected by the president but accountable to the majority in parliament. In practice, the French president has usually been the dominant figure, with the prime minister whom he appoints administering policies set by the president. As long as the parliamentary majority is the same as the party affiliation of the president, there are few problems. But the terms do not coincide. Early National Assembly elections may lead to one party controlling the parliamentary majority and thus providing the prime minister while another party holds the presidency. As a result, sometimes elections produce a different majority coalition in parliament from the partisan commitments of the president. For example, the Socialist president François Mitterrand was forced to govern with a conservative National Assembly on two occasions. More recently, from 1997 to 2001, a conservative president, Jacques Chirac, had to cooperate with a socialist majority in the National Assembly and a socialist prime minister. This cohabitation can be tense since the president must cooperate with a rival prime minister and a hostile parliamentary majority. Usually, the French president tries to maintain his influence on foreign policy matters where his constitutional mandate is clearest. But he has felt free to criticize the government in all its acts.

Conflict between the two executives is greatest as presidential elections approach. For example, Chirac wanted to run for reelection in 2002, and his socialist prime minister, Lionel Jospin, harbored similar ambitions. Their clashes became more frequent and intense as the presidential election approached.

There are parallels between this pattern of "divided" government in France and other countries with mixed presidential-parliamentary systems and what occurs in the United States when the president is from a different party than the majority in Congress. The situation is usually more tense in France, where party discipline and greater party polarization generally impede the kind of cross-party coalitions that pass laws in the U.S. Congress.

While at one time unique, the French pattern has proven popular among new democracies in a number of postcommunist regimes. Russia, for example, has a constitution patterned on the French mixed system. The Russians and other countries seeking to establish democracies in former authoritarian settings see the need for a strong president to provide guidance and continuity in an era of rapid social, economic, and political change. They want strong presidential leadership to provide stability at a time when their party systems are still new, weak, and fragmented. In most of these cases, as in France, the mixed system has resulted in powerful presidential rule. For example, both Presidents Yelsin and Putin exercised extensive decree powers during their terms of office.

The Advantages and Disadvantages of Parliamentary and Presidential Systems

Each of these frameworks for organizing political power has its advantages and disadvantages. The parliamentary system usually offers a speedier and more efficient legislative process than does a presidential system. But such speed may lead to faulty laws. Government legislation tends to be more coherent in the parliamentary system than in a presidential system, where the separation of power may lead to entirely different approaches by the president and congress. The existence of checks and balances in a presidential system may lead to better concern for the interests of diverse constituencies in the adoption of legislation, but it can also produce legislative gridlock. It is easier to dispose of national leaders who have lost the confidence of others in government or the electorate in parliamentary systems, but that same ease of ousting leaders can produce frequent changes in government and the resulting uncertainty in government policy and action. Leaders who emerge out of the lengthy parliamentary apprenticeship may be better skilled in governing and more reliable, but they may also be lackluster and unable to innovate.

Parliaments in parliamentary systems, despite this name for these kinds of regimes, usually lack political power. Party discipline and firm parliamentary majorities usually mean that the seat of power shifts from parliament to the government. As one historian notes: "When the party system regulates, [parliamentary] debate addresses the deaf."[7] As a result, many of the features that have prominence in American presidential-congressional interaction—such as congressional committees and their hearings, confirmation votes, and interest group lobbying—are less important or nonexistent in parliamentary systems. However, parliament retains the ultimate powers of censure over the government. Members of parliament seek to represent the views of their constituents even in such strong government states as Britain.[8] Major decisions may be made elsewhere, but parliament is a major site for politics. Its politics shapes policy through the influence of its individual members and through its debates.[9]

Americans often worry about the concentration of power that occurs in the parliamentary system, where prime ministers enjoy considerable power based on their support by cohesive legislative majorities. This comes from an American pre-occupation with the fear that concentrated power inevitably leads to absolutism and the end of democracy. In fact, the parliamentary system has proved to be entirely consistent with successful democracy and limited government. In practice, it is the presidential system that has more often yielded to autocracy than the parliamentary system.[10] This is because powerful leaders win election to the presidency and then use their popularity and position to acquire greater and greater power at the expense of the other branches of government. As a result, the American success with presidential democracy is an exception; most practicing democracies are parliamentary systems.[11] However, a parliamentary structure is no guarantee that democracy will prevail. Autocrats often use the parliamentary system as a façade for their authoritarian rule. For example, China has a parliamentary structure for its formal political institutions, but it is ruled in fact by the Communist party elite.

Parliamentary systems are generally thought to be more accountable to the electorate. This is because when a party or coalition of parties controls both the parliament and the government, voters can more readily identify who is responsible for government action or inaction. In the presidential system, the president and congress can blame each other for failed government policy or stalemates within a congress that fails to pass legislation that is acceptable to the president. Since both branches of government share political power, it becomes much more difficult for the voters to assign responsibility for good and bad government policies. In contrast, in a majority-based parliamentary system, it is always clear who is accountable, and citizens can reward or punish the parties in power by their vote. For example, in Britain, where there is a single-party government, or in Germany, where there is a durable two-party coalition, voters can hold their governments accountable for their acts: Voters who dislike the government's policies can vote for the opposition; those who approve of the government can vote to return it to office.

If there are too many parties who share power in parliament and are unwilling to form durable coalitions, parliamentary systems may experience instability and frequent changes in government. The classic case is Italy, where there are so many parties present in parliament that it takes four or five of them to build a majority. That majority is often fragile as the various parties in the coalition defect on issues of concern or maneuver in the hope of obtaining better ministerial posts. As a result, Italy had fifty-eight governments between 1946 and 2001, with the average government's life being less than eleven months. Italy's record is unusual but not the only such case. Both France and Germany have experienced similar difficulties in the past. In these unstable situations, the usual advantage of the parliamentary system in assuring accountability to the voters is lost as successive governments muddy the issue of who is responsible for what. However, multiparty coalition governments in many settings have proved durable and facilitated the government's accountability to the electorate.[12]

The parliamentary system can offer better linkage between government and people. This does not mean, however, that it is the superior form of organizing for democracy. No governmental framework ensures democracy. Indeed, the effects of specific constitutional structures are less important in building effective democracy than are political culture and traditions, elite attitudes, party structures, and the socioeconomic setting. Even the best set of political institutions cannot impose democracy in a hostile environment.

This is difficult for many people to understand. As a result, countries with troubled polities often resort to *constitutional engineering* by tinkering with or completely replacing the basic institutions of government. More often than not, constitutional engineering is a failure. Old patterns or problems tend to reassert themselves whatever the institutional arrangement.

THE CENTRALIZED STATE AND FEDERALISM

Constitutions not only arrange power among different branches of the national government; they also dictate a vertical division of power between the national level and other levels of government. There are three basic patterns: centralized states, federal states, and confederations. Americans, often preoccupied with the need to divide power in order to prevent absolutism, usually see federalism as necessary for democracy. However, the majority of today's successful democracies are centralized states rather than federations or confederations. Examples of successful democracies with unitary frameworks include Britain, Japan, France, and the Scandinavian countries. Federalism is more related to the size of a country than to the democratic or nondemocratic character of its government.

Constitutions in centralized or unitary states confer all political power to the national government. The national government can devolve some of its powers and duties to lower levels of government, but the definition of the responsibilities and prerogatives of local or provincial governments is established by the national government.[13] In most cases, the local governments become simply the administrators of decisions and policies made at the central level. The central government establishes national laws and guidelines that are imposed uniformly throughout the country with little allowance for adjustment by local governments. Local governments may have some responsibilities such as local roads, sanitation services, zoning laws, and maintenance of public buildings. But their powers and finances are controlled by central guidelines.

When local governments are involved in implementing centrally made policies, they can still have important influence. They are composed of individuals who are elected by the people and have some standing as representatives of local interests. Wise central governments pay heed to their concerns. In the last resort, however, it is the unitary state that prevails. A good illustration of this came during the 1980s when Margaret Thatcher faced resistance by the Labour-dominated Greater London Council (GLC). Thatcher simply won enactment of legislation that abolished the council. This was an extreme case, but it demonstrates that in unitary or centralized systems, political power ultimately is exercised at the national level. On the other hand, central control cannot always be used to overpower local authorities as is shown by another example involving Prime Minister Thatcher. A few years after her abolition of the GLC, she was forced to resign because of her high-handed efforts to impose an unpopular tax scheme on local governments.

In contrast, federations are based on specific divisions of powers between the central government and local or regional governments.[14] The regional and local governments have responsibilities and powers in their own right by constitutional fiat. The national government cannot infringe upon these prerogatives of lower level governments. The powers accorded to local and regional governments are extensive and in some cases, as in the United States, include all governmental duties not specifically assigned to the central government.

Most federations are found in populous or large countries. In many cases, federal structures are effective ways of linking together diverse peoples who happen to end up in a single political entity.[15] The federal divisions into provinces or regions mirror historical political units that were once independent but now joined together. Examples of federations include the United States, Canada, India, and Germany, all of which follow democratic traditions. However, federal structures offer no hindrance to authoritarian rule as in past regimes in Russia, Nigeria, or Brazil.

Under confederal arrangements, political powers are in the hands of the regional or provincial governments except where they have specifically accorded usually limited powers to a central government. Typically, the confederal institutions handle foreign affairs, defense, and the control of a common currency. Confederations are less common in the contemporary world for this reason: Modern polities need a strong, central state to contend with the international nature of economics and defense. The best example of a successful, contemporary confederation is Switzerland.

Confederations are inherently unstable. The Swiss confederation is a rare exception, due to its small size and unique international position. Elsewhere, confederations often yield to the secession of the member states or their acceptance of more intense cooperation in federal or unitary frameworks. After the collapse of the Soviet Union, several of the member republics joined together in a Confederation of Independent States (CIS). The CIS began as an umbrella organization. By the mid-1990s, the CIS began to acquire broader importance as several of the now-independent former Soviet republics found growing value in coordinating economic and security matters. The fear of a reabsorption into a Russian empire has waned, and countries such as the Ukraine, Belarus, Georgia, and others find cooperation to be valuable. Confederal political institutions have not yet emerged in the CIS. Interaction remains more like international relations than a confederation.

The Advantages and Disadvantages of Federalism and the Unitary State

Unitary systems offer as one of their most important advantages the uniformity of policy throughout the country. This brings an equality in governmental services among all citizens regardless of where they live. On the other hand, federalism, as in the United States or Canada, allows wide differences from state to state on policies from speed limits to school content, health regulations to recreational facilities, and from court structures to social welfare benefits. Such diversity allows federal states to accommodate regional differences, but it also means that citizens may have unequal access to important government resources simply because of where they live.

Federalism, however, can lead to duplication of government services. For example, in the United States, there are fifty separate state offices administering food safety regulations in addition to the federal Food and Drug Administration, separate state and national environmental protection offices, multiple state, local, and national educational bureaucracies, and so on. Unitary states can bring economies of scale by providing one national set of government offices and employees for key government services.

Unitary states have the disadvantage of taking policy-making powers to far-off capitals. Centralization thus brings the sense that government is "distant" from the people and unaware of problems at the grass-roots level. Federalism bridges that distance and brings more sensitivity to local needs and concerns. Federalism also creates many more opportunities for citizen political participation through state elections and public offices. It allows experimentation on a limited scale with new policies. For example, in the United States, several different welfare programs were tried out in different states, allowing national policymakers the benefit of seeing how changes might work out in the real world before implementing a nationwide reform.

Centralized systems tend to be less vulnerable to control by single, large interests. Smaller units often are dominated by single interests that are very important in the local economies. For example, in British Columbia, the timber industry has very strong influence over natural resource administration; in the prairie provinces of Manitoba and Saskatchewan, grain producers wield unusual power over public policy. By shifting policy-making power to the more diversified national level, such regional interests counter each other and allow for a greater concern for the broader national interests rather than regional economic powers. In effect, centralization brings greater diversity and that diversity produces crosscutting economic and social cleavages. As I argued in Chapter 3, this pattern of cleavages tends to result in lower social conflict and more balanced public policy.

This same dynamic can also work to reduce discrimination against ethnic or religious minorities. The larger the polity, the more cleavages and the greater the need to build coalitions across cleavages. That dynamic tends to reduce the danger of one group oppressing another. To the contrary, when the unit is small and one group confronts another, the danger that the majority will abuse its power and oppress the minority is greater. That is what happened, for instance, in Northern Ireland. Until 1972, considerable autonomy in Northern Ireland allowed the Protestant majority to dominate the Irish Catholic minority. When the Northern Irish government was dissolved and London took over in 1972, the police and government in Northern Ireland offices gradually became more impartial. The government in London was largely uninvolved in the Northern Irish ethnic conflict and was therefore able to bring greater equality of treatment to Northern Irish

Catholics. A similar phenomenon can be seen in Nigeria where ethnic homogeneity at the state level often leads to discriminatory action against minorities; this has been countered by shifting more policy control to the central government where the multiple and diverse ethnic groups counterbalance each other and lead to less racially oriented public policy.

If the greater diversity achieved in unitary polities hinders the development of explosive social cleavages, federalism has the advantage of facilitating the isolation of conflict when it does break out. A useful contrast can be seen in the student revolt of the late 1960s that hit most industrialized countries. In France, the highly centralized policy system brought all protest to bear on the national government in Paris. Even a change in dormitory visiting hours required the assent of the national minister of education. The result was a very volatile situation of demonstrations, strikes, and riots that almost toppled the French regime. In the United States, even more violent student protests posed no threat to the regime because they were diffused geographically and institutionally. Students in Berkeley battled against the California National Guard; in Chicago, demonstrators fought Mayor Daley and the city police; in New York, students attacked Columbia University's private board of trustees; in Washington, protests against the Vietnam War were directed at national political institutions. The fact that there were numerous targets lessened the impact on the national institutions and facilitated isolation and control of the unrest.

Federalism is particularly useful in providing a framework for governing geographically large and diverse countries. Most federations are either very large units or ethnically diverse. Federalism facilitates the rule of the vast territories and diverse societies of Canada, India, Mexico, Nigeria, Russia, and the United States. (China is one of the very few large states with a formal unitary structure.) However, the federal framework can also facilitate secession. Canada, for example, continues to struggle to maintain its unity against strong separatist inclinations in Quebec and growing demands for autonomy in the Western provinces. Nigerian federalism promoted the secession of Biafra and a tragic civil war. Postcommunist Russia continues to struggle with secessionist tendencies among its federal units.

What this section suggests is that there is no universal ideal arrangement for the vertical division of powers. Nor is either framework better than the other in ensuring democracy or defending human rights. Unitary structures are often successful and compatible with democracy; other centralized systems are authoritarian and stifle the expression of popular concerns. Federal systems are also successful in certain settings and operate democratically; other federations promote division or are unable to sustain democracy.

Decentralization

In the past twenty years, there has been a strong movement in many countries to devolve central powers to regional and local governments. This is explained by the growing involvement of government in the everyday lives of people. As the impact of government is felt more directly and frequently, people want those who exercise these powers to be aware of local needs and special conditions. As a result, major efforts at decentralization have taken place in many countries, both those that have always been highly centralized–such as France and Italy–and in those that have decentralized or federal traditions such as Canada, the United States, and India.

What is surprising in almost every case is the limits of decentralization. For example, the Reagan drive for greater state powers did little more than shift the financial and administrative burdens of federally mandated programs to state and local governments. In France, reform only gave formal sanction to limited powers that department and regional authorities have long enjoyed. In Russia, decentralization in the 1990s was due more to the collapse of central authority than to a purposeful reform. President Putin's reimposition of central authority in 2001 demonstrated that Russian Federation republic governments have little chance of holding on to their powers when the central government asserts itself.

Where decentralization has occurred, it has not necessarily brought more responsive government. Voters are less interested in regional and local politics; they vote less frequently in these elections. Regional and local governments are not as visible as national governments. It is true that citizens have greater opportunity to know first-hand local officials, but they generally have less knowledge of what these officials do in the performance of their public duties. National officials usually have many groups demanding attention that can be played off against each other. Local-level elected officials are often more vulnerable to the powers of narrow special interests who dominate local economies and politics. As a result, there is a beginning of a sense that decentralization is not the panacea to the ills of modern society that many thought it would be ten years ago.

BUILDING DEMOCRACY THROUGH CONSTITUTIONAL CHANGE

The wave of democratization that began in the 1980s has renewed the search for appropriate institutions to promote and perpetuate democracy. Often, the new democracies are established in settings where there are no traditions of democracy, no democratic institutions in place, and no ideas of how to give institutional reality to the democratic aspirations. As a result, Russian, Polish, Nigerian, and other political leaders have sought models for their new institutions in successful Western democracies. However, constitutions do not travel well; they are not easily moved to alien settings. It is only where there are exceptional leaders and unusual conditions that democratic institutions can be imported and then become successful.

There are some exceptions where constitutional changes have succeeded in bringing new and more democratic forms of government. After World War II, occupying military forces imposed democratic constitutions on Germany and Japan. Even though these institutions were alien to their past traditions, they took root and succeeded in providing the basis for effective democracies. Their success derived from the highly unusual conditions of total military defeat and then an exceptionally rapid economic recovery that gave legitimacy to the democratic institutions and leaders. But there are far more examples of failure: Weimar Germany (1918–1933), which provided the means for Hitler to come to power legally; the many presidential regimes modeled on the United States that have collapsed into presidential dictatorships or military regimes; the short-lived parliamentary structures patterned on former colonial masters that yielded to autocracy in Africa and Asia. And we are witnessing this failure of imported institutions again in most of the former communist countries in Central Asia.

It is not only new democracies that resort to constitutional engineering to remedy past political problems. In the past ten years, Italy and Japan have contemplated drastic revisions in their constitutions in order to face problems of corruption and governmental failure. Occasionally this has worked in the past. An example of successful constitutional engineering was the constitution of the Fifth French Republic, adopted in 1958, that has provided France with a durable and effective democratic system. But more often, old political practices resume under the new institutions. This has been the case in many of the institutional reforms in both Italy and Japan during the 1990s.

CONCLUSION

The most visible forms of politics—national political institutions such as prime ministers and parliaments—are important to understanding political life in all governments of the world. They are the sites of power and policy making in many countries. They help us in identifying the key political actors.

Institutions alone, however, do not determine the political game. The many countries now trying to build democracies in former communist states or in the third world need a good set of political institutions. But the key to the success of these institutions is the ability of leaders and institutions to draw support from the existing social and cultural values.

NOTES

1. Cited by James Q. Wilson in a lecture entitled "The History and Future of Democracy." Pepperdine University, School of Public Policy, Malibu, California, November 15, 1999, p. 12.

2. Keith G. Banting and Richard Simeon, eds., *Redesigning the State: The Politics of Constitutional Change* (Toronto: University of Toronto Press, 1985).

3. The classic definition of constitutionalism is found in Carl J. Friedrich, *Constitutions and Constitutionalism*, rev. ed. (Boston: Ginn and Company, 1950).

4. See Giovanni Sartori, *Constitutional Engineering: An Inquiry into Structures, Incentives, and Outcomes*, 2nd ed. (New York: New York University Press, 1997), and Arendt Lijphart, *Parliamentary Versus Presidential Government* (Oxford, England: Oxford University Press, 1992).

5. Mark Franklin and Philip Norton, eds., *Parliamentary Questions* (New York: Oxford University Press, 1993).

6. Thomas A. Baylis, *Governing by Committee: Collegial Leadership in Advanced Societies* (Albany: State University of New York Press, 1989).

7. Barbara Tuchman, *The First Salute* (New York: Knopf, 1988), p. 104.

8. Bruce Cain, John Ferejohn, and Morris Fiorina, *The Personal Vote: Constituency Service and Electoral Independence* (Cambridge, MA: Harvard University Press, 1987).

9. Frank Baumgartner, "Parliament's Capacity to Expand Political Controversy in France," *Legislative Studies Quarterly* 12 (February 1987): 33–54.

10. Juan Linz and Arturo Valenzuela, eds. *The Failure of Presidential Democracy* (Baltimore, MD: Johns Hopkins University Press, 1994), and Arendt Lijphart, ed., *Parliamentary versus Presidential Government* (Oxford, England: Oxford University Press, 1992).

11. Matthew Soberg Shugart and John M. Carey, *Presidents and Assemblies: Constitutional Design and Electoral Dynamics* (Cambridge, England: Cambridge University Press, 1992).

12. Arendt Lijphart, *Democracies: Patterns of Majoritarian and Consensus Government in Twenty-One Countries* (New Haven, CT: Yale University Press, 1984).

13. For discussions of central/local relations, see E. C. Page and M. Goldsmith, eds., *Central and Local Government Relations* (London: Sage, 1987), and Yves Meny and Vincent Wright, eds., *Center-Periphery Relations in Western Europe* (London: Allen and Unwin, 1985).

14. Daniel J. Elazar, ed. "Special Issue: New Trends in Federalism," *International Political Science Review* 17 (April 1996).

15. Ronald L. Watts, *Comparing Federal Systems,* 2nd ed. (Montreal and Kingston, Canada: McGill-Queens University Press, 1999).

Chapter 10

Policy Implementation and Adjudication

In 1993, the long-dominant Liberal Democratic party was ousted from power in Japan, bringing a new party coalition to power for the first time in Japan's forty-five years of democracy. The new government came to office with ambitious plans for political and economic changes. Within less than a year, however, the prospect of change had virtually disappeared. Among the major reasons for the collapse of reform efforts was the power of an entrenched bureaucracy that remained in place in spite of the change in political leaders. A leading Japanese statesman bemoaned the failure of change:

> The Japanese are, unfortunately, the most conservative people in the world, and perhaps the bureaucrats are the most conservative among the Japanese. Face it. We are not accustomed to change.[1]

Every modern state requires a vast bureaucracy of professional civil servants to carry on the tasks of government. The policy-making leaders have to rely on others for the actual implementation of their policies. This bureaucracy is the face of the state as it interacts with the populace. In theory, the bureaucracy simply implements the decisions of the elected or autocratic political leaders, taking whatever policies are set by the politicians and putting them into action throughout the country. In reality, the bureaucracy shapes and distorts policy decisions in the process of implementing them.

Some of this shaping of policy decisions is a natural and appropriate adjustment of policy to the real world. However, the bureaucracy's interpretation of policy decisions may be quite different from and even at odds with the purposes of the political leaders. The Japanese bureaucracy is not alone in being the most conservative force in that country; bureaucracies everywhere are renowned for their resistance to change. They all have the means and the will to avoid political decisions when the policies do not meet the civil servants' own definition of the needs of the country or, even more narrowly, when the policies conflict with the bureaucrats' own self-interests.

THE MODERN CIVIL SERVICE

All governments need extensive personnel for their activities. Until the last century, most government activities centered on law enforcement or military actions. Only as governments moved beyond these activities did they need the large civilian bodies of government administrators that we now find everywhere. In earlier periods, most countries conferred government administration to small groups of individuals holding public offices because of their loyalties or family ties to the rulers. Governments had limited roles and the few people involved in the administration of government were generally selected on the basis of heredity or their personal or partisan ties to the political leaders. Tax collectors, customs officers, and diplomats were often lesser nobility, partisan supporters, or personal friends of the political leaders who were in need of a public sinecure to sustain themselves. Until the nineteenth century, such patronage-based administrations worked reasonably well. Then, two trends brought the need to reform public service: the growth in government responsibilities and democratization.

First, government responsibilities began to grow with new activities such as postal delivery, telegraph services, public sanitation and utilities, public education, and eventually work safety and welfare programs. These new services required a much larger and more active body of public employees. As the size of the bureaucracy grew, so did the need to bring rational procedures for selecting, promoting, and directing the public employees.

Secondly, rulers began to sense the need to develop extensive popular bases of support. Accordingly, political leaders often built large systems of supporters based on the exchange of government benefits (such as jobs or contracts) for political support. In North America, such relationships between political leaders and their followers characterized the early years of American and Canadian party organizations.[2] Local party bosses built large political "machines" to organize support for their candidates. Many supporters were ensured jobs in exchange for their votes, participation in political rallies, and campaign contributions. Vast patronage powers were used by those who ruled to reward their supporters with public jobs ranging from senior administrator to postal worker, street cleaner, and chauffeur.

In many settings, democratic as well as nondemocratic political leaders seek to develop public support through the creation of extensive networks of patron-client relationships. As described in Chapter 5, political clientelism develops as a local political leader (or "patron") recruits followers ("clients") who are willing to provide political support at the polls or in rallies. In exchange, the clients expect material rewards, notably public jobs. In elaborate clientelist systems, there are vast networks linking patrons from local to top-level national political leaders, with each level able to provide public jobs to their valued supporters.

Such practices helped build strong political parties in such diverse settings as the United States, Canada, Italy, Japan, Mexico, and the former Soviet Union. But these patronage systems were inefficient and inequitable means of conducting government business. Individuals held public posts on the basis of their partisan or personal ties with politicians rather than on their abilities to perform their government tasks. Continuity of government policy was hindered because public officials at all levels changed frequently as parties or leaders came and went. Citizens seeking government services would find their access varied according to whether or not they supported the dominant politicians. Patronage often resulted in corruption and diversion of public resources to private or partisan ends. Reformers soon identified the bureaucracy as a major target of their efforts.

By the nineteenth century, the need to develop more efficient means of administering government policies became compelling. Early in the century, Napoleon brought a modern bureaucracy to France and to many of the countries he conquered. The hierarchically structured and centrally controlled bureaucracy became the key element in maintaining cohesive policies throughout a vast empire. Then later in the nineteenth century, the Prussians created a modern civil service that became a model for many other countries. Recruitment and promotion were based on merit as determined through competitive examinations—a tradition that had long prevailed in the much less modern but highly structured bureaucracies of the Chinese dynasties. Such a professional and technically competent staff would ensure a government of able administrators to carry out its operations. The civil servants were expected to accept and implement without hesitation or disputation whatever policy decisions were made by the politicians. They were expected to follow established procedures that would ensure that all citizens were treated evenhandedly. Lines of responsibility were hierarchical to promote control from the top of all levels of the bureaucracy. All these elements together would bring about the ideals that the German sociologist Max Weber found in a rational bureaucracy: merit-based recruitment and promotion, uniformity by adherence to rules and procedures, expertise through specialization, and rationality.[3] These bureaucratic virtues would bring rationality and efficiency to government administration and help develop the bureaucracy's legitimacy in the eyes of those it served.

While the principles of a modern bureaucracy are widely accepted, in practice most countries still have some elements of the old patronage or clientelism. In the United States, there are large numbers of senior administrative posts that are distributed by election winners at the local, state, and national levels. Although patronage is less extensive in Britain, France, and Germany, it is widespread in Italy, where patronage was seen as a root cause of the corruption that discredited the democratic regime in the early 1990s. Clientelism is especially common and often the dominant form of bureaucratic recruitment in developing countries. Mexico, India, and Nigeria have vast systems of clientele relationships based on either political attachments, as in Mexico, or communal ties, as in Nigeria. In past and present communist countries, such as China, clientelist links often underlie the party's system of naming public officials to strategic social and economic positions.

The Ills of Modern Bureaucracy

Government employees have long been the subject of popular derision. A century ago Mark Twain defined bureaucracy as 50,000 ants on a log floating down the Mississippi River and every one of them thinking that they are running it. Even where the Weberian ideals are attained, there are many causes for complaints about the civil service in nearly every contemporary political system. Most common is the complaint about the bureaucracy's ever growing size. In the United States, for example, public employment has nearly doubled since the mid-1950s, with nearly all the growth in public employees occurring at the state and local levels while the federal workforce has remained constant. Similar increases in the number of civil servants are found in nearly all other countries, no matter what political form they have. But the bureaucracy's growth is not so much due to an innate tendency for government administration to increase in size as it is to the continued expansion of what people expect government to do. As government's responsibilities have grown, so has the size of the administrative force needed to fulfill those duties.

While many protest about the size of government and even its intrusion into some parts of their lives, they want government present in other areas. For example, conservatives are among the loudest critics of the size of the bureaucracy needed to carry out public welfare programs, but they call for more police officers and jailers, more government protection for the small investor, more air controllers for safer airports, and smoother highway systems. In short, while the notion of smaller government is attractive, it has few supporters when specific government services are identified for possible elimination. Instead, governments are usually asked to add new functions. From environmental protection to disaster relief, from public safety to care for the homeless, governments of all types and in all settings are expected to provide ever more services for their citizens.

Another frequent complaint is that bureaucracies are remote from the people and unresponsive to local and personal needs. In part, this is endemic in institutions that are hierarchical and that must follow regular procedures (in common parlance, "red tape") as is the case in most modern bureaucracies. In many societies, bureaucrats see themselves as socially superior to the citizens they are supposed to serve. The resulting aloofness causes resentment. In some former colonial states, such as India and Nigeria, the old colonial bureaucracy's state of mind and aloofness have persisted long after the European civil servants were replaced by native inhabitants. In many countries, citizens see bureaucrats as responsive to individual needs and cases only when the citizens have bribed them. Much of the public's disillusionment with the communist regimes at the end of the 1980s came from the extravagant benefits enjoyed by public employees and by their corruptness.

Modern bureaucracies tend to be highly complex. This often results in lack of coordination and compartmentalization. One part of the bureaucracy may not be aware of what other parts are doing and may even be working at cross purposes to government actions elsewhere. Cabinet deliberations are supposed to address such problems. But, as an example, it is common for a ministry of industry to press for a new industry in a region where the ministry of environment is struggling to reduce air pollution. Specialization of government offices is useful in promoting efficiency and expert attention to policy matters, but it also leads to disjointed policy making.

Furthermore, the specialization of government bureaucrats can lead to frustration for citizens trying to find where a particular government service is provided. A common example of this can be seen when a customer enters a French post office. Each of the windows offers specific services: stamps, parcels, postal savings accounts, or telephones. Even when lines for stamps are long and no one is in the other lines, the French know that they cannot get the employee at another window to provide them with a postage stamp. Such frustrations produce public disenchantment with the bureaucracy and the government that tolerates them.

While the need for civil service reform is acknowledged in virtually all polities, such reform rarely occurs. Civil servants tend to be conservative in that they prefer to maintain the existing patterns of action and relationships rather than experiment with new ones. Few politicians have the courage to attack their own bureaucracy with fundamental reforms. Those who do usually find that the civil servants are able either to block the reform or to distort the changes to serve their own interests. A good example can be seen in the case of Britain's Margaret Thatcher, one of the most powerful democratic leaders of the past twenty years. Prime Minister Thatcher was successful in achieving a number of major reforms, but her hopes to reform the civil service and to reduce its size were blocked by bureaucratic inertia and overt resistance.

Civil servants nearly always prefer to continue doing things the way they have in the past rather than to experiment with new policies or procedures. This resistance to change—and especially to changes in the bureaucracy's own structures and activities—is why bureaucracies are nearly always leaders in defending the status quo. Hence, in many settings, reform-minded leaders find themselves thwarted by an uncooperative or openly hostile bureaucracy more interested in continuity than change.

The positive side of this is that bureaucracies provide an element of stability in states where political leaders or even regimes change often. The civil service continues in spite of dramatic political changes. The same people are usually present in government offices from the national to the local levels to administer government policies and ensure that the mail gets through, that laws are enforced, and that pensions are paid. This is important in polities where there is great instability or major political changes. For example, in spite of the dramatic changes in political direction in Russia, the same bureaucrats are around providing services to the population as they did under the former communist regime.

POLITICAL CONTROL OF THE BUREAUCRACY

Underlying the notion of a modern civil service is the principle that government is divided between those who make policy (the political leaders) and those who implement it (civil servants). Ideally, the bureaucracy acts as an automaton simply carrying out the will of the politicians *sine ira et studio* (without anger or passion). But these ideals are difficult to achieve: It is impossible to separate all policy making from implementation; bureaucrats are influenced by their own feelings as they carry out their tasks. A central concern, then, in all types of political settings is the need to ensure that the administration carries out the policies dictated by the political leaders. Nearly all civil services are founded on the principle of political neutrality and the commitment to execute loyally the decisions of the political masters. In practice, however, there are many cases where bureaucracies subtly alter or blatantly ignore the wishes of the political leadership.

All political leaders want control over the administration so that their policies are implemented loyally. Otherwise, their directives and policies mean little. Democratic leaders want that control so that they can try to fulfill the campaign pledges that got them elected. Nondemocratic regimes are also interested in maintaining control over the bureaucracy. Their motives are based less on notions of public accountability than on the wish to have a civil service that is obedient to the autocrat's directions. Even powerful dictators are ultimately reliant upon the obedience of the bureaucracy in carrying out their will.

Political control is an important issue because it is the means by which a permanent civil service is held accountable to the needs of the public it is supposed to serve. This is what makes the issue of bureaucratic obedience to elected political officials particularly important in democratic countries, where government is supposed to be accountable to the citizens.[4] Unelected, career civil servants can be held responsible only through the elected leadership, who can be changed when the public is dissatisfied. Citizen control over the bureaucracy then must pass through elected leaders. That line of accountability between the bureaucracy and the citizen hinges upon the ability of the elected officials to get the bureaucrats to do what the democratically responsible leaders want them to do. Only if the bureaucrats do what the elected officials tell them is democratic accountability maintained.

The challenge of maintaining political mastery of the administration is a big one. Civil servants have a number of characteristics that make it difficult for politicians to control them.[5] They enjoy the benefits of permanence and stability that elected officials who rotate in and out of public office lack. While politicians who are supposed to direct the bureaucracy must devote much of their time and energy to partisan activities, the civil servants spend full time on their administrative duties. Government employees who have been hired and promoted on the basis of their training and merit may be skeptical or openly contemptuous of the ideas of politicians who lack expertise. As a result, there is a natural and inevitable tension between politicians who want to maintain their control and bureaucrats who "just want to do their jobs."

In the United States, monitoring the civil service is a multifaceted affair.[6] It starts with the appointment by presidents of their political allies to top-level positions throughout the bureaucracy. The political appointments go deep into the senior ranks of all departments and agencies. Presumably, these political friends will fill those positions that may affect policy content and in doing so ensure that the president's will is accomplished. The next control mechanism is legislative oversight by congressional committees and subcommittees that observe the civil servants' compliance with laws and established policies. Finally, individual legislators check on the performance of the civil service in response to individual complaints or requests for assistance from their constituents. Despite, or maybe because of, this elaborate and multilevel system of control, the American civil service is not noted for its obedience to political leadership. The multiple checks often offset each other since the preferences of the president may differ from those of the appropriate legislative committee or individual legislator. In a setting of political monitors who disagree with each other, the interpretive and discretionary powers of the civil servants acquire great latitude.

In most other democracies, the structures are simpler. Only a few political appointees in each administrative department or agency are expected to control those underneath them. Other senior-level administrators are all career civil servants. For example, the British minister of home affairs is assisted by two or three junior ministers who are also members of Parliament and the same party, but the permanent secretary who runs the ministry is a civil servant. Permanent secretaries have made their career in a department and stay on as ministers come and go. Even the minister's private secretary who handles the minister's appointments and political contacts is a civil servant, although usually one drawn from another department.

In France, ministers often have a small group of political appointees to advise them on policy and politics. Known as the minister's *cabinet,* these officials assist the minister in developing new ideas and in ensuring political control over the bureaucracy. Britain and other democracies have also experimented with the use of such small bodies of political advisors for ministers. But the practice is restrained and does not compare with the vast patronage system at the top of the U.S. bureaucracy.

Legislative oversight of the bureaucracy in other democracies is less pervasive than in the United States. Of course, legislators stand ready to assist their constituents in their problems with the administration. But in other democracies, the parliamentary committees are smaller, less active, and less powerful than in the United States. The committee system in Germany, one of the strongest, does do some oversight of the bureaucracy. The British House of Commons has instituted "select committees" with some still embryonic oversight powers.[7] In Britain and in most other countries, parliamentary committees usually lack the ability to require civil servants to report to them; instead, the minister provides the sole link between parliament and the department. The discipline and cohesion of the government majorities usually serves to reduce the desire of committee leaderships to embarrass their own party's government with an inquiry into one of its departments. The presence of a minister who alone represents the government and who in parliamentary systems is usually also a member of parliament establishes a clear line of political accountability: It is the minister, not the civil servant, who is responsible to parliament and the voters for the conduct of the ministry.

While ministers do attempt to supervise their staffs to keep them in line with the government's directions, they are often distracted by their own multiple political duties. They can focus only on a few key issues in their efforts to impose political leadership on the vast bureaucracy. As a result, bureaucratic subservience to the political masters usually depends upon the voluntary compliance of civil servants with what they believe to be the will of the government. Loyalty is the product more of a powerful norm that the civil service should defer to the wishes of the political leaders than it is the actual enforcement of those wishes by the politicians. Americans versed in the notions of checks and balances and constitutional precepts tend to be uneasy about relying on something as vague as the civil servant's acceptance of a norm of subservience to political leaders. But that norm is well established in the civil services of most democratic countries. The British civil service, for example, accepts this norm and is widely regarded for its evenhanded and loyal implementation of the government's policies.[8] This is true also of the French and German bureaucracies and the senior civil service in India. The norm is much less well established in Japan, and the bureaucracy takes advantage of the relatively weak prime minister and cabinet to impose its own views.[9]

Civil servants are expected to remain aloof from partisan concerns. In some countries, such as the United States and Britain, bureaucrats are barred from partisan politics of any kind beyond the private act of voting. In others, such as France and Germany, civil servants are allowed to take leave of their state positions in order to participate in partisan politics and even to run for or serve in elected offices. In still other settings where a single party dominates politics over a long period, as in Japan or Mexico, for example, close ties between politicians and civil servants are common and lead to the politicization of the civil service.

The real test of the loyalty of the bureaucracy comes when a reform-minded government comes to power and challenges the status quo. The bureaucracy is a natural and formidable defender of the way things are. This usually is complicated when the reformers are from the Left since the predominant political biases of senior civil servants are conservative.

THE COURTS AND POLITICS

In the United States, the Supreme Court plays a very important political role. Some of the key political issues of the second half of the twentieth century were resolved by the Court rather than by Congress: desegregation, voting rights, fair apportionment, rights of the accused, division of power between states and the federal government, religion in public schools, and abortion. The Court did so by determining that the Constitution established a principle or right that the federal or state government had failed to observe. In some instances, the Supreme Court declared laws that failed to observe these principles and rights to be unconstitutional. In other cases, the Court ordered the federal or state governments to take steps that would bring existing practice into compliance with the Constitution.

Judicial Review

The power of a court to declare duly enacted laws to be unconstitutional is known as *judicial review*. It emerged in American political practice when the Supreme Court declared that the doctrine of checks and balances endowed the Court with the right and obligation to determine whether or not the government's acts and laws were in compliance with the Constitution. There is no specific clause in the Constitution that grants the Court that power. The Court and Chief Justice John Marshall declared that power on its own in the historic *Marbury v. Madison* decision of 1803. The Court declared itself to have special obligations to defend the integrity of the Constitution. By the middle of the twentieth century, the U.S. Supreme Court had become a major political actor through the use of its powers of judicial review.

In most parliamentary systems, judicial review has been limited by the fundamental notion of parliament's supremacy. With all sovereign powers conferred upon parliament, there is no theoretical justification for courts or any other body to review legislation or government action to verify its compliance with the constitution. In such settings, the courts are limited to reviewing specific actions to see if they are in harmony with the laws. They cannot review the constitutionality of the laws themselves. An additional concern in many other democracies is the wisdom of endowing unelected judges serving long—sometimes lifelong—terms with too much say in political decision making. To do so is to lose the heart of representative democracy—the accountability to the people of the key political leaders.

A final obstacle to the development of judicial review has been the more conservative approach to law that is characteristic of most countries. Courts in most parts of the world are limited to the narrow application of codified laws, unlike the prevalence of precedence (reliance on prior decisions), judge-made law, and common (sometimes unwritten) law found in Britain, the United States, and other Anglo-Saxon countries.

Constitutional Courts

Since the end of World War II, a number of other countries have begun experiments with judicial review. Canada is the state whose experience most closely parallels the U.S. practice of judicial review. As in the United States, the Canadian Constitution says nothing about judicial review, but through ongoing practice and precedent judicial review has emerged as an important power of the courts. The

Canadian courts have exercised significant powers in the interpretation of federalism and, to a lesser degree, in the defense of civil liberties.

After World War II, the new constitutions in Germany, Italy, and Japan all included provisions for constitutional courts. These courts were empowered to rule on the constitutionality of acts of parliament. After slow starts in all three countries, these constitutional courts have begun to exercise their powers of judicial review only in the last twenty years. They have emerged as powerful defenders of human rights and interpreters of the constitutions. In Italy especially, judicial activism has had an important political role. In these three countries, individuals, local governments, and social groups all have the ability to bring cases alleging unconstitutionality or abuse of human rights to these courts.

In several other countries—notably India, Israel, and Spain—constitutional courts play important and legitimate roles in the governing process. For example, in India, the Supreme Court pressured the federal police into action against corrupt politicians. The impact of these constitutional courts in countries where judicial review is developing goes beyond the courts' decisions. Their presence has a deterrent effect on governments and legislators. Rather than facing the embarrassment of a reversal of their actions, governments avoid ahead of time policies that may be challenged and overruled in the constitutional courts.[10] Indeed, even with a strong Supreme Court in the United States, in 210 years the Court has stricken down parts of only 135 federal laws.[11] But its presence and readiness to act deters leaders in Congress and the presidency from taking actions that might be deemed unconstitutional.

The French have a more restricted Constitutional Council.[12] This body can review the constitutionality of laws only prior to their promulgation. In addition, appeals to the Council can be made only by the president, prime minister, or groups of at least sixty members of Parliament. The Council has not emerged as a defender of civil liberties as have the Constitutional Courts in Germany, Italy, and Japan.

Despite the parliamentary tradition's hostility to judicial review, European countries are increasingly developing their courts' ability to review the constitutionality of laws and government actions. One reason is that their membership in the European Union obliges them to accept the rulings of the European Court of Justice (ECJ).[13] EU treaties stipulate that the Union's statutes prevail over national laws. National laws that conflict with treaty obligations and European Union regulations can be declared null and void by the ECJ. In addition, European countries have accepted the jurisdiction of the European Court of Human Rights as the final arbiter of claims that a country violated its citizens' human rights. To avoid such international action, European states have increased the power of their own courts to review the laws and actions of the government.

Many of the constitutions in former communist countries have created constitutional courts with powers of judicial review and the ability to defend individual civil liberties. It is still too early to determine the effectiveness of these courts.

They are handicapped by the lack of traditions of strong, independent courts and the rule of law. The same is true in many third world countries where there have been efforts to create supreme courts patterned on the U.S. example. Nigeria is one such case where the supreme court's independence has been limited by years of military rule. Most Latin American governments also have supreme courts patterned on the U.S. court, but their effectiveness as agents of judicial review and as defenders of human rights varies with the nature of the overall political regime. Authoritarian rulers usually find ways to limit or eliminate criticism from the courts. On the other hand, in some countries where the rule of law has become entrenched, as in India, supreme courts have been effective in using judicial review and defending civil liberties. India's experience, however, illustrates the tenuous nature of constitutional courts in the developing world. While the Indian Supreme Court functions, there is a provision that allows parliament to stipulate that certain laws are not subject to the Court's review. This provision has been used over forty times, often to protect repressive laws that the Court was likely to invalidate. Through such measures, the Indian government seeks to acquire the laws needed to promote stability in a troubled country—but at the cost of limiting the Court's ability to protect human rights.

At the beginning of the century, the greater preoccupation with protecting civil liberties and the establishment of effective democracies are spreading the notions of powerful and independent courts capable of defending these new values. Even in Britain the philosophical resistance to judicial review has seen some movement toward judicial review. Since the 1970s, British courts have begun to claim and exercise the power to review the constitutionality of government acts and laws of Parliament. Courts in many countries are increasingly seen as important guarantees of democracy and human rights.

CONCLUSION

Decision making in all countries of the world includes many more institutions than the legislature and political executives. This chapter has focused on two important sets of institutions that are not always visible participants in policy making but that, in fact, are major decision makers: the bureaucracy and constitutional courts. Both these sets of institutions pose challenges to the more visible and publicly accountable political leaders in that the power they exercise over the policy-making process is difficult to control. Nearly all political leaders, democratic and authoritarian alike, complain about their difficulties in getting the bureaucracy to carry through and implement their programs. Where there are constitutional courts, political leaders are often exasperated by the court's actions and complain about the undue influence of nonelected judges. The challenge of maintaining political control will always exist, but bureaucrats are indispensable and courts are usually important protectors of civil liberties and constitutions.

NOTES

1. *The New York Times,* 1 March 1994.

2. On the United States, see Michael Johnston, "Patrons and Clients, Jobs and Machines: A Case Study of the Uses of Patronage," *American Political Science Review* 73 (June 1979): 385–393. On Canada, see S. J. R. Noel, *Patrons, Clients, Brokers: Ontario Society and Politics, 1791–1896* (Toronto: University of Toronto Press, 1990).

3. The classic statement of the nature of the rational bureaucracy is found in Weber's work. See "Bureaucracy" in *From Max Weber: Essays in Sociology,* ed. by H. H. Gerth and C. Wright Mills (New York: Oxford University Press, 1978), and Max Weber, *The Theory of Social and Economic Organization,* trans. by A. M. Henderson and Talcott Parsons (New York: Free Press, 1964).

4. See Eva Etzioni-Halevy, *Bureaucracy and Democracy: A Political Dilemma* (London: Routledge & Kegan Paul, 1983).

5. B. Guy Peters, *The Politics of Bureaucracy,* 3rd ed. (New York: Longman, 1989), pp. 182–217.

6. James W. Fesler and Donald F. Kettl, *The Politics of the Administrative Process* (Chatham, NJ: Chatham House, 1991), pp. 317–336.

7. Gavin Drewery, ed., *The New Select Committees: A Study of the 1979 Reforms* (Oxford: Clarendon Press, 1985).

8. R. Pyper, *The British Civil Service* (London: Harvester Wheatsheaf, 1995), and Peter Hennessy, *Whitehall* (London: Secker & Warburg, 1989).

9. Lonny E. Carlile, "The Politics of Administrative Reform," in Lonny E. Carlile and Mark C. Tilton, eds., *Is Japan Really Changing Its Ways? Regulatory Reform and the Japanese Economy* (Washington, DC: Brookings Institution Press, 1998).

10. Alec Stone Sweet, *Governing with Judges: Constitutional Politics in Europe* (Oxford, England: Oxford University Press, 2000), p. 202.

11. "The Gavel and the Robe," *The Economist,* 7 August 1999, p. 44.

12. Alec Stone, *The Birth of Judicial Politics in France: The Constitutional Council in Comparative Perspective* (New York: Oxford University Press, 1992).

13. Martin J. Shapiro, "The European Court of Justice," in Alberta M. Sbragia, ed., *Europolitics* (Washington, DC: Brookings Institution Press, 1992).

❖❖❖❖❖❖❖❖❖❖❖ PART IV ❖❖❖❖❖❖❖❖❖❖❖

EVALUATING POLITICAL PERFORMANCE

People expect their governments to do more than simply hold power. Political leaders should accomplish community goals rather than simply serve their own narrow and selfish interests. The collective power exercised by the state should be used to accomplish desirable tasks. What it is that people expect the state to do and the priorities attached to these goals differ from one society to another. But there is a growing consensus among peoples everywhere that the state should provide a setting in which economic necessities can be met, a minimal level of care or services for its citizens is assured, basic human rights are respected, and protection is provided against external enemies and internal disorder. The real challenge is determining more specifically, country by country, sometimes era by era, what these ends are in practice, who defines them in detail, and how well the political leaders are doing in meeting them.

Evaluations of political performance lead to the issue of political change. Where regimes are performing poorly and failing to meet the expectations of their peoples, there may be calls for change. Change may come through gradual or rapid reform, or even tumultuous revolutions; it may not come at all when inept or oppressive regimes hold on to power because there is no challenge or effective body to force change. But change is not linked only to poor performance. All polities evolve with changing socioeconomic patterns; many states undergo evolutionary changes of varying degrees in response to changing popular expectations and new policy challenges. Indeed, political order or stability often requires such adjustments.

Chapter 11

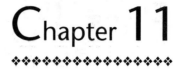

Political Performance

In his list of seven sins, the great Indian leader Mahatma Gandhi included "politics without principle." In the real world of politics, principles must often be adjusted to meet actual conditions and limitations; those who insist on achieving the ideal or nothing usually end up with nothing. But true leaders are those who can inspire hope among their followers in a set of limited but lofty goals and then use that hope to build support to achieve those goals.

While many leaders are guided by principles and policy goals, all elected leaders take office with the intention of doing those things that will bring their reelection or the reelection of their party. Few political leaders look forward to losing power and becoming subject to rivals whom they once ruled. In open societies, politicians generally sense that their goal of reelection is intertwined intimately with the need to satisfy the political expectations of their electorate. Such a recognition leads them to temper their electoral stratagems with efforts to achieve the policy demands of the people. They come to believe that reelection depends not only on their political wile but even more on their performance in policies and deeds.

Authoritarian leaders are similarly concerned with doing those things that will allow them to stay in power. Authoritarian leaders are especially loath to consider loss of power to rivals whom they often have oppressed; they can expect the same treatment if they lose power. As a result, in both democratic and autocratic settings, most political leaders believe that their continued hold on power depends upon their meeting certain expectations of the people. The leadership's continued hold on power and sometimes the very existence of the regime depend upon the government's ability to provide for its society's needs: a growing economy; basic social services such as education, retirement benefits, and public works; respect for some individual rights; protection from external enemies; and maintenance of public order at home.

The preoccupation with holding on to power is not necessarily inappropriate when it takes the form of meeting popular expectations. For those political leaders who are honestly convinced that they can better govern their country than their rivals—and that is usually the case—it is normal for them to see staying in power as a natural and desirable end. In serving society they hope to perpetuate their rule. In democratic systems, periodic elections work well to ensure that those in power do in fact please the public. While voters may not always be able to assess the qualifications and policies of challengers, they are very good at knowing whether or not they approve of what the incumbents are doing, as demonstrated in 1994 and 2000 by Americans and in 1993 and 2000 by Canadians.

In practice, many regimes are so weak that their entire strength is devoted to the task of hanging on to power. Lacking legitimacy and effective control of the state's institutions and facing overt challenges from powerful rivals, all these political leaders can do is try to hold on to their power. Under such unstable circumstances, it is not unusual for the political leaders in fragile states to divert public resources to their own bank accounts or to their friends while they still have power rather than promote the interests of the society as a whole, reflecting the attitude of "get what we can while we can."[1] This explains in part the widespread graft and corruption endemic in many developing countries with weak and unstable regimes. The billions of dollars siphoned off the Nigerian economy by General Abacha and his coterie and from the Indonesian economy by General Suharto and his sons are extreme but not isolated examples of this problem.

The total preoccupation of leaders with staying in power is often found in developing countries but also in some well-developed countries that are undergoing rapid change, such as Russia and other successor states of the old Union of Soviet Socialist Republics (USSR). There, the disappearance of the old institutions and procedures has not been followed by the establishment of effective new ones. Their leaders calculate that without the institutional base needed to achieve reforms, they had best concentrate all of their efforts on the retention of power. While the obsession with holding power is particularly common in developing and changing polities, it can also be found in very highly developed countries. This is especially the case when political leaders face criticism or scandals that pull their attention away from their policy goals in order to defend their hold on power. For example, during the Clinton presidency, several scandals diverted the attention of the president and his aides from working for the policy goals that they believed they were elected to achieve. Even more trouble was faced by President Richard Nixon during the eighteen months of the Watergate crisis when the White House did little else than try to save the president.

HOW CAN WE EVALUATE POLITICAL PERFORMANCE?

If there is agreement on the need for government to do more than hang on to power, there is much less accord on how to assess what governments do accomplish. Most citizens of a country can develop some sense as to whether or not their government is meeting the needs and wishes of "people like me." Often, however, their judgments are far from being accurate or unbiased. Evaluations of political performance may be influenced by partisan ties; by group affiliations such as churches, labor unions, and interest groups; by media interpretations; and by comments and reactions of friends and family. Even supposedly objective observers—news analysts or scholars—are influenced by their own feelings; in spite of a desire for evenhanded objectivity they often fail to applaud accomplishments for fear of appearing favorable to the government.

The challenge of assessing government performance becomes even more difficult when observers from one country try to evaluate the operations of the government of another country. Even among countries of similar backgrounds and levels of development, important cultural differences affect judgments on each other's state policies. For example, Canadians, enjoying their own popular state-provided medical care, have long found it impossible to understand why Americans do not censure their government for failing to provide universal, low-cost medical care to all Americans. And these are quite similar peoples. When the cultural differences between countries are greater, that makes fair evaluations of one country's political performance by careful observers from another country even more difficult. For example, how can an American fairly assess the human rights record of Islamic courts in northern Nigeria?

I leave that question unanswered. And indeed that is the challenge that all thoughtful citizens should have in approaching the evaluation of other political systems (and their own, too). In trying to assess the validity of someone else's evaluation of political performance, we should seek to understand what the evaluator uses as the basis of evaluation. As we make our own evaluations, we should be aware of the grounds for that evaluation and recognize the limitations of that evaluative approach. We should be aware and tolerant of other evaluators who may use different but no less valid bases for their assessments.

POINTS OF PERFORMANCE EVALUATION

In the next few pages, I will suggest several areas of government action and public policy that might be used in evaluating the performance of a country's political system. They reflect my personal feelings regarding what a country's leaders should be trying to do in a variety of different settings. Your bases for evaluation may be different, and in reading about the ones I present you should do so critically. Measure them against your own standards of evaluation and see how much you agree or disagree with my efforts and conclusions on evaluating political performance.

Security Issues

In nearly all societies, people look to their governments for protection against violence from within and without the country's borders. Indeed, there are some who argue that such needs to protect against external threats are the very basis for the creation of the modern nation-state.[2] People expect their government to protect them against violent attacks from neighboring countries as well as against foreign efforts to control what is happening within the country's borders. With such an expectation, it is not surprising that when a country loses a war there is often a change in regime. The old leaders who allowed defeat at the hands of enemy neighbors are replaced by new leaders who may be better able to defend the country. France's Third Republic toppled as German armies invaded France in 1940; Germany experienced regime changes after military defeats in 1918 and 1945; Japan also changed its polity after its loss in World War II. In some circumstances, it is not necessary for a regime to lose a war before it is toppled; even small military defeats may discredit a regime and bring its replacement. A series of defeats in colonial wars provide at least part of the explanation for the fall of the French Fourth Republic in 1958.

Regimes also need to provide domestic security. People usually expect their governments to prevent continuing, large-scale disruptions of society through rioting or terrorism. Regimes that experience considerable political violence over extended periods of time lose the confidence and backing of their citizens. The public comes to feel in danger of personal or property damage from the political disruptions and withdraws support from leaders or governments that seem unable to prevent domestic turmoil. In democratic settings, such failure to provide domestic order leads to electoral defeat of the incumbents as, for example, the defeat of the U.S. Democratic presidential candidate in 1968 at the peak of civil unrest related to the war in Vietnam. Weak democracies are often overthrown by autocrats promising to end political violence and restore the domestic peace that the democratic leaders seemed unable to achieve. For example, in India, domestic turmoil was used to justify Indira Gandhi's suspension of democracy and rule by decree in 1975. When given the choice, most peoples prefer order to domestic turmoil even when the cost of achieving that tranquility is the sacrifice of democracy. In nondemocratic settings, extended political turmoil can lead to the overthrow of the regime by civil or military revolts. Thus, ethnic unrest and violence produced Nigeria's first military coup in 1965 and contributed to several others over the next thirty years.

The close link between political turmoil and the legitimacy of a regime is why terrorism is such a potent tool for opponents of a regime. By disrupting domestic order, carrying out well-publicized violent incidents, threatening even more disorder, and demonstrating the inability of the government to prevent such outrages, a handful of terrorists or guerrillas can bring an otherwise strong government into question. A good recent example was the 1994 guerrilla uprising in the southern Mexico state of Chiapas. The dispute was isolated, but government troops were not able to prevent the guerrillas from carrying out an attack on their supporters and buildings and then disappearing in the jungle. The uprising coincided with national elections, which brought greater visibility to the guerrilla cause and opposition parties that sought to address the socioeconomic discontent at the roots of the guerrilla cause. The apparent impotence of the government in responding to the threat damaged its legitimacy and weakened the governing PRI's reelection campaign. When the opposition party headed by Vicente Fox took over the Mexican national government in 2000, one of its first acts was to appease the Chiapas rebels so as to restore order in that part of Mexico.

Governments can also be damaged by nonpolitical disorder. Increased crime and the apparent inability of the police to control it can also produce disaffection among the public. Rarely does this contribute to the collapse of a regime, but democratic governments in recent years have seen many of their supporters abandon mainstream parties and support "law and order" parties of the far Right. Today, in Germany, France, Britain, and elsewhere extreme right-wing parties or movements base their appeal on the growth of crime, open drug abuse, and urban decay. Demagogues can promise draconian and impossible solutions to crime that they do not have to carry out. Responsible politicians are not free to do so. As a result, the collapse of public morals and order can produce destabilizing tensions even in well-established democracies. And in new, would-be democracies such as Russia, where popular roots for democratic principles are still shallow, crime and urban decay threaten to fatally undermine public support for democracy.

Economic Growth

As I have argued earlier in this volume, governments find themselves under ever-increasing pressure to make certain that their countries' economies perform well. Even in countries committed to free enterprise and a minimal economic role for government, political leaders are aware that excessive unemployment, inflation, or economic stagnation will weaken their political positions. Democratic leaders know from past experience that voters vote the parties in power out of office when the economy sours, whether or not that government or any government is responsible for the economic problems. As a result, whatever their ideologies, governments are concerned with keeping the economy healthy and the people prosperous.

Governments encourage investment in promising areas by tax concessions or outright subsidies. They try to manipulate currency and monetary controls to facilitate economic growth. Governments underwrite basic research that will ultimately provide information and inventions needed for the flourishing of the private and public portions of their economies. They provide benefits to protect those who are unemployed, disabled, or elderly. Above all, governments are expected to build and maintain the infrastructure necessary for the economy to perform: public education, highways, airports, seaports and canals, mail services, waste disposal, irrigation and flood control, and often public utilities such as water, gas, and electricity.

It is easy to agree that political leaders are expected to promote their countries' economies, but it is much more difficult to measure that performance. On the face of it, it seems simple. We have a wealth of uniform, international economic statistics that allow us to measure and compare economic growth, inflation, unemployment, investment, and so on. But the statistics themselves may be misleading. For example, in 1994, the United States replaced Japan as the world's leader in industrial productivity. But was the Clinton government responsible for that success or was the Japanese government accountable for its country's slippage? Did this shift do anything to redress the long-standing imbalance of trade between the United States and Japan? It is hard for economists to establish what meaning, if any, there is in such a change, much less whether any government played a role in it.

Let me give another example. For many years, economic growth in India and China was compared, usually to India's detriment. China was more adept than India at solving the problems that had produced famine in both countries' past. China was more successful in developing its own heavy industry; its economic growth rate usually exceeded that of India; China's compulsory birth control programs were more successful in preventing rapid population increases from eroding the gains of economic growth. The Chinese economy was free from the inflation and currency problems that plagued India. As a result, some analysts claimed that China illustrated the advantage of a centralized, monolithic, and authoritarian regime in organizing for economic transformation compared with India's efforts at maintaining democracy, a mixed economy, and a pluralist society. Is such a judgment accurate? Is it fair? Again, it is hard to answer just on the basis of statistics and economics.

Similar questions are raised today about the different approaches of Russia and China as both countries have moved toward more market-driven economies. Russia has moved simultaneously toward both economic change and democratization; China has opened its economy to private entrepreneurs and foreign investors but defiantly opposed internal and external pressures to open its politics to allow free expression of dissent. Again, the cold statistics favor China: Over the past decade it has had one of the highest rates of economic growth and industrialization while avoiding inflation and currency problems. Post-communist Russia has been plagued with economic decline, hyperinflation, rising foreign debt, and currency crises. But there are economic and political factors at work that might affect this first assessment. Relatively underdeveloped economies (as in China) can usually grow more rapidly in early stages of growth than can more developed ones (such as Russia). And many would question whether the improved Chinese economy adequately compensates for the social and political repression still suffered by its people.

The problem of evaluating economic performance becomes even more difficult when we move to the underdeveloped portions of the world. Many of these countries are ruled by leaders so uncertain of their hold on power that they seek to divert the state's resources to their own bank accounts. It is not surprising that where leaders are dishonest, corruption is widespread throughout the country. Not only does such corruption drain the economy of its resources and strength but it also disguises much of the economic activity that does occur. In states with considerable corruption, there are extensive "gray" economies based on black markets, payoffs, unreported production, and tax evasion. The official economic statistics then are often highly inaccurate measures of what is going on in the economy and underreport economic activity.

Often there is the assumption that economic development is always desirable. That assumption is now challenged on two grounds. Some insist that more attention be paid to the environmental costs of development and criticize rapid industrialization in poorer countries for sacrificing the environment in the pursuit of rapid economic growth. But those who express such criticism are usually enjoying a very comfortable standard of living and issue their pleas for respecting the environment from air-conditioned offices. It is not surprising that those struggling to eke out an existence in Mexico, Nigeria, or India and their governments are not impressed by such arguments that they should abstain from economic development to rescue the global environment.

A second and less common criticism is that economic development often destroys existing traditions and values that differ from those in the West but should be preserved. In a parody of nineteenth-century notions of the "noble savage," such critics point to the damage to the traditional family, communal feelings, and traditional values wreaked by rapid socioeconomic change. Some will even claim that the traditional lifestyle that is imperiled by economic growth, modern education, and medicine is superior to what is achieved by change. Indeed, there is some support for such concerns. For example, prior to independence, Nigeria was largely self-sufficient in meeting the food needs of its peoples. The redirection of the economy and population toward modern industry and commerce has made Nigeria now a food-importing country. In balance, however, it is usually Westerners who object to the changes rather than the third world peoples actually affected by the decline of traditional values. Indeed, it is the extreme of self-centered paternalism for us to suggest that children in poorly developed countries should go without education, modern medical care, and economic opportunities in the interest of preserving traditional values.

How much politics matters in economic affairs is a matter of debate. Some contend that in developing countries democracy lends itself to economic growth; others see the explanation for the rapid economic growth of Southeast Asian countries as due to the stability of their often authoritarian regimes.[3] One empirical test of the relationship between types of political regimes and economic performance found that out of 16 cases studied, 3 supported the notion that democracy was correlated with economic growth, 3 supported the opposite: that democracy was linked with economic decline, and 10 showed no relationship at all between the performance of the economic system and kind of political regime.[4] More important than type of regime was overall stability and the confidence of investors in the political future of the country. In mature democracies there is little evidence that the specific party that holds power makes much difference in economic outcomes. Limits imposed by independent central banks, the need for stability and continuity by business interests, and international considerations leave little latitude for a party to make significant changes in its country's economic policies.

Social Policies

Americans often react very strongly when social welfare policies are raised. For some, such public policies waste tax revenues on ill-guided exercises in "social engineering" and are doomed to failure. Others see public policy as a way to respond to the causes and results of widespread poverty in an otherwise wealthy country. There are few issues that raise stronger or more emotional responses in U.S. politics than those associated with welfare policies. However, in most other industrial democracies, social welfare policies are much more positively viewed. They are seen, and correctly so, as successful policies that have not only eased the sufferings of many but have also helped win the allegiance of less-advantaged people who were alienated from the market economy and sometimes from democracy as a result of the harshness of early capitalism.

As a result, most industrial countries have extensive social welfare states whose expenditures amount to about one-fourth of the nation's gross domestic product. (See Table 11.1.) These social programs provide citizens with subsidized housing, public transportation, medical care, social security and retirement programs, unemployment insurance, income supplements, payments for children, and other benefits. Some of these programs are based on needs as determined by an individual's or a family's income; others, such as medical care and social security, are provided to all regardless of need or income. Depending upon the country and the specific program, they are funded through insurance payments by employers and employees (as in the American social security programs) or by direct payment from the country's general tax revenues (as in subsidies for low-income housing in the United States).

As these programs have grown in size and extent, there has been increasing concern about their costs. This is especially the case in countries where aging populations reduce the number of income earners who pay taxes or insurance premiums and increase the number of benefit recipients. However, even where there are cost concerns, the benefit programs remain very popular, and few politicians are prepared to face the public's ire by reducing social security benefits or most of these other social welfare programs. Even conservative leaders such as Ronald

TABLE **11.1**   Social Expenditures as a Percentage of GDP in 1980–1981

Country	With Education	Without Education
Britain	24.5%	19.0%
France	35.9	30.6
Germany (West)	27.2	22.3
Italy	27.0	21.1
The Netherlands	43.0	32.1
Sweden	37.9	30.7

Source: Michel Peillon, "Welfare and State Centralization," *West European Politics* 16 (April 1993): 110.

Reagan and Margaret Thatcher who called for such reductions shrunk from actually cutting these popular programs. As a result, states occasionally trim some benefits or increase the shares paid by the individual. But they rarely abolish or substantially reduce social welfare programs.

With the exception of the lack of universal coverage in health services in the United States, the differences in benefit packages from one industrial democracy to another are relatively small. The costs of these programs and how they are financed, however, often vary substantially from one country to another. It is possible to evaluate performance by measuring costs with benefits on a comparative basis among industrial democracies. Table 11.2 does this with 1997 data on medical care. It shows that there is very little difference in life expectancy among leading industrial democracies but that costs vary sharply. Note that per capita medical care in the United States is four times what it is in Spain even though Spaniards have a longer life expectancy. Britain's nationalized health service seems to provide the same life expectancy as much more costly national health insurance programs in Canada, France, and Germany.

Such cost-benefit analysis may provide some insights, but there are other less readily measured indicators of how well a social benefit is provided by govern-

TABLE **11.2**   Medical Costs and Life Expectancy in Selected Countries, 1997

Country	Per Capita Costs of Medical Care (in U.S. dollars)	Healthy Life Expectancy in Years*
Japan	$2,373	74.5
France	2,369	73.1
Sweden	2,456	73.0
Spain	1,071	72.8
Italy	1,855	72.7
Canada	1,783	72.0
United Kingdom	1,303	71.7
Germany	2,713	70.4
Israel	1,385	70.4
United States	4,187	70.0
Mexico	240	65.0
China	20	62.3
Russian Federation	158	61.3
Brazil	319	59.1
India	23	53.2
Nigeria	30	38.3
Sierra Leone	11	25.9

*The WHO calculates life expectancy based on the expected years of healthy life. To figure the Disability Adjusted Life Expectancy (DALE) the number of years of ill-health are weighted according to severity and subtracted from the expected overall life expectancy. Figures include the combined life expectancies of men and women.

Source: World Health Organization website: www.who.int/whosis/statistics/dale

ment. For example, to continue with the case of medical care, there may be hidden "costs" in terms of the individual's choice of doctor or waiting periods for elective surgery that offset the strict financial accounting. For some beneficiaries of the service, these noncost concerns may be of great importance.

In developing countries, there is less government concern with the provision of social welfare benefits. Often, relief for the poor and aged is left to relatives, communal groups, churches, and other volunteer programs. For example, in Nigeria, extended family members and communal groups care for their own in the southern portions; in the North, the Islamic tradition of almsgiving provides relief for the poor. As a result, there are substantial differences from one part of Nigeria to another.

There are also important differences in such welfare services from one developing country to another. The level of services varies greatly depending on the country's level of development and cultural background. The process of modernization generally increases pressures for state-provided benefits. As the family and communal groups decline in importance, these traditional sources of care for the disadvantaged lose the ability to care for the aged and poor. By and large, developing countries face such urgent demands to provide for the immediate needs of their peoples and economies that they are not able to provide the extensive array of public welfare programs expected of governments in more developed settings. There are simply not enough state resources for governments to meet the basic requirements and also to provide social welfare protection.

In developing countries, the inadequacies of state welfare programs hinder the achievement of other goals, such as ensuring potable water and adequate food supplies and promoting economic growth. Often developing countries encourage programs of family planning in order to prevent population growth from overwhelming economic progress. When governments try to limit population growth as part of a development program, there is greater need for government pensions for the aged since there are fewer children to care for the parents. When such pensions are not provided or where the people do not believe that the programs will still be available when they need them, population growth tends to increase as parents try to provide for their old age by the only means available.

In most advanced democracies, social welfare is a key issue in contemporary political debate.[5] Many countries that have large social welfare programs have entered an era of "permanent austerity" in that governments face multiple pressures to reduce government expenditures. Expensive social welfare programs appear as tempting areas for cuts. These programs, however, are very popular and cutting them is full of political risks for the governments that make efforts to reduce them. During the mid-1990s, in France, Germany, and Italy, proposals to cut social welfare costs stimulated the largest demonstrations in decades; the parties supporting the governments that made these proposals were tossed out of power in the next election. Nevertheless, pressures to reduce social welfare expenditures are likely to grow. Most of these countries have aging populations, and fewer active workers will have to pay state pension costs for the increasing numbers of retirees. International competition with countries having fewer benefits and lower wages will pressure entrepreneurs in the mature democracies to seek cuts in their labor costs. This is an issue that will continue to dominate the political scene in democracies for the next decade and beyond.

Education

Government support for universal education is an older and less controversial part of government social policies. By the end of the nineteenth century, most West European and North American countries had developed programs for universal education, first for boys and later for girls, through the early teen years. The state first made primary and secondary education available and later made it compulsory for a set number of years. In the United States, this involved the creation of local-based public schools; in other countries the central government kept education under its control and set up public schools that often competed with private, religious schools.

In many settings, especially countries with strong Roman Catholic traditions, the process of bringing the state into education paralleled struggles to limit the role of the Church in society and the state. As a result, it was a highly politicized and sensitive issue. In some countries, state versus religious education remains a sensitive subject with continuing controversies over state subsidies to private, church-operated schools—as in France—or over state directions on curriculum in countries where the separate schools exist and remain under the control of Catholic and Protestant churches—as in some German states and parts of Canada. For example, in the 1980s, there were massive demonstrations in France bringing literally millions of people into the streets, first in support of church schools and later to back public schools when the government proposed ending and then increasing subsidies to private schools.

Unlike in the United States where there are many private universities, higher education is usually provided only by the state. Britain is a partial exception where private institutions dating to medieval times—such as Cambridge and Oxford—provide the elite education. Elsewhere, private universities are uncommon and usually less prestigious than the state universities. For example, in Germany, with the exception of a few church-owned institutions, the universities are state facilities funded and directed by the lander (regional-level) governments. And in Japan, most institutions of higher education—and all the prestigious ones—are state universities.

Everywhere in Europe and North America, the numbers of students attending universities have dramatically increased, often by as much as ten times the numbers of twenty-five years ago. This has placed severe strains on universities to provide adequate classroom space, laboratories, libraries, and instructors for the larger number of students. These shortages often result in poorer-quality educational experiences and the devaluation of the university degree. In the past, university degrees were passports to successful careers; today in many countries so many people have university educations that the degree no longer has the same ability to ensure good employment opportunities. As a result, even though more young people from modest backgrounds now go to university, the degrees they earn do not provide assurance of the kinds of jobs that the more privileged few in the past were able to find after completing university educations.

Developing countries have more challenges in allotting limited resources for public education. The most important task is providing greater literacy. Whereas well over 90 percent of the population is literate in developed countries, the literacy level is much lower in developing countries. (See Table 11.3.) As a result, priority is usually given to primary and secondary education. But there is also pressure for state support to higher education in order to provide university education for students who cannot afford to go abroad. Often, universities are seen as symbols of achievement in development. As a result, there is often regional competition to establish new universities. For example, in Nigeria each of the twenty or so states wants its own university as a prestige symbol of its standing. But there are not enough resources (money, qualified instructors, students) to support such a large university system. As a result, funds that might have been used to improve primary and secondary schools are devoted to propping up uneconomical and unneeded universities. Nigeria is not alone in facing the problems of allocating scarce state funds for the most needed types of education. Throughout the developing world, educational needs from the primary level through universities still go wanting.

Education has great value for the modern state because it is the most important element in enabling its citizens to become active participants in the political process. The better educated a person is the more likely that person is to become involved in politics. Literacy not only creates good workers for modern economies, it also is essential for good citizens. As one scholar noted: "[Public

TABLE **11.3**　Literacy Rates in Selected Countries

Country	Literacy Rate of Adult Population
Britain	100%
Germany	100
Japan	100
France	99
Russia	99
Canada	97
Italy	97
United States	97
Mexico	90
Brazil	85
China	82
Nigeria	57
India	52

Source: The World Almanac and Book of Facts 2000 (New York: World Almanac, 2000).

education] enables individuals to become citizens capable of discovering common ground and rendering sound political judgment."[6]

Environmental Protection

In 1985, lethal gases escaped from a Union Carbide pesticide plant in Bhopal, India, killing nearly seven thousand people and blinding or seriously injuring several hundred thousand other residents. Indian government officials accused Union Carbide of negligence. Fifteen years later the catastrophe still marks the people and economy of Bhopal. Many environmental activists argued that the Bhopal disaster was the kind of abuse possible when Western corporations escape environmental protection laws in developed countries by building plants in third world countries, where laws are less strict or poorly enforced. Eager for the economic benefits of new industries, third world countries sometimes tolerate environmental dangers or damage that would not be allowed in developed countries. As the new century begins, environmental awareness is very strong in developed countries and becoming greater even in developing countries as a result of accidents and abuses such as those at Bhopal.

Environmental protection has become a central issue in the politics of most industrial nations.[7] Influential environmental interest groups and smaller but still important ecology political parties now press democratic governments throughout the world to consider the environment as a valuable and endangered part of our lives. More and more, governments are expected to play a leading role in cleaning up pollution and preventing the further degradation of the environment we all live in.

Environmental concern is a priority in already developed countries that have achieved a certain degree of prosperity. In such settings, governments can "afford" to pay attention to the protection of the environment. Their citizens have had basic needs satisfied and have attained a degree of economic well-being. They are increasingly concerned that government now devote efforts to promote control of potentially unsafe food additives, more ecologically harmonious sanitary waste disposal, less-polluting factories and cars, and a pleasing countryside. But it is the comfortable who are most likely to call for greater government involvement in such environmental protection, and they do so more often when environmental protection will not affect their livelihoods. For example, in Britain air pollution legislation was poorly enforced at the grass-roots level because the local authorities knew that the cost of installing cleaners might force the closing of factories their voters depended upon for their employment. As a result, in Britain and in other democratic governments, environmental legislation is usually more effective when it comes from and is enforced by national governments that are more insulated from local economic pressures. Citizens may protest against the location of new installations such as water treatment plants, power stations, or dumps out of the NIMBY (not in my backyard) effect, but they are equally uneasy about new environmental controls that affect their existing jobs.

In industrialized, democratic societies, governments have generally responded to environmental concerns by establishing new air quality standards, food inspection and nutritional requirements, water treatment programs, and many other new ecologically motivated programs. The governments of many countries have reacted to environmental concerns by curtailing what were once rather ambitious plans for nuclear power production as a replacement for costly coal- and oil-fired generators. Nearly every government now has a ministry of the environment to direct such programs and to defend an environmental agenda in government deliberations. But there are often surprising gaps in the environmental programs. They come from the economic concerns about the impact on jobs and also out of traditions that people do not want to abandon. For example, the Germans are generally supportive of protecting the environment, but those in the eastern states resist the closing of plants that pollute the air; Germans in the west are defiant of suggestions that they adopt laws to limit the speed on their autobahn even though the 90–100 mph speeds produce more air pollution and consume more precious petroleum than would be the case at lower speeds.

In a way, the concerns of industrialized nations with their environmental problems seem out of proportion when compared with the unchecked damage to the environment in developing countries. New Delhi, Mexico City, and Lagos are among the most polluted cities in the world. An estimated 1.3 billion people in the less developed world live where air is highly polluted. Four million children under the age of five die each year from respiratory disease linked to unsafe air in these urban areas or in rural huts heated by cow dung or wood fires; another 3.8 million die from intestinal disease resulting from unsanitary conditions.[8] In the crowded suburbs and less populated rural areas of developing countries, people wash in the same water they drink and have primitive, open sewage facilities or no sewage treatment at all.

Beyond this absence of even the most basic environmental care in third world countries is an even more strident clash between environmental concerns and the need for industrial development than characterizes similar debates in the developed world. Peoples in the developing world have urgent needs for factories, power plants, and new agricultural land in order to support growing populations and build stronger economies. They see these needs as more pressing than concern for air pollution or protecting endangered species. And there is some logic behind it. A new coal-fired power plant providing electricity that makes possible new jobs, lighted schools, clean heat for houses, and refrigerators to keep food safe, makes sense for these peoples even if the power plant is environmentally "dirty."

Westerners complain, and rightly so, about development and deforestation of tropical areas in Brazil or Africa, the spread of polluting factories and power plants, and destruction of endangered species in the developing world. But those in the developing world respond, correctly too, that westerners can afford to make such complaints only because they have already achieved prosperity and solved the far more basic environmental challenges of clean water, safe heating, and sewage and trash treatment. There are westerners who recognize the link between economic development and pollution and who are willing to accept a simpler, less materialistic world. Few of them, however, are willing to accept poverty or impure water, loss of sewage treatment, and unsafe foods in exchange. Yet that is what is often asked of people in the developing world when environmentalists press their concerns on them. And third world requests for additional development funds to enable them to practice more environmental protection fall on deaf ears.

Human Rights

The measuring of a country's protection of human rights is even more difficult than assessing its success in providing for security, economic growth, and social programs. The standards of measurement are even more diverse, and the relative importance of basic rights varies from one setting to the next. Americans pride themselves on their extensive civil liberties and the legal system that enforces them. But many Americans encounter racial, gender, or religious discrimination that undermines these rights. What count as important rights for the majority are not always shared by minorities in our midst. There are many controversies that surround such issues. Recently, for example, many university and college campuses have tried to find the balance between the First Amendment right of free expression and the need to prevent racist and sexist slurs that create hostile environments and hinder learning for many. Americans cherish freedom of the press, but those who advocate unorthodox ideas are unable to find forums in newspapers and electronic media that are attuned to advertisers interested in avoiding controversial programs. These issues are not easy to resolve for ourselves.

If we cannot fairly judge ourselves, it is even more difficult to make judgments on the human rights records of other countries. Even among countries with very similar backgrounds, the value and importance placed on human rights varies widely. For example, Americans place religious freedom at the top of their lists of rights to be defended; the British and French place free expression at the top of their lists. Many peoples in other developed and democratic countries are less insistent on the rights of the individual and more interested in community rights than are most Americans.

Of course, the contrasting priorities in human rights become even more dramatic when we compare our American notions of liberties with those in other parts of the world. The American preoccupation with the rights of private property and free enterprise is not shared in many parts of the world where people are more concerned with community rights and collective goals. People in many countries, such as Russia, China, and many developing countries, feel that economic rights such as the right to work and social justice based on equality are more important than the individual liberties and political rights that Americans stress. Often, developing world leaders complain about Western tutelage on human rights agendas that differ from their own cultural background. During a visit to Washington a few years ago, the Malaysian prime minister reminded his hosts that Asian countries often value social harmony over personal freedom and criticized the Western world for trying to impose its values on less developed countries.[9]

The protection of human rights involves three requirements. First, there must be a statement of the basic rights to be protected in a country. Second, there need to be independent courts that enforce these rights against abuses by individuals and the government. Finally, the state must abide by the rule of law, accept the courts' decisions, and seek to comply with the formal guarantees of civil liberties.

Nearly all countries in the world have accepted the United Nations Declaration of Human Rights. This document includes a long list of what most Americans would consider to be essential rights. In addition, most European countries have accepted a similar catalog of civil and personal liberties as signatories of the European Convention of Human Rights. They accept the jurisdiction of the supranational European Court of Human Rights as an ultimate appellate body for alleged human rights violations in their countries. It is clear that many countries that accept these human rights pledges simply do so in order to be regarded as good citizens in the world community. In practice they do little more than pay lip service to these international human rights standards and feel little obligation to observe these rights in actual domestic politics. However, at the start of the twenty-first century there does appear to be more international moral consensus on basic human rights than has ever before been the case.

Serious abuses of human rights by governments still are found in more than half the countries of the world. This comes from the absence of independent courts that are able to issue decisions that might go against the will and preferences of those holding power. In many countries, courts lack independence and exist to serve and protect the interests and choices of the rulers rather than the ruled. Access to courts may be limited by formal or informal restraints on individuals with human rights grievances against the state, the courts themselves biased against the individual, the entire legal system designed to impose laws on the people and not on the state or its leaders, or all three of these problems may exist, effectively closing off opportunities for the redress of civil rights abuses. For example, such a tight control over the courts prevents citizens in China from seeking relief from human rights violations. The mass arrests and mysterious deaths of detained members of the Falun Gong religious sect in the early years of the twenty-first century demonstrate China's continued repression of groups and ideas thought to be challenges—even remote ones—to the Party's dominance.

Finally, governments need to accept and abide by court rulings on their conduct in the area of civil liberties. They should not only accept court jurisdiction and rulings but also strive to behave according to the law and the courts' interpretation of the law even when cases are not adjudicated. For example, during most of the eras of military rule in Nigeria, the authoritarian military leaders abided by the decisions of the courts and generally accepted judicial limits on the exercise of state power. However, in 1993, the government of General Sani Abacha left the courts in place but ignored their rulings on civil liberties, closed down critical newspapers, deported foreign journalists, and intimidated or arrested Nigerian civil rights advocates. Nigeria's generally good reputation for human rights, even when under authoritarian regimes, soon suffered.

Despite such problems, some contend that the overall picture of human rights is improving. The end of the cold war and the fall of the rigid authoritarian

TABLE 11.4   Measures of Freedom in Selected Countries

Country	2000			1980		
	Political Rights	Civil Liberties	Status	Political Rights	Civil Liberties	Status
Brazil	3	4	Partly free	4	3	Partly free
Britain	1	2	Free	1	1	Free
Canada	1	1	Free	1	1	Free
China	7	7	Not free	6	6	Not free
France	1	2	Free	1	2	Free
Germany	1	2	Free	1	2	Free (West)
				7	6	Not free (East)
India	2	3	Free	2	2	Free
Italy	1	2	Free	2	2	Free
Japan	1	2	Free	2	1	Free
Mexico	1	2	Free	3	3	Partly free
Nigeria	4	3	Partly free	2	3	Free
Russia	4	5	Partly free	6	6	Not free (USSR)
United States	1	1	Free	1	1	Free

1 = Most free; 7 = least free

Source: Freedom House, *Freedom in the World 1980* (New York: Freedom House) and Freedom House website: www.freedomhouse.org.

communist regimes has generally reduced the extent of government oppression in many parts of the world. According to Freedom House, a U.S.-based organization that measures democracy and human rights throughout the world, there are many more "free" and "partly free" countries now than two decades ago. (See Table 11.4.) On the other hand, monitors of human rights, such as Amnesty International, still find considerable evidence of abuses even among countries with generally good records. There appears to be stronger international public opinion against the most extreme abuses as evidenced by the world community's reaction against human rights violations in Rwanda, Somalia, Haiti, and elsewhere. But international pressures can be ignored or offset. China, for example, was able to deflect international pressures against its limits on the freedom of its people despite attempts by the United States to link improved trading conditions with commitments to greater Chinese respect for human rights. Countries like the United States, France, and Britain are strongly committed to human rights, but they also want access to China's rapidly growing markets.

CONCLUSION

This chapter includes my own assessments, which you may not share. More so than other parts of political science, the task of evaluating policies and polities is fraught with personal biases and subjective judgments. Yet such evaluations are needed as we, as citizens, judge our own government's performance and prepare to reward or punish those in office when we go to the polls. It is also important to evaluate the records of other countries to see if they have policies or procedures that are better than ours and should be emulated in our own country. I invite you to make your own evaluations based on your own informed value preferences of political performance at home and abroad.

NOTES

1. Mancur Olson, "Dictatorship, Democracy, and Development," *American Political Science Review* 87 (September 1993): 567–576.

2. John Herz, *International Politics in the Atomic Age* (New York: Columbia University Press, 1959).

3. "Measuring the Price of Politics," *The Economist*, 27 January 1996, p. 72.

4. Silvio Borner, Aymo Brunetti, and Beatrice Weder, eds., *Political Credibility and Economic Development* (London: Macmillan, 1995).

5. Paul Pierson, ed., *The New Politics of the Welfare State* (Oxford, England: Oxford University Press, 2001).

6. Benjamin R. Barber, *An Aristocracy of Everyone: The Politics of Education and the Future of America* (New York: Oxford University Press, 1992), p. 267.

7. Sheldon Kamieniecki, ed., *Environmental Politics in the International Arena: Movements, Parties, Organizations, and Policy* (Buffalo: State University of New York Press, 1993).

8. See Gregg Esterbook, "Forget PCB's, Radon, Alar." *The New York Times Magazine,* 11 September 1994, pp. 60–63.

9. Agence Française de Presse, 22 May 1996.

Chapter 12

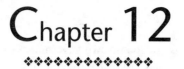

The Politics of Change

The world we live in is one of constant change, and the changes in society, culture, and economics bring political transformation as well. The relationship is reciprocal: Often political transformation leads to social, cultural, and economic changes. At times, the changes are almost imperceptible and it requires observation over lengthy periods of time to take note of the direction and extent of change in our societies. At other times, revolutionary change disrupts the lives and beings of virtually everyone.

As the new century begins, there is much to suggest that the beginning decades of the twenty-first century will be times of unprecedented change. This rapid change is less likely to be caused by violence, as were the changes at the beginning of the twentieth century, but more likely to be the result of the closer interaction of all parts of our globe. Vast world wars brought most of the major changes—both good and bad—during the twentieth century. But in the new century, change is likely to occur simply because of new technologies that at once bring causes for adaptation and spread the new technologies and one area's responses to them more rapidly throughout the world. Communications and transportation enhance change by allowing transformations, which in the past would have been restricted to a small area or a country, to affect the entire world.

It appears unlikely that the kind of worldwide violence that characterized much of the twentieth century will recur in the next few decades. Comprehensive world wars between powerful, large world powers seem less menacing now, but the dangers to people in many parts of the world may be equally great in smaller conflicts and civil wars. Such conflicts are nihilistic in that they are often devoid of idealism and ideology. Even today's small wars that seem driven by ethnic nationalism or religious fundamentalism are conflicts where "violence has freed itself from ideology."[1] In such settings, combatants seem as likely to destroy themselves and their supporters as they are to defeat their enemies and bring meaningful change. Even if global war recedes as a danger—and a source of change—and the nihilism is isolated to remote regions, there remain other crises that will need to be faced through global cooperation. Among them is the obvious need to respond to the political, economic, and social challenges of an infinitely growing world population and finite world resources. In responding to this need, not to change at all is clearly unacceptable, but some changes may worsen rather than ameliorate the crises faced by the world today.

Despite the need for major adaptations, people in general fear the unknowns that might be unleashed by visible change. Psychologists and anthropologists have discovered a yearning for order, continuity, and predictability as a near universal human instinct.[2] In politics, this is reflected in the search for *political stability*. The concept of political stability, however, is often rather vaguely defined. In most usages, political stability refers to a polity characterized by a durable political regime, continuity in power of a set of leaders, popular acceptance of the regime and leaders as legitimate, and absence of politically driven violence. As desirable as political stability may often be, political scientists are able to give only vague explanations as to what brings stability: There are poor and wealthy countries that experience long periods of stability and countries at all levels of prosperity that succeed or fail to achieve political stability. Many democratic regimes are stable but others are not; many authoritarian regimes are unstable but others are quite stable.

Indeed, it is often difficult to determine whether or not a country is stable when we try to apply a definition based on durability, continuity, maintenance of public order, and legitimacy to real-world situations. For example, most observers of the Soviet Union believed their communist regime to be stable as late as 1990. The regime was over seventy years old; the same leaders held power without challenge for decades; people accepted the regime for the exceptional scientific advancements, economic progress, and international position it had brought; they appreciated the order that it provided and the virtual absence of domestic violence. Knowledgeable observers held that view right up to the last moment, when events proved that the communist regime was in fact so unstable that it could not sustain itself against even a poorly organized and divided opposition. On the other hand, many people have looked at the constant turmoil in Japan and labeled it as unstable because of its short-lived governments, endemic political corruption, skeptical public, and occasional violent demonstrations. But the Japanese regime continues to muddle through one crisis after another. In short, often regimes that look durable and legitimate fall while others that look shaky and illegitimate endure one challenge after another.

Perhaps these errors come because we neglect a crucial and paradoxical element in stability: change. Although change is the logical opposite of stability, some change appears to be necessary for political stability. To endure and enjoy continued legitimacy, regimes must adjust to changing circumstances in their own societies, cultures, and economies and also to a changing world setting. Political stability, then, does not mean rigidity but ordered change.

In some societies the economic, social, and political status quo becomes so insufferable that many people may be willing to endure disorder and violence in order to alter their conditions. In recent years, violent struggles for change have occurred in many parts of the world as peoples concluded that even the risk of injury or death was not enough to make them accept the status quo: Indians in southern Mexico, Muslims in India, advocates of democracy in Nigeria, Russia, and China. Such peoples have fallen so far into despair that any change—even one that may be disruptive or violent—is better than a continuation of existing conditions. There does not have to be a solution in sight or clear alternatives; despair over deep-seated and enduring inequities produces a lack of respect for existing institutions and the urge to destroy them even if the path to improvement is not clear.

CHANGE, REFORM, AND REVOLUTION

Political change can take at least three distinctive forms, and it can do so simultaneously or separately.[3] Political change may be little more than almost unconscious adjustments to gradual alterations in technology, citizen attitudes, and socioeconomic structures. A second and greater degree of change involves shifts in the personnel of government or in their policy priorities as one set of leaders replaces another or as the same set of leaders reconsiders its programs. A third and even greater level of change results from deliberate efforts to transform existing political structures and economic systems. In most countries, the first two of these types of change are usually always at work; the more comprehensive systemic transformations of the third type are less frequent in developed democracies but not absent even there. For example, some in the United States seek radical solutions to the institutional deadlock that has characterized Washington politics for over a decade. Even more serious efforts at institutional reform are under consideration in Japan, where endemic political corruption has undermined public support for democratic institutions and parties.

Reform

The most common form of change comes through reform. Reform involves the gradual adjustment of existing social institutions or public policy to respond to technological, social, economic, or political changes. The pace of change may be so gradual as to be almost imperceptible; it may even be unconscious or undirected as institutions and people adapt automatically and almost imperceptibly to new settings. For example, over the past two decades the position of women in politics and society has radically changed in nearly every country, not always because of concrete policy reforms but rather because of shifting attitudes and cultural values that emerged from higher education levels, new work patterns, and changing family relationships. In Chapter 3, in discussing the gradual decline of social class and the political transformation it has brought, I pointed to another example of un-conscious political change brought about by technological and economic changes.

There is little doubt that other such forces for change are at work now shap-ing patterns of further political transformation. For example, technologies of the last decade have radically altered patterns of communication and seem likely to do so for the coming decade. Out of the new electronic superhighways are likely to come new patterns of political participation and decision making based on the new forms of communication. It does not take a great leap in imagination to think of a nearby future where every television would not only receive public affairs broad-casting on the lines of C-SPAN but also have a panel of buttons for citizens to enter their policy preferences as a way of direct involvement in making public policy de-cisions. This and other changes will come without much planning or direction as the result of changing technologies and citizen attitudes.

On the other hand, reforms may be deliberate as leaders or their rivals rec-ognize needs and try to devise new approaches or institutions to meet them. Such change may be relatively limited in scope, such as the recent efforts in the United States to develop a national health system. Other reforms may be more compre-hensive in their consequences, such as the debates in Canada over the nature of the confederation and the impact of the possible secession by Quebec or perhaps other provinces. In such cases, change is planned and deliberate, although the reform often will not work as expected. The actual consequences of the changes may turn out to be unpredicted and even damaging to the goals sought by the reformers.

There are other still more sweeping efforts at fundamental change of political and economic institutions. Among the best examples of this is the current recon-struction of Russia in the postcommunist era. Since 1989, Russia has struggled with simultaneous efforts to bring radical change to its political structures, shift its eco-nomic system to a market economy, alter civic values from those established during centuries of autocracy, and overcome the consequences of decades of state oppres-sion in dealing with its citizens. Russian leaders opted initially for the fast track to re-form with efforts to simultaneously and immediately move to a free enterprise econ-omy, democracy, and respect for individual civil liberties. Progress toward all three of these goals was limited by the scope of the operation and the inability of the regime to focus on any single area of change. As a result, Russia is still far from dem-ocratic; civil rights abuses continue by police forces that no one controls; and the economy is in shambles. The once powerful Russian economy suffered especially as reformers pushed a "big bang" approach to economic change with immediate cur-rency decontrol, an end to price controls, rapid privatization, and opening the once closed Russian economy to foreign investors.[4] The result was a sharp drop in in-dustrial output (with the 1993 figure less than 50 percent of output in 1990), hyper-inflation, shortages of basic products, and the flourishing of a criminal black market. The versions of democracy and capitalism that have emerged in Russia have re-flected the old communist propaganda that democracy is dominated by ruthless eco-nomic monopolists and that "making money in a free society is a purely predatory and criminal activity."[5] As a result, democracy was discredited and Russians began to yearn for a strong leader to reimpose economic order; citizens cry now for the abridgement of civil liberties that seem to have been more successful in unleashing a crime wave than in improving the quality of their lives.

One of the crucial factors in understanding the effects of change in meeting expectations and in avoiding disruption of existing patterns is the pace of change. Obviously, slow change occurring over decades is less likely to be disruptive of existing patterns and politics than is sudden change. An illustration of change through slow reform can be seen in the case of the development of British democracy over several centuries. Historians differ on when the threshold was passed and the old autocracy gave way to democracy: The ascension of parliament over the monarch in the seventeenth century? The extension of the electorate to most males in the nineteenth century? The 1911 law granting the popularly elected House of Commons supremacy over the aristocratic House of Lords? The achievement of full adulthood suffrage in 1924? Or the further extension of the franchise to young adults eighteen and older in 1970? It was a slow process that was prodded on not only by reformers but by conservatives who hoped to preserve their influence and what traditions they could by co-opting change from their rivals. The evolution was often unnoticed until much later. For example, at some time in the mid-twentieth century, an understanding developed that the prime minister must always be from the House of Commons rather than from the unelected House of Lords. But that understanding was never fully recognized until an aspirant for the prime ministership in the 1960s, Lord Home, confirmed it by renouncing his hereditary aristocratic rights to become a commoner, Sir Alec Douglas-Home, and eventually prime minister.

The recent Russian experience stands as an illustration of the opposite approach to slow reform. Since 1985, changes affecting all parts of Russian society have been occurring simultaneously and without much central control. So too does the French historical pattern of rapid change over many different parts of the state and society in short periods of time. Many of the issues that had been resolved over centuries in England were addressed at once and in the charged setting of a revolution: membership in the "nation," economics, social structures, church-state relations, rights of citizenship, and the definition of democracy. Out of this explosion of violence and change has come a string of revolutions, insurgencies, uprisings, coups, and near revolts as a constant feature of French history for over two hundred years. They leave a legacy of unpredicted and uncontrolled change that makes future revolts a very real possibility even as the country has acquired stable and effective democratic government. Even today, French governments often back away from modest planned changes because they fear that those opposed will take to the streets in a process that may escalate into a civil revolt.[6]

In today's industrial democracies, reform comes more frequently through deliberate and gradual efforts to adjust the existing policies and institutions to meet new or continuing demands without disrupting the overall pattern of things. In this sense, change is incremental and gradual, with often minor adjustments of the status quo as governors seek to respond to new circumstances. Over time, such incremental change may lead to extensive transformations, but they have come step by step, a little at a time. There is always the danger that the reforms will occur so slowly that they will be outstripped by demands for change from new technological, attitudinal, or social demands. Incremental change may also be too slow for those who feel that the process is unacceptable. As an example, peoples of Los Angeles, Johannesburg in South Africa, and Lagos in Nigeria have all taken to the streets because the rate of change was so slow as to be of little or no value to them in responding to their senses of deprivation and oppression.

Revolution

In this discussion of change through reform, two sets of alternatives can be seen at play: the pace of change and the presence or absence of violence. For the most part, reform involves nonviolent, gradual change. But there are episodes of violence that motivate reforms and eras when change is very rapid and comprehensive. Sometimes such thorough, fast-paced, and even violent change is labeled as revolutionary. Revolutions involve more than simply the change in a regime, which is often accomplished by a coup d'état that involves only a handful of elite-level participants and may even be accomplished with little or no violence. Revolutions are usually thought of as involving all of the following characteristics: a change in entire regimes in addition to leadership or party changes; a mass uprising of the people; extensive violence; and efforts (not always successful) to achieve extensive, rapid, and concurrent changes in values, social structures, and economic institutions.

Many scholars have tried to identify the causes of revolution, but there is little consensus. Indeed, what explains one revolution does not necessarily explain another. Conditions that brought revolution in one country exist in other countries without the occurrence of revolution. It is likely that the causes are multiple in any given country, and the conditions that bring revolution in one country may be different from what produced revolution elsewhere. Many revolutions have been driven by peasant uprisings;[7] others are urban-based. Some seem to occur when social and economic conditions are actually improving, but a slowing in the pace of improvement may mean that expectations exceed accomplishments.[8] Some see revolutions as the product of modernization,[9] while others argue that modernization is not the key factor.[10]

In addition to these other factors, some societies seem more inclined to conflict—and thus to revolution—than do others.[11] Aspects of the political culture—such as trust in others, sense of security and well-being, and perceptions of the ability of individuals and groups to shape their futures—that are developed in youth and cultivated by adulthood experiences affect a people's willingness to push conflicts to violent levels.

The difficulty of explaining revolution is well illustrated by the recent revolution in Eastern Europe and Russia that ended communism and brought two dozen new states into being. Even the most perceptive observers of communism failed to see the strength of the revolutionary forces that were welling up in these countries, and specialists in revolution are still struggling to explain why the revolt occurred at the time it did. One observer discusses a number of alternative explanations for this revolution and concludes that the revolution occurred because a new generation of young people emerged who did not realize that revolution was impossible.[12] This new generation therefore tried to revolt and found the communist systems to be surprisingly vulnerable. If these young people had believed as did their parents that revolution was impossible, the mighty changes that occurred in Eastern Europe and the Soviet Union may well not have taken place.

One analyst compared our efforts to explain revolution to efforts to understand when earthquakes occur:

> When one occurs, scholars try to make sense of the data they have collected and to build theories to account for the next one. Gradually, we gain a fuller understanding of revolutions and the conditions behind them. And yet the next one still surprises us.[13]

The twentieth century is often referred to as the era of revolutions. Indeed, there were several major revolutions that punctuated this century: the Irish revolt of 1916–1923; the Mexican Revolution of 1910–1917; the Chinese Revolutions of 1911 and 1949; the Russian Revolutions of 1917 and 1918; the Kemalist revolution in Turkey in 1923; the Spanish Civil War of 1936–1939; the decolonization revolutions of 1947–1967 throughout Asia and Africa; the Iranian Revolution of 1979; and the antiapartheid revolution in South Africa of 1983–1994.

Most recently, there have been the anticommunist revolts of 1989–1991 that brought regime changes, new leaders, fundamental and comprehensive socioeconomic transformation, and major shifts in social and civic values. These revolts have very literally redrawn the world map and entirely restructured international relations at the beginning of the new century. They were broad-based, popular revolts that started nearly spontaneously. They lacked, however, the widespread violence that is usually associated with revolutions.

The absence of mass violence in most of these anticommunist revolutions suggests one reason to believe that old-style revolutions with mass violence may not be as common a feature in the future as they have been in the twentieth century. States usually have enormous power capabilities to keep their people in line and limit civil disobedience. This in itself is a major deterrent to revolution. But the power of modern armies also deters governments from using that power to suppress dissent. Even autocratic leaders are usually reluctant to use such power against their own people, and their military and security forces are similarly disinterested in using their full power on a mass of their fellow citizens. The August 1991 coup by supporters of the crumbling communist regime in Russia failed in part because the military was unwilling to fire on the pro-democracy crowds that jammed Red Square and other sites in Moscow, Leningrad, and other cities.

There are exceptions to this: The tragedy of Tiananmen Square in China is clearly a case when the full force of the state was employed against unarmed student advocates for democracy. However, at the end of the century of revolutions, the spreading sense of the need for democracy, the state's capability for repression, and respect for the rights of individuals restricted the use of violence by the state to protect oppressive regimes.

There are still peoples who will want to revolt, but they are not as likely to need the extensive violence that characterized revolutions of the twentieth century. A case in point is the reaction of the Mexican government to the revolt in Chiapas state in early 1994. In the past, such revolts would have been ruthlessly put down by the Mexican army. This time, a regime concerned with its international reputation and democratic aspirations responded with much greater care and with considerable effort to understand and respond to the grievances that incited the revolt.

But the disinclination among the discontented to resort to violent revolt and the state's hesitation to use its full repressive powers do not necessarily mean that we are entering a more peaceful era of politics. The Mexican example also suggests another consequence of the reluctance to engage in full-scale civil war or revolution: Those opposed to the regime often resort to guerrilla warfare and terrorism in order to express their vehement dissatisfaction with both their socioeconomic conditions and their inability to find other effective means of expressing that dissent. And states unwilling to use their full capacity for violence on their own people resort to state terrorism against their domestic enemies. Hence, in many parts of the world guerrilla warfare is endemic as the discontented seek change in the only ways possible. We tend to see this as a problem of the developing world, but many industrial democracies—including Britain, France, Germany, and the United States—experience terrorist violence from very dissatisfied groups. Such violence from small, isolated groups on the fringes of society is often nihilistic and without clear or realistic goals. Thus, we enter an era of "molecular civil war," which may be as troubling and as difficult to control as the revolutions and global wars of the past.[14]

DEMOCRATIZATION

If the consequences of the ending of the era of revolution are not bright, there is some consolation in the opening of what many see as a new era of democratization. Over the past twenty-five years, a number of once autocratic regimes have embarked on democratization. The achievements are still partial and fragile in many settings.[15] But those who see democracy as the best practical form of government and as a potential source of a more peaceful world can take satisfaction in the shifts away from dictatorships to democracy.

This is part of a general trend toward democracy that began in the mid-1970s. Freedom House, an independent organization committed to promoting democracy, calculated that in December 2000, 86 countries were "free" in the sense of providing for the basic political rights and civil liberties of their peoples.[16] That accounted for 2.5 billion people or 40.7 percent of the world's population. More people lived in freedom than ever before in world history. Another 59 countries, with a total population of 1.4 billion people, 23.6 percent of the world's total, were "partly free." Nearly two-thirds of the world's population lived under free or partly free conditions. An earlier Freedom House report found that in 2000 there were 120 electoral democracies (63 percent), more than ever before in history. In 1900, no country would have met today's standard for democracy; in 1950, only 22 (28 percent of the independent countries of that era) were democratic.[17]

This movement has occurred in all parts of the world: In Western Europe, long-standing dictatorships in Spain and Portugal and a shorter-lived military dictatorship in Greece have been replaced by stable democracies. In South America, only three of the twelve countries could be regarded as democratic in 1983; in 2000, eleven were democratic. The fall of communism in Eastern Europe and the former Soviet Union produced over twenty new democracies—although in many of these former communist states the long-term success of democracy is by no means certain. In Asia, democracy replaced the autocracy in the Philippines and new pressure for democratic change was felt in Taiwan, South Korea, Indonesia, and many other countries. In Africa, South Africa at long last replaced its repressive system of apartheid with a fledgling democracy for everyone. Nigeria began civilian rule in 2000 following competitive elections.

But the movement to democracy is by no means complete or successful. The tragedy of the pro-democracy movement in China is an example of the resistance of many authoritarian regimes to the new wave of democratization. None of the eleven Arab countries can be classified as democratic or free; of forty-one predominantly Muslim countries, only eight hold democratic elections and only one is regarded as "free."[18] Many of the newly established democracies in Asia, Eastern Europe, and South America must struggle to endure with political cultures, ethnic mixtures, and economic situations that are hardly conducive to democracy. As a result, many of the new democracies are still in the delicate stage of consolidating and developing political and social institutions that will support democracy.

Some contend that these broad assessments of democratization overemphasize the actual spread of democracy. They focus too much attention on the achievement of "electoral" democracy in the form of competitive and basically free elections. Elections are an important feature of democracy but by no means the only or the most important gauges of the presence of democracy. One African observer notes the emergence of "virtual democracy" in parts of Africa where the rituals and symbols of democracy are present but not its substance. There, illusory democratic practices and institutions exist "to satisfy prevailing international norms of 'presentability.'"[19] To make democracy real, countries need also to accept and implement the rule of law and human rights. The "rule of law" involves the existence of a body of known statutes or practices. The equal enforcement of these laws on all—ruled and rulers, rich and poor—is vital in democratic regimes. This requires an impartial and effective judiciary and the willingness of the political elite to accede to judicial rulings. Full democracy also requires the effective enforcement of civil and social rights, again by an impartial judiciary committed to the values of human rights. Finally, democracies need the support of active and well-developed "civil societies" where autonomous groups exist to share powers with government and to offset the weight of governmental power.[20]

Economics and Democratization

Certainly, economic prosperity facilitates the establishment of new democracies. Germany provides a good example of both democratic failure and success based on economic performance. In the 1920s and early 1930s, the troubled German economy, hyperinflation, and the worldwide recession discredited the fledgling democracy established in 1918 and paved the way to Hitler's rise. In contrast, the economic miracle of the 1950s sustained democracy in West Germany even when a supporting political culture was still developing and provided a climate in which people came to associate their economic success with their democratic practices.[21]

But the relationship between economics and democracy is by no means deterministic. There are many countries that experience economic prosperity and remain autocratic; there are other poorly developed countries that sustain democracy without prosperity. But there does appear to be some relationship between prosperity and democracy. Leaders of newly established democracies certainly benefit when they do not have to contend with economic crises and when they do have economies with sufficient strength to satisfy the needs of many of their citizens. Many years ago, a political sociologist demonstrated the link between democracy and development.[22] Over the decades there have been some "statistical outlyers": wealthy countries that become or remain autocratic and impoverished countries that nevertheless succeed in building democracy. But the general relationship remains: Economically developed countries are more likely to be democratic than are underdeveloped ones.[23]

There is no reason in the abstract why democracy cannot thrive in a variety of economic settings—free enterprise or capitalism, socialism, mixed state and private sector economies, and perhaps even a brand of communism that is free from the authoritarianism of Lenin and Stalin. In practice, democracy performed well during the twentieth century in three of these economic settings: capitalism, socialism, and mixed economies.

There are many who argue that capitalism has inherent traits that promote democracy. Capitalism fosters pluralism or the presence in society of many independent groups with power to make economic decisions that have political and social consequences. Under a free enterprise system there are many autonomous actors who together are able to make decisions that otherwise would need to be made by government: decisions on wages, prices, what to produce, management styles, much of labor relations, and so on. The mere division of this decision-making power among private economic actors serves to place restrictions on the power of government as demanded by democratic principles of limited power. The free flow of ideas that is important to successful competition in economic matters is important in promoting democracy. As a society opens up for exchanges of ideas and technology needed for international commerce it is also exposed to political and social ideals from surrounding democratic countries.[24]

There are some apparent contradictions to the association of democracy and free enterprise capitalism. A number of countries have succeeded in building strong capitalist economies without consolidating democracy. This is seen in the slow progress toward democracy in many of the Asian newly industrialized countries (NICs), such as Taiwan, Singapore, Thailand, and South Korea. It is even more the case in China, where the leaders have pursued the privatization of the economy with energy while at the same time demonstrating equal or greater enthusiasm for political oppression and autocracy. Perhaps the time frame for evaluating such cases needs to be extended to allow time for the economic system to have an impact on political reform. There have been pressures for democracy in the NICs and even in China; it may be too soon to see the resistance of these capitalist and industrialized countries to democracy as a refutation of the general linkage between democracy and free enterprise.

There are also features of capitalism that seem inimical to democracy. Economic decisions are not always amenable to democratic policy making. For example, voters everywhere favor lowering taxes but maintaining the services that government provides them. Incumbent political leaders are tempted to prime the economy just before elections to gain support from voters who everywhere tend to "vote their pocketbooks." Both of these inherent tendencies in democracies result in large, uneconomic budget deficits and inflation. As a result, nearly every large industrial democracy bestows large amounts of power on undemocratic bodies like the American Federal Reserve or the European Central Bank to prevent some of those abuses that would have long-term consequences on inflation. In countries moving from state-dominated to free enterprise, such as Russia and other former communist states, this very process of privatization and freeing the economy requires a strong, central, even authoritarian government to press change on reluctant beneficiaries of the old system and to keep the process orderly during the transition. In this sense, economic liberalization (or moving toward market economies) may actually promote authoritarianism.[25]

Capitalism also leads to economic inequalities. Free market competition results in some getting more than others. Many are concerned that such economic inequality leads to the undermining of the fundamental democratic tenet of political equality: one person, one vote. The notion of political equality is difficult to maintain when there are excessive economic differences. Can anyone doubt that media mogul Rupert Murdoch has more political influence in Britain or the United States than an automobile worker in Detroit or a coal miner in Wales? Or believe that the president of the French electronics multinational Thompson has the same political clout as the owner of a small bookstore?

Democracy emerged in postwar Germany, Italy, and Japan in times of relative equality; everyone started out with little in the aftermath of the war. U.S. democracy was born and developed its roots in an era when economic differences were minor. One of the challenges facing large democracies such as Britain, France,

Germany, and the United States as we move into the new century will be making democracy work in societies that are divided by growing economic inequality.[26]

"Third Wave" Democratization

One author correctly notes that the current trend toward democracy marks the "third wave" of democratization in modern history.[27] The first "long" wave of democratization began with the American and French Revolutions, continued at a slow pace through the period just after World War I, and was succeeded by a reverse wave and the failure of democracy to fascism and communism. Then in the aftermath of World War II there was a "short" wave of democratization: Japan, Italy, West Germany, and new countries in many of the former colonial countries as they acquired independence. A second "reverse wave" saw the expansion of communism in many parts of the world and the rapid collapse of new democracies in the newly independent states, Latin America, and elsewhere as military coups and other forms of autocracy supplanted the new democracies.

A third wave of democratization began in the mid-1970s with the restoration of democracy in the Mediterranean regions of Europe (Greece, Portugal, and Spain). It included renewed efforts at democratic rule in Latin America and the transition to civilian rule in several Asian and African countries. The third wave reached its crest in the tumultuous end of the 1980s with the fall of communism in Eastern Europe and the establishment of new democratic successor states to the Soviet Union.

The sweeping democratization of this "third wave" has meant that new democracies have often been established in countries without much or any prior experience in limited and democratic government. The new democracies have untested leaders with little or no past acquaintance with the nuances and limits of democratic politics or indeed any experience in governance of any kind. Democracy requires, as one author notes, "patience, forbearance and moderation—qualities not common among political leaders."[28] Yet these new democratic leaders face exceptional economic and social challenges that would try even experienced leaders and well-entrenched democracies.

The economic challenges are particularly important for two reasons. First, many of the new democracies are trying to rapidly reform their economies, which inevitably brings confusion and reduced economic performance. Such economic disruption discredits the democracies as they start out. Second, many of those who called for democracy in Eastern Europe, Africa, Asia, Latin America, and elsewhere did so because they saw the prosperity enjoyed by the industrial democracies of North America and Western Europe and hoped that democracy in their lands would bring economic change and consumer societies. They want democracy more because they expect it will make them rich than because it is a means of giving power to the people.

There is little hope that such economic rewards of democracy will be arriving soon. Indeed, the immediate economic results in most of the new democracies that replaced communist regimes have been disappointing. Russia, for example, had a solid if troubled economy under communism, and it has experienced extraordinary economic distress as it has tried to build democracy. Table 12.1 shows how the Russian economy suffered in its first four years of postcommunist government by measuring the length of time an average worker had to work to earn enough to purchase various staples. The economy is finally improving in Russia, but with the still important increases in the cost of basic necessities and widespread corruption, one can readily understand why many Russians are now skeptical about the value of democracy. The economic failures so often occurring with democratization disillusion many of those who backed democratization more because they thought it would bring quick prosperity than for its intrinsic values as a form of government.

Many of the new democracies also face severe challenges in controlling ethnic violence unleashed by the disappearance of autocratic governments. To maintain the integrity of the country, pacify those with long-standing grievances, and preserve domestic peace in settings where centuries-old conflicts are reviving would try the skills and patience of even the best-established democracies. New democracies will find it difficult to avoid returning to the repression of old when ethnic conflict persists and even increases. Even where new democracies establish themselves, they may not be successful in disarming or weakening revolutionary or guerrilla movements within their borders.[29] This too will complicate the task of establishing order and thereby building democratic legitimacy.

Facing such severe challenges, it seems likely that some of these new democracies will not last. Even if many of the new democracies fail, the current trend toward democracy will leave important legacies for future experiments with democratization. One such legacy is what now appears to be a general sense throughout most parts of the world that democracy is the desired form of government. A second legacy may well be that even these brief democratic episodes in many countries that lack prior democratic experience will provide examples and build aspi-

TABLE **12.1**   Costs of Selected Items in Time Worked in Russia

Item	Amount of Time Worked to Earn Enough to Purchase Item		
	1990	*1992*	*1994*
Pound of sugar	13 minutes	61 minutes	29 minutes
Pound of bread	3 minutes	17 minutes	14 minutes
1/2 gallon milk	19 minutes	76 minutes	70 minutes
Pound of sausage	54 minutes	197 minutes	147 minutes
Gasoline (gallon)	49 minutes	187 minutes	76 minutes
Woman's dress	6 days	9 days	6 days
Man's suit	12 days	22 days	11 days
Television	54 days	253 days	71 days

Source: New York Times, 16 October 1994.

rations that future leaders can draw upon to construct more durable democratic regimes. Finally, the embracing of democratic norms by peoples everywhere will make it more likely that even those who rule autocratically will claim to be democratic. Such "pretend democracy" may be worse than no democracy at all if it discredits the democratic ideals.[30] On the other hand, some leaders who might otherwise be inclined to authoritarianism may be forced by national and international expectations of democracy to pay more heed to some democratic niceties and civil liberties. For example, some claim that this need to meet the heightened expectation of democracy among Mexican citizens and their international partners is part of the reason for Mexico's endeavors for greater democracy during the last decade.

Alternative Models of Democratization?

Democracy in the modern era has been defined by the values, experiences, and institutions of the Western world. I earlier defined democracy (see Chapter 1) as based on free and competitive elections, the rule of law, and effective guarantees of basic human rights. This is the democratic pattern that has succeeded in North America and Western Europe. There are examples of successful "Western" democracies in non-Western settings. In India and Japan "Western-like" democracies have succeeded with only minor modifications to fit different cultural heritages. However, the Western model is also the pattern that has been tried and failed many times in other settings where Western values and traditions are weak or nonexistent.

In Africa, Asia, and South America the Western version of democracy has more often faltered in the past than it has succeeded. These failures have prompted some scholars from non-Western countries to urge searches for new models of democracy that would be more compatible with their traditions and cultures. Twenty years ago, it might have been possible to propose that such an alternative might be found in democratic forms of communism, but the collapse of communism in Eastern Europe and the Soviet Union has destroyed most hope for a reconciliation of communism and democracy. Revelations of the brutal nature of Leninist and Stalinist versions of communism leave few who still see democratic communism as a possible alternative to Western democracy.

Elsewhere the hunt for third world alternatives has also been disappointing. African intellectuals decry Western democracy's reliance on the ballot box form of democracy and call for new forms of democracy based on Africa's "historical mosaic of economies and modes of social organization."[31] However, it is far easier to point to the limitations of the Western model of democracy than it is to uncover new democratic patterns that conform to the special conditions that exist in Africa or other parts of the developing world. And perhaps it is too much to expect that such a model should be developed ahead of time. After all, Western democracy evolved over many decades, and sometimes centuries, before it fit the circumstances of Western Europe and North America. An African intellectual, Claude Ake, writes:

> A unique African democracy is not something that will emerge from a rational blueprint: it will emerge from practical experience and improvisation in the course of a hard struggle. . . . But it will be quite different from the contemporary version of liberal democracy, indeed, different enough to elicit suspicion and even hostility from the international community that currently supports African democratization.[32]

Ake writes about his own continent, but the thrust of his argument applies to other non-Western areas: Democratization in such settings will emerge gradually and in new forms compatible with traditions and cultures of the setting. Otherwise, democratization will fail or produce what Ake calls the "democracy of alienation." His call for understanding of non-Western variations on democracy is important for us as peoples in Africa, Asia, and Latin America seek to build their versions of democracy. It should also be remembered by people in the developing world, who often measure their polities against Western democracies and withdraw their support when the non-Western versions fail to meet expectations drawn from Western models.

Clearly, viable forms of democracy for the developing world must meet the aspirations of peoples in these countries for relief from their oppression. That oppression is only in part political. Oppression also comes from the grinding poverty and despair that many people in the developing world face in their struggle for existence. Successful democracy in these parts of the world will have to take those forms that will allow the state to address these economic and social problems. Oscar Arias, the Nobel Peace Prize winner from Costa Rica, captured well the challenge of democracy as we move into a new century:

> If democracy as a form of government cannot improve the conditions of the many impoverished and destitute people on this planet, mere electoral legitimacy and its formalities will not sustain it.[33]

GLOBALIZATION

At several points in this book, I have talked about tendencies toward greater interdependence of peoples and countries around the world. Often, those who talk about this globalization point especially to the economic interdependence imposed by international trade and free movement of investment capital around the world. There are also important political and social effects as a result of the global spread of ideas, decisions, and actions. Modern communications makes this particularly important. In a matter of seconds, a laptop computer can link you up to news, information, sales sites, and positive and perverse ideas anywhere in the world. Blocking such communications, essential to authoritarian regimes, is very difficult, if not impossible. It is not unusual, for example, to find satellite dishes on the roofs of huts in remote villages in China. North Korea has tried to cut its people off from the rest of the world, but this has been at the cost of the economic well-being of its peoples. In other cases, countries may try to cut off such communications to and from "rogue" states, as in the attempts to isolate Iraq, Libya, or Cuba. Such ventures are usually unsuccessful.

The issue of globalization has elicited varying responses. There are some who see only its advantages and inevitability. Thomas Friedman extols globalization in *The Lexus and the Olive Tree*.[34] He describes globalization as the undirected and unstoppable spread of the American way of life—its economic, social, and political values—throughout the world. Lester Thurow, with little criticism of globalization, focuses more on the importance of knowledge in achieving economic success in a global society.[35]

Globalization certainly has its critics. Some question its reality. They argue that the degree of economic interdependence measured by the importance of imports and exports in national economies and the integration of capital movement are no greater now than they were a century ago.[36] Others have shown how nation-states are able to block or reshape global tendencies to meet their own national needs.[37] Often those who deny the reality of globalization focus on economics and miss the important homogenization of cultures that is taking place and the ease of spreading new social and political ideas throughout the world. But others stress the importance of cultural differences in limiting globalization. Samuel P. Huntington, for example, argues that there are seven or eight major civilizations that are distinct from each other, that limit convergence or globalization, and that will be the source of conflict in the new century.[38]

Others accept the reality of globalization but have questioned the desirability of globalization in a world still characterized by deep differences between modern economies and developing states. Inequities are perpetuated and exploited by interdependence. Globalization also poses dangers for democracy. There are few counterbalances or democratic controls over the enhanced roles of international organizations such as the World Trade Organization (WTO), World Bank, and International Monetary Fund (IMF). Others are more skeptical of the extent of globalization and its inevitability and desirability. William Greider accepts the likelihood of continuous globalization but bemoans its effects in his book *One World, Ready or Not: The Manic Logic of Global Capitalism*.[39] He worries about the social dislocation and economic uncertainties that it produces. He and others also see globalization as a way that the long-enduring pattern of the rich exploiting the poor continues and is extended worldwide. There are clearly parts of the world that have been left out of much of this process of global interdependence and progress, notably the less developed countries of sub-Sahara Africa.

Over the last few years, opposition to globalization has emerged at the popular level as well as among scholars. For these grass-roots opponents of globalization, the questions are less those of its reality and speed than of its desirability. Nationalist groups have taken on new importance in many countries to protect cultural values, traditional languages, and customs threatened by homogenization as global culture spreads. Popular manifestations of concern over globalization also include the demonstrations against those organizations seen as embodying globalization: the World Bank, the International Monetary Fund, and the World Trade

Organization. In Seattle (1999), Prague (2000), and Switzerland (2001) such demonstrations expanded beyond complaints against these nongovernmental bodies to sometimes violent protests against the ills of liberal democracy and modern society.

This debate over globalization is a continuing one.[40] There are many complaints about globalization's economic effects and especially its purported support of economic inequalities between rich and poor countries. But there is much more support for the kind of internationalization that promotes the spread of democracy and the observance of human rights.

CONCLUSION

Will we see more democratization and globalization as the twenty-first century moves along? If democracy continues to spread, will it retain its current form of liberal democracy founded on the people's selection of their leaders in free election, the rule of law, and protection of human rights? Will Western countries that have been the source and strongholds of liberal democracy overcome their problems of corruption and disaffected publics?[41] Will globalization bring reduction in the economic gap between rich and poor countries?

North Americans have long found the diversity and size of their own countries great enough that they have often failed to look at the world around them. This can no longer be the case. Americans must see our own economic and political activities in the broader context of a shrinking world. In such an environment, there is a need for the study of comparative politics. There is also a need to apply what we find in looking elsewhere to the understanding and possible solution of our own society's problems and challenges.

Political science can become a "laboratory science" if we are willing to use the experience and examples of countries around the world as our "experiments" in governing. By finding and explaining different approaches to common problems and by using comparative analysis of politics in many settings, we can better understand our own political system, policies, and practices.

NOTES

1. Hans Magnus Enzensberger, *Civil Wars: From L. A. to Bosnia* (New York: The New Press, 1994).

2. Abaham Maslow, *Toward a Psychology of Being* (Englewood Cliffs, NJ: D. Van Nostrand, 1962), and Abraham Maslow, *Motivation and Personality,* 2nd ed. (New York: Harper & Row, 1970).

3. Charles Andrain, *Political Change in the Third World* (Boston: Unwin Hymin, 1988).

4. Marshall I. Goldman, *Lost Opportunity: Why the Economic Reforms in Russia Have Not Worked* (New York: W. W. Norton, 1994).

5. Paul Klebnikov, *Godfather of the Kremlin: Boris Berezovsky and the Looting of Russia* (New York: Harcourt, 2000) p. 323.

6. Frank L. Wilson, "Political Demonstrations in France: Protest Politics or Politics of Ritual?" *French Politics & Society* 12 (Spring-Summer 1994): 23–40.

7. Theda Skocpol, *States and Social Revolutions* (Cambridge, England: Cambridge University Press, 1979).

8. J. C. Davies, "The Varieties of Revolution," *American Sociological Review* 27 (1962): 5–19, and T. R. Gurr, *Why Men Rebel* (Princeton, NJ: Princeton University Press, 1970).

9. Samuel P. Huntington, *Political Order in Changing Societies* (New Haven, CT: Yale University Press, 1968).

10. Charles Tilly, "Does Modernization Breed Revolution?" *Comparative Politics* 5 (July 1973): 425–447.

11. Marc Howard Ross, *The Culture of Conflict: Interpretations and Interests in Comparative Perspective* (New Haven, CT: Yale University Press, 1993).

12. Zbigniew Brzezinski, *The Grand Failure: The Birth and Death of Communism in the Twentieth Century* (New York: Charles Scribner's Sons, 1989). See also Ralf Dahrendorf, *Reflections on the Revolution in Europe* (New York: Random House, 1990).

13. Jack A. Goldstone, "The Comparative and Historical Study of Revolutions," in Jack A. Goldstone, ed., *Revolutions: Theoretical, Comparative, and Historical Studies* (Fort Worth, TX: Harcourt Brace, 1994), p. 17.

14. Enzensberger, *Civil Wars*.

15. Larry Diamond, "The Global State of Democracy," *Current History,* December 1992, pp. 413–18.

16. Press release of December 2000 by Freedom House at its website: www.freedomhouse.org.

17. Adrian Karatnycky, "The 1999 Freedom House Survey: A Century of Progress," *Journal of Democracy* 11 (January 2000): 187–200.

18. Ibid, pp. 196–97.

19. Richard Joseph, "Africa 1990–1997: From *Abertura* to Closure," *Journal of Democracy* 9 (April 1998): 3–17.

20. Larry Diamond, *Developing Democracy: Toward Consolidation* (Baltimore: Johns Hopkins University, 1999).

21. Kendall A. Baker, Russell J. Dalton, and Kai Hildebrandt, *Germany Transformed* (Cambridge, MA: Harvard University Press, 1981).

22. Seymour Martin Lipset, "Some Social Prerequisites of Democracy: Economic Development and Democracy," *American Political Science Review* 53 (September 1959): 69–105. For a critical assessment of this argument, see Philip Cutright, "National Political Development: Its Measurements and Social Correlates," *American Sociology Review* 28 (1963): 253–264.

23. Larry Diamond, "Economic Development and Democracy Reconsidered," *American Behavioral Scientist* 15 (March–June 1992): 450–499.

24. For a discussion of these issues, see the special issue on "Economic Reform and Democracy," *Journal of Democracy* 5 (October 1994) and Larry Diamond and Marc F. Plattner, eds., *Capitalism, Socialism, and Democracy Revisited* (Baltimore: Johns Hopkins University Press, 1993).

25. Adam Przezworski, *Democracy and the Market: Political and Economic Reforms in Eastern Europe and Latin America* (Cambridge, England: Cambridge University Press, 1991).

26. Robert A. Dahl, *A Preface to Economic Democracy* (New Haven, CT: Yale University Press, 1985), and Robert A. Dahl, *Democracy and Its Critics* (New Haven, CT: Yale University Press, 1985).

27. Samuel P. Huntington, *The Third Wave: Democratization in the Late Twentieth Century* (Norman: University of Oklahoma Press, 1991).

28. Dennis Austin, "Reflections on African Politics: Prospero, Ariel and Caliban," *International Affairs* 69 (April 1993): 219.

29. Jeffrey J. Ryan, "The Impact of Democratization on Revolutionary Movements," *Comparative Politics* 27 (October 1994): 46–66.

30. Austin, "Reflections on African Politics," p. 212.

31. Adebayo Adedeji, "An Alternative for Africa," *Journal of Democracy* 5 (October 1994): 119–132.

32. Claude Ake, "The Unique Case of African Democracy," *International Affairs* 69 (April 1993): 243.

33. *Mershon Memo,* Spring 1992, p. 3.

34. Thomas Friedman, *The Lexus and the Olive Tree* (New York: Farrar, Strauss, Giroux, 1999).

35. Lester Thurow, *Building Wealth: The New Rules for Individuals, Companies, and Nations in a Knowledge-Based Economy* (New York: HarperCollins, 1999).

36. Kenneth N. Waltz, "Globalization and Governance," *PS: Political Science and Politics* 32 (December 1999): 693–700, and Robert Wade, "Globalization and Its Limits: Reports of the Death of the National Economy Are Grossly Exaggerated," in Suzanne Berger and Ronald Dore, eds., *National Diversity and Global Capitalism* (Ithaca, NY: Cornell University Press, 1996).

37. Linda Weiss, *The Myth of the Powerless State: Governing the Economy in a Global Era* (Cambridge, England: Cambridge University Press, 1998).

38. William Greider, "The Clash of Civilizations?" *Foreign Affairs* 72 (Summer 1993).

39. William Greider, *One World, Ready or Not: The Manic Logic of Global Capitalism* (New York: Simon & Schuster, 1997).

40. For an interesting collection of essays covering many sides of this debate, see Patrick O'Meara, Howard Mehlinger, and Matthew Krain, eds., *Globalization and the Challenges of the New Century: A Reader* (Bloomington, IN: Indiana University Press, 2000).

41. Susan J. Pharr and Robert D. Putnam, eds., *Disaffected Democracies: What's Troubling the Trilateral Countries?* (Princeton, NJ: Princeton University Press, 2000), and Pippa Norris, ed., *Critical Citizens: Global Support for Democratic Governance* (Oxford, England: Oxford University Press, 1999).

Index